No Grass Grows Under Our Feet

A SOUTHERN LEGACY

JEFFREY DAVIS PAGE

Copyright © 2023 by Jeffrey Davis Page

All rights reserved. No part of this book may be reproduced in whole or in part without written permission from the publisher, except by reviewers who may quote brief excerpts in connection with a review in a newspaper, magazine, or electronic publication; nor many any part of this book be reproduced, stored in a retrieval system, or transmitted in any form or by any means electronic, mechanical, photocopying, recording, or other, without written permission from the publisher.

ISBN: 978-1-960146-70-0 (hard cover)
       978-1-960146-71-7 (soft cover)

Edited by: Monika Dziamka and Melissa Long

Published by Warren Publishing
Charlotte, NC
www.warrenpublishing.net
Printed in the United States

To Gordon Davis Page; Hazel Turbeville Page; my loving and supportive wife, Diane Marie Triggs Todd Page; Patrick Wayne Page; Emma Victoria Page; Sereny "Rena" Page; Anna Elizabeth Hathaway (Prince) Page; Daniel Return Page; Patience Carolina Fowler Hathaway; Amelia Ann Fowler Wright; Stephen Wright; Ann Wright Fowler; Isaac Fowler; Mourning Van Pelt Lewis; William Lewis, Elizabeth Cartrette; Mitchell Davis Page; Dollie Monteen Williamson Page; Kimberly Michelle Page; Eddie Leekota Williamson; Denise Lawson Prevatte Williamson; Joseph Nathan Williamson; Ara Mae Worley Williamson; Brittany Elizabeth Page, Captain, USAF; Tiffany Victoria Page; Cora Reagan Page Petrovich; Ava Ruth Page Petrovich; Lydia Davis Page Petrovich; Bobbie Jean Page Lunsford; Herman Lunsford, MSgt, Retired, USAF; Pattie Sue Page Powell; John Fowler; Elizabeth Rackley; Elizabeth Fowler Spivey; Edmund Caleb Spivey; Daniel Fowler Jr.; Peter Fowler; Lancey Fowler Cartrette; Charles "Chris" Mitchell Powell Jr.; Terry Gene Jacobs; Unsuk Yim Page and Family in South Korea; Karl G. Cahoon III, USAF; Trista Paige Daniell, USAF; Ms. Debbie Strickland Green (sixth grade teacher); Ms. Church (first grade teacher); C.J.B. Shearouse, LtCol, Retired, USAF; Darrell Richard Charbeneu, Captain, Retired, USAF; Kenneth Joseph Thibodeau, CMSgt, Retired, USAF; a friend "Fanny"; and the extended families of South and North Carolina and those family members who migrated to Alabama, Mississippi, Louisiana, and Texas.

AUTHOR'S NOTE

Gordon and Hazel Page and my brother Patrick Wayne Page eternally rest upon an unusual piece of high ground outside Fair Bluff, North Carolina. I had often returned there while I researched this book and would tell my grandparents I was learning more and more about the family history. Thus, my conversations with them did not stop with their deaths but began anew at Powell Cemetery in Fair Bluff, North Carolina, not far from the banks of the Spanish moss clinging from cypress trees caressing the Lumber River. I knew neither of my grandparents wanted me to go rummage through the family history, so I begged for Granddaddy Gordon's forgiveness for learning of things he did not want to speak of, but regardless, I was desperate to learn about my family's history and think anything I uncovered would no longer be damaging to anyone still living. In relating these things, I must make it a point that many may be angry at my attempts to uncover the facts. Many of the items in this story are like old sheets covering furniture. While they remain covered, I do not know if there is a piece of gorgeous furniture or a monstrosity of wood underneath. I intend to remove those sheets in order to uncover the hidden, both ugly and beautiful, and in doing so, dust will fly all over and irritate some people. My objective is not to offend, nor do I intend to pass judgment on those who will occupy these pages. Judgments of people's character are for the Lord to render. I will be judged, so I do not plan to judge others. I see my role as a gatherer of facts. As best as I can, I want to discover them so I can learn. I am not a jury weighing the facts and determining who is guilty or innocent, but rather, I am an audience who wishes to gain a better knowledge of forgotten things. History passes its conclusions on our individual actions. To elaborate on this, history is fixed, and it cannot be changed; only the way we view history may be changed and altered. But, in changing our interpretation of history, we must not fall into the trap of passing judgment upon others who may have lived contextually in a different era. We may view their decisions as ones we would not make, but what those people who lived before us did during their lives cannot be altered. It is up to us as individuals to do what is morally right today in this moment and not be concerned about someone else's judgment in the future. While researching my ancestors, I have seen many who did what was morally right and others who fell short. Can I divorce myself from either?

I also must make it understood that from the beginning, neither Grandpa nor Grandma ever expressed any anger toward anyone or anything. After learning what I have learned, that in itself is undoubtedly surprising. Gordon and Hazel Page lived on the farm of the childless Vanuel and Minnie Edwards Strickland from 1931 until about 1952. The agreement between them was that Gordon would stay on the farm and assist the Stricklands, and in return, their farm—or part of it—would be given to him. According to my aunts, Vanuel would not allow Gordon to have his own mule but had Gordon to use his mule. This meant that Gordon had to purchase his fertilizer from Vanuel. The other agreements were a typical tenant-farmer arrangement which required Gordon to give Vanuel 50 percent of the crops. I assume Gordon stayed on the farm in hopes the childless Stricklands would honor their promise. But if it is not in writing and recorded at the courthouse, no promise is worth the breath it took to say it. Sometime around 1952, Guilford Edwards and his brother Fred, the nephews of Minnie, persuaded the Stricklands to sign over the farm to them. Fred never married nor had any children; thus the beneficiary of this deal was Guilford Edwards and his descendants. I'd like to note here that Guilford's wife was Clara Turberville, the sister of Grandma Hazel. I never heard my grandparents say a cross word about either Clara or Guilford. Aunt Bobbie once stated that shortly after she left home in 1952, "Daddy moved. Grandma Minnie begged him to stay and was crying when he stood in front of her. Daddy said, 'I can't.' Then he turned and walked away."

Therefore, this work is not intended as random arrows aimed at targets in the past. I cannot change what was done. Instead, it is the pouring out of emotions and facts which are my history. My Granddaddy Gordon and Grandma Hazel occupy the central point of motivation for this journey. As I stated previously, they continued to do what was morally right. They harbored no hatred, no plans of vengeance; they simply continued to make the best of what they were given. Grandpa lived his life with greater assurance in the trust of the Lord's benevolence than his fellow man. He forgave all and asked God to bless all. If these memories should cause enmity between present generations who are descendants of the people now dead, I, as Granddaddy would desire, pray for all your blessings and ask your forgiveness, if I will offend, and love. But these facts will be known because they are what made me and my descendants.

This book is an amateur attempt to breathe life back into the people who were once small children, grew into adults, and lived lives, which I wish to make known so they are not forgotten. I have found many bones scattered along what the early settlers called Drowning Creek, and my hope is those people will not forever recede beneath the Spanish moss and sandy soil of southeastern North Carolina. Their story could be similar to those of people who moved into Illinois or Colorado. In researching this, I have attempted to be as accurate as the records I have found have allowed me to be. For example, there may be instances of different spellings of names found in the records from time to time, depending upon the educational level of the recorder. The story is never finished, and my desire is that one day in the future this work will be of benefit to someone who has questions about their people and their story. I alone bear responsibility for any errors and ask forgiveness for these honest mistakes.

For my part, I have concluded that the Declaration of Arbroath from the Scots to Pope John XXII, dated 6 April 1320, summarizes the character of the people in this book. In pleading with the pope to intervene on Scotland's behalf against Edward II of England, the Scots state, "As long as a hundred of us remain alive, never will we on any conditions be subjected to the lordship of the English. It is in truth not for glory, nor riches, nor honours that we are fighting, but for freedom alone, which no honest man gives up but with life itself." Perhaps this love of freedom of those that follow will remain as long as there are a hundred allied together.

PART I
Beginnings

CHAPTER 1
Cerro Gordo, North Carolina

I was born in 1965 in Columbus County, North Carolina, on what was then a dirt road. When my parents brought me home from Whiteville—the county seat and where the hospital was—I was coming home to a trailer that sat next to my paternal grandparents' home. My parents owned the trailer, but the land upon which it and my grandparents' home sat belonged to a Mr. Monroe Powell. His wife was a Blackwell, and perhaps the land was originally hers since, when the county named the road, it became Blackwell Road. Grandpa Gordon and Grandma Hazel had moved to the place in 1955 when my father was ten years old. About 1968, Grandpa persuaded Mr. Monroe to sell him a half acre of land on the farm. It was at this juncture when both my parents and grandparents built homes financed by the Farmers Home Administration about two thousand feet from where the trailer and old house were located. Thus, I spent my first fifteen years living beside my paternal grandparents. Dad did shift work, so the time that was not spent with my mother was spent at my grandparents' house. There were not, and still are not, many homes on Blackwell Road. Thus, my opportunities at having a fun childhood consisted of playing cowboys and Indians with the few kids nearby, riding my bicycle, or spending time at my grandparents', which was often. Sometimes, when my dad's sisters, Marjorie, who lived in Delaware, Bobbie in Georgia, or Pattie in Cerro Gordo, came to visit, I usually was at my grandparents'. I never recall any of them coming to my house.

I must have been ten years old when I asked my paternal grandfather, Granddaddy Gordon, "Where are we from?"

He replied, "Virginia." And not anything else.

I later learned why Granddaddy Gordon wouldn't talk about his family much. Granddaddy Gordon's father and mother were both born out of wedlock due to the circumstances surrounding the Civil War. Granddaddy was embarrassed by that fact. Of course, they could not have prevented this, and in many respects, their mothers probably were caught in a whirlwind of history that pays little respect for the desires of individual wishes, especially those of women.

When I asked him this question, it was autumn, and it was during this time he would wake up before daylight and get the tractor from Uncle Lee Turberville's house and hook it up to a plow. Granddaddy had a 1950s Farmall tractor he kept under Uncle Lee's shelter attached to his warehouse. Uncle Lee was the elder brother of my Grandma Hazel, and he and his wife, Ethel, had moved to their home from South Carolina sometime in the 1950s. Granddaddy had received permission to clear about an acre of land behind our houses from Mr. Monroe, and each year, he would plant various vegetables to sell to locals. In the fall, after the first frost, it was time to harvest the potatoes. Granddaddy would cut the vines, and then I would meet him out in the field behind his house and drive the tractor as he negotiated the plow through the sweet potato vines. I would move along the ground holding the hog feed sack open as he would toss the potatoes into the bag. After I completed unearthing the potatoes, I'd wait for the school bus, and he would spend the remainder of the day collecting the sweet potatoes. In the afternoon, the potatoes that were not big enough to eat were collected and stored for seeding the following year.

I repeated my question that afternoon after school, but again, Granddaddy Gordon gave me his one-word response: "Virginia." I had been hoping for more information on the family and who we were. As far as I knew, there was my dad's sisters, Marjorie, Bobbie, and Pattie, and Grandma's sister, Aunt Clara, and her brother, Uncle Lee. When I started school, most people seemed to be related to someone else in the community. Sometime in elementary school, I realized my last name, Page, was unique and rather rare in the community. I once desired my last name to be my mother's maiden name of Williamson for no other reason than there seemed to be many of them in the community. After all, I was half Williamson as much as I was half Page.

The only subject I developed any interest in at school was history. Yet, despite the books I read, I seemed to have none when it came to my family tree. How had my family wound up on Monroe Powell's farm on Blackwell Road? Why did my grandparents not discuss their parents? What role had my family played in the history of Columbus County and the state of North Carolina? For those questions and many others, the answers remained hidden for a long time.

I became a voracious reader of history books and biographies and yearned to learn more about my family and our history. The one book that began my quest to read as much as I could was a biography of Napoleon. I think what I identified most with was Napoleon was an outsider and yet became the man the established monarch of Europe feared when the French Army appeared. Similarly, the lessons of overreach were impressed upon me when I read of Napoleon's disastrous Russian Campaign. Thus, from an early age of about twelve, I learned the ends of any pursuit must match the means to accomplish the desired end. Great undertakings must be planned and replanned, and then the element of boldness must not silence caution but moderate it. Similarly, all I knew about my mother's parents was that her father, "Pa Joe," had fought in World War II against the Japanese, and her mother's family was only known as The Worleys from Cherry Grove. My grandparents on both sides of the family said little concerning family; they didn't even talk much about their own parents. Despite all my nagging questions, I knew not much else other than "Virginia." There was not much concerning the Pages, very little concerning the Turbervilles, only that the Williamsons were very numerous in the western part of the county, and the Worleys were from the Cherry Grove community. My history seemed to be the sphinx of Egypt covered in sand. There was a base to their head which protruded from Columbus County, but no one was readily volunteering any information about it, which was extremely disappointing to a ten-year-old filled with questions.

Most days growing up, I came home from school, dropped my stuff, and then walked over to my grandparents' house. Most of the time, Grandma was in the kitchen or sitting at the table. There, she would take a pair of scissors, fold a piece of paper several times, and then cut out paper dolls for me to draw faces on. She told me this was what they did to have something to play with when she was young. One weekend when I was looking for something to do, I found myself sitting at the table with Grandma. I recall telling her how bored I was. She told me, "Jeffrey, you need to find things to do to entertain yourself." This was when she showed me how to make those paper dolls. As we worked, I thought it a good time to inquire about the family, and I asked Grandma Hazel about the Pages and why Grandpa did not speak of them. Grandma Hazel was a very stoic and serious person, and she never lifted her eyes from those scissors as she said, "Jeffrey, your grandpa does not like talking about his parents because his father was illegitimate."

Of course, at ten years old, I was not sure what being "illegitimate" meant. I wanted to know more, but I could tell from her tone that the conversation was over and stopped asking questions about my great-grandparents after that day.

As the number of my remaining family members started to dwindle down, the history they knew from firsthand accounts and the emotions connected to that history returned to cemeteries not far from Drowning Creek (Lumber River), and I lost my only access to my family's history. After the internet came upon the scene, my interest in the family history was rekindled, and I once again sought to finally find the answers by using information that was more readily available. While I can never sit and speak to those people who passed, who contributed to the person I am today, the knowledge I gained has helped me get to know them better. I have learned their history is intertwined with voyages across the Atlantic, the risks of revolutions, the story of migration, the ravages of war, and the heartache of what it means to have a family, lose a child to war or disease, fall in love, and perhaps do what is forced upon a person to survive. Their story is my heritage; I wish it had not been hidden for so long.

The one thing I have learned over my five decades of living is that families spread out, and distant cousins may pass each other in the grocery store and not even know who each other is. Similarly, when there may be an aspect of embarrassment or disgrace upon the family's name, time and distance are used to bury any knowledge of what may have happened and the original circumstances that may have brought about the "disgrace" to the family name. In many ways, my quest to know more about the family was buried by Granddaddy's acknowledgement that the past cannot be changed and it was better to move forward and leave any knowledge of the past embedded in his memory. Since neither I nor my father ever interacted with any of the Pages or any of the relatives in and around Tabor City, our knowledge of that side of the family had been like a cancer, cut off and removed. Yet the evidence of that cancer, like the notes of a surgeon, was there to be discovered by me in the form of death certificates, wills, others' research, and DNA evidence, which would connect me to Return Page Jr. Additionally, discovering the name of Anna Elizabeth Page's father on her death certificate was another mystery I had never even expected. That was a mystery Granddaddy kept locked away and took with him to the grave.

Granddaddy Gordon died in 1981, and in the summer of 2000, I received a call from Aunt Pattie stating my father and I needed to come home because Grandma was diagnosed with cancer. When Grandma Hazel discovered she had cancer, she told the hospital staff, "I am going home, and there will not be any treatments or effort to stop it." Grandma's actions came as no surprise to me; she was a person filled with determination. She had lived without Grandpa for nineteen years and dutifully carried on with a dignified degree of independence other than relying on someone to drive her to her appointments and the grocery store. She felt she had lived long enough, and it was time to see Gordon.

During Christmas of 1999, she had given me a picture, stating, "I think this is a good picture of me, and I want you to have it." Today, that picture rests next to my bed. There are three other pictures of her that are special to me. One is of her standing in front of her home decorated for Christmas and holding a wooden cutout of a snowman. In Columbus County, this was as close to making an actual snowman as one could achieve in the balmy weather of December in eastern North Carolina. The other one is of her holding a beer bottle with the biggest grin I had ever seen light up her face. One of my cousins persuaded her to hold it and then surprised her by taking a picture. Grandma did not approve of alcohol; thus the mere fact she was holding the bottle had been a miracle. The last photo is of her standing on the back porch of the tenant home, holding her skirt hem up, with my father of about two years old standing next to her.

Dad and I drove home to Cerro Gordo from Rock Hill to see her when she was sick, and once again, she gave me information that left me puzzled. When I visited Grandma in the past, she always kept the door locked when she was alone. Thus, when I knocked on the door, at first, a gray head would appear and then slowly a set of eyes as she stood on her toes to see who was at the door. If the door was unlocked, it meant someone was there with her. When Dad and I arrived, the door was open, and we walked into the house. Aunt Pattie was there, the son of Granddaddy's brother, Norman Page, Norman's wife, and his son Randy Page. Dad and I said hello, and I walked over to the green vinyl couch where Grandma was lying. This was the same couch where I took many naps while I was living next door and the one Granddaddy had instructed me not to "flop down in."

As I leaned over and kissed her goodbye, I said, "I love you."

She replied, "I love you more, and I have a secret I have not told anyone."

"Oh my," I said. I thought she would finally tell me more about the family or something she and I would only know.

But no.

After a pause, she said, "I should take it with me."

I have since asked my aunts and my father many times if they have any idea what she may have kept hidden. No one knows. That secret rests on a sandy slope of land in a cemetery outside of Fair Bluff. I loved and will forever love Hazel and Gordon Page, but as I grew older and obtained a degree from Winthrop University and traveled with the air force, I thirsted to know more, and that thirst was with me for ten more years until I finally decided to research what I was looking for. I have discovered much since that time but do not know if I have uncovered Hazel's secret, and if she divulged it to anyone, they are not revealing it.

When Grandma was in her last days, she had many relatives come visit her. One of these was Norman Page, son of Jesse Page and thus Gordon's nephew. I learned that Norman's son Randy Page had done a lot of research into our family and was assisted by Pansey Louise Page Jensen, who proved to be a valuable resource. Pansey was a retired school teacher, and she was the granddaughter of William Page and daughter of Edward Walker Page. William Page was the twin of Return Page Jr., my great-great-grandfather.

Soon after my grandma passed away, I connected with Randy, and the research he and Pansey provided gave me more information on the Pages. Still, many questions remain unanswered, and even as of this writing, I believe many of these answers will be hidden away from me until I meet these people in heaven.

Despite the fact I have unearthed much, there are still many questions remaining. What happened to Kinion Cartrette? Why did he disappear? Why were Kinion and Lancy's children sent to live with relatives? How did their daughter Elizabeth meet my great-great-grandfather Return Page? Why did they not get married? Who was Solomon Prince, and did he acknowledge my great-grandmother Anna as his daughter? What did the Fowler brothers do at the Battle of Moore's Creek Bridge in the Revolutionary War? What happened to Abraham Page during the American Revolution that shows him as being killed during it? Why were the Pages Quakers? The more I discovered, the more questions there were to answer, which could not be.

In trying to discover more about my lineage, I have found little left by anyone concerning a written diary or records that reveal my family members' past and present lives and how their lives relate to the history of the United States. What I discovered was a very enlightening tale of a mixture of British peoples who left the British Isles. Many had come to Britain from France, the Low Countries, and the Rhineland area, and then they collectively ventured across the Atlantic and settled in the British colonies because they sought opportunity, adventure, and wealth, and surprisingly, many came seeking religious freedom. Some were even sent over as bonded passengers—a.k.a. prisoners. My concrete research and sleuthing through English parish records and documents in the United Kingdom would be needed to prove this, but records on genealogical sites show ordinary people momentarily intersecting with nobility and historic events.

What I have learned has given me a greater appreciation of who I am and has improved my self-esteem, considering I knew nothing about my family and lived on such a small portion of land. When I lived on Monroe Powell's farm, I did not have a history. It was as if I had been dropped in 1965, as the Beatles had been, and history began at that moment. I desired to know the story behind 1965 and how I came to be. I have discovered that there were many people and events to take pride in for what they had accomplished. Many were woven in the pages of the events of history I had studied in college and school. They may not have been the general upon the horse, but they were there, making their contribution and often giving their lives.

Because of the media and historical events, when people speak of "the South," images of oak trees, plantation houses, and privilege usually come to mind, or the institution of slavery and the depredation against humanity and the worth of an individual. Margaret Mitchell's *Gone with the Wind* was not my South but the vestiges of the history of slavery and its consequences. The South I knew consisted of my granddaddy being a tenant farmer and my Pa Joe owning around sixty acres of land, with about twenty some acres of it being swampland, one side of the family owning land but not much else, and the Page side providing much of the food we ate from the garden Granddaddy Gordon kept. Grandma Hazel and most of the people I knew as older people back then canned vegetables all summer and then ate sweet potatoes and collards and killed hogs in the winter.

Growing up on a quarter acre of land next to a big canal that kept the property drained and not knowing anyone except your immediate family was bewildering. But since my childhood, I have discovered I am related to many of the families in Columbus, Brunswick, Robeson, Marion, and Horry Counties. In most instances, these families came from England, Scotland, Wales, Ireland, Holland, and France, first to Virginia, with some exceptions, and then into North and South Carolina. After two generations, they did as the United States as a whole did and moved their families west, first to Alabama, Mississippi, and Texas, and then finally as far away as California. Despite this spread across the southern states, my extended family stayed near the land drained by the Lumber River, the Little Pee Dee, the Great Pee Dee, and the Cape Fear Rivers. In between these black-water rivers, which empty into the Atlantic, are many creeks dissecting dry land once filled with longleaf pine, creeks onto which hardy people moved and began to cultivate.

The goal of researching my family history is an attempt to make known what I have found. During my research, I stumbled into the lives of people who lie buried in Columbus County, who had walked the same roads I did and had fallen in love beneath the same Spanish moss–draped trees of the Lumber River. Those people who lived both in triumphant and tumultuous times, in peace and war. If I can provide any benefit to my three granddaughters or any others who share our history—and I believe I have relatives numbering in the thousands—I have done my duty, as have those before me who added their part to this pageant of history. Among my many discoveries, I have found that human nature is the same today as it was one hundred years ago. By this, I mean humans are driven by the same passions today as they were at any time in the past. I, too, learned that no matter the relationship, when land or wealth is involved, there is always a Judas lurking in anyone's soul. I have found ancestors who owned slaves and those who did not; it is difficult to grapple with seeing wills in which human beings are transferred to family members like any other property. I immediately think, *What happened to those people? What are their stories?*

I cannot change the past, but I can learn from it. The Roman statesman Marcus Tullius Cicero states, "To be ignorant of what occurred before you were born is to remain always a child. For what is the worth of human life, unless it is woven into the life of our ancestors by the records of history?"[1]

Alice Walker, the author of *The Color Purple*, writes, "To acknowledge our ancestors means we are aware that we did not make ourselves, that the line stretches back perhaps to God, or to Gods. We remember them because it is an easy thing to forget: that we are not the first to suffer, rebel, fight, love, and die. The grace with which we embrace life, despite the pain, the sorrow, is always a measure of what has gone before."[2]

I know one day I will not walk this earth, but I will leave a part of me in the hearts and DNA of my children and grandchildren. Further, whatever decisions and history I have made will be passed as a legacy to those who follow me, just as I was born into the decisions and past of my ancestors. One does not have the option to select who they are nor who their family is. Likewise, my granddaughters will live and make decisions both wise and unwise; perhaps this story will enlighten those choices and decisions they will make. I do not know what trials, sorrows, triumphs, and happiness will be their companion, and I sometimes wonder what we are to do here among the limitations of mortals and why we were called to do so.

In researching this story, I kept looking for some link to another part of the country and, thus, another history other than the one associated with the South. I found a plausible link to New England through Return Strong of Massachusetts but cannot explain what he'd been doing in North Carolina. I even uncovered a link to *Mayflower* passenger George Soule, who came to New England as an indentured servant and signed the Mayflower Compact. Some of his later descendants, seeking relief from Puritan rule, migrated to North Carolina and became known as Soles. Given the choice, I'd originally hoped the story of my ancestors would be filled with principled decisions and life's choices, but that was not the case. And I realized it is not the case for anyone. We live by many of the choices made before we were born. I did not get to choose to be a Southerner any more than I chose to be an American. This was where I was put, and I have had to accept this and do the best I could. To be a Southerner is to be born with baggage I had nothing to do with. I would love to have found someone who rode against the tide and took a stand against certain historical wrongs in the past, but the past exists as something unchangeable by me or anyone. I am morally responsible for the life I live, not the decisions of my ancestors. As they say back home, "You will have to hoe your row." You as a person must make the conscious decision to clear the weeds from the seeds you plant. If you do not stay vigilant, the weeds will overtake the seeds, and the fruits of your efforts in life will result in turmoil, chaos, and a reputation of an unjust person. I cannot imagine the difficulty many of the women I descend from faced when burying dead sons or husbands from the ravages of the Civil War, or how many stood the bombardment of cannons, the whizzing bullets across battlefields, only to die of dysentery in a Union prison camp. My great-grandmother Patience did not ask her husband to go fight in the Civil War and die of smallpox in Virginia, but that was what life had handed her. Would any of us choose heartache?

So why write this book? Because there was once a young boy who thought he was no one special and yearned for something other than the sharecropper legacy he knew. This journey has shown me there was indeed much more to know.

The story starts in a place called the Old North State or the Tar Heel State, in a place laced in my day with tobacco, corn, and soybean fields dissected by Dunn Swamp and Porter Swamp.

About a year into writing this memoir, God sent John Hybert Williamson of Davidson, North Carolina, into my life. John was kind and shared a similar interest in the family's past. After retiring from Davidson College, John, in his retirement, did extensive research into the Williamson family of Columbus County. He had material on many of the other old families of Columbus County and had acquired many photos of Cerro Gordo and the lumber mill in the early 1900s. When I was young, I had heard of the lumber mill at Cerro Gordo but never knew it was called the Brown and Williamson Lumber Company and was connected to the Williamson family. Unfortunately, the mill caught fire, and after its demise, Cerro Gordo was not the same place it once was. The lumber mill provided jobs and kept families close, but once the mill and jobs disappeared, the families that made up the community moved away, and the town suffered accordingly. Family connected Uncle Eddie's wife, Denise, to the Brown side of the lumber mill through her great-grandmother. It is pretty amazing how all of these connections are still there in the community.

CHAPTER 2
My Bucket Fell Here

Booker T. Washington made a speech in 1895 in Atlanta, Georgia, called the Cast Down Your Bucket speech. Washington was specifically addressing the African American experience in the United States and the South. However, I think the analogy of "casting down your bucket" is applicable to anyone who is desirous of change for the better.[3] A person who casts down their bucket is a person ready to seek opportunities and contribute to the positive growth of both themselves and their community. If I walk around with my bucket in my hands, it will never be filled. I only wind up with an empty bucket. If you are standing under an apple tree and desire apples, they will not just fall into the bucket. I have to reach for and pull them from the tree. Similarly, seldom will anyone help you with anything; you must take your bucket and start filling it yourself. Be it planning or taking one course at a time to receive a college degree, you must start filling your bucket and not wait on others to do it for you.

I first learned of this speech in college, and it still lingers with me as a reminder that everyone begins life in a place and into a given set of circumstances that are all different. Naturally, some have more opportunities than others. The ones who are not as fortunate to be born into wealth have to start somewhere to move forward. Thus, wherever you may be, you do need to cast down the bucket and get started.

These places and the people in this story are mine. No matter their faults or merits, I come from them. I am not ashamed of them, nor do I stand in judgment of them. I was not there as they made their decisions in life, and I cannot ask them to speak from beyond the grave. But I do wish to one day gather with them and fill in the spaces time and death have taken from me. I know time is the thief of us all, and it is seemingly unstoppable. No matter how far I have traveled—be it to South Korea, Europe, Afghanistan and other places in the Middle East, or Whidbey Island in Washington State—those places and people are with me. My voice and philosophical outlook are intertwined with my neurons and the sinews of my muscles. Columbus County and the swamps that dissect it remain in a corner of my memory, where I long to revisit but not to linger.

The people of Columbus County are the objects of my affection, admiration, bewilderment, and range of passion from disappointment to love. Some, not all, of the people I knew will fall short, while others remain true to this principle as stated in the 1599 Geneva Bible version of Romans 12:9–10: "Let love be without dissimulation. Abhor that which is evil, and cleave unto that which is good. Be affectioned to love one another with brotherly love. In giving honor, go one before another."[4] In many ways, this passage has been honored, and in other ways, it has been disavowed by those people I loved.

The places of my youth in Columbus County are still there. The names of towns and communities exist on the map, but the faces of the people are no longer the same. Many of the people I knew were from the generations of World War I, the Great Depression, World War II, and baby boomers. Those I knew as teenagers and young adults are now in their sixties and seventies and are increasingly fewer and fewer. The buildings I remember along the country roads have been torn down. Some are still there but have succumbed to the passage of time and vines of wisteria and kudzu that have pulled them apart and are slowly swallowing them, only to be visible in the winter. I have come to realize that the places I love and cherish so much may not still exist long after I have departed this world. However, the land is still there; the dirt that sustained generations with food, fed livestock, and grew crops remains, along with the names given by those first settlers.

For me to not be consumed by the regret of admitted wrongs is a trying process of patience and an admonishment to honor one another with love above my limited knowledge, indeed a difficult task. I gather the thoughts and memories of those moments of revelation when I reflect back on my time in Columbus County. Weighing those times, I realize there are good memories, and then there are disappointments. For example, I am still perplexed how human nature ebbs with love and indifference toward other people, especially family. Those emotions are like the water on the banks of Cape Fear during the passage of the day. Perhaps indifference and love are cozy neighbors. In the end, I suppose, I can only cling to what was good and see how all these places and their associated people and stories have shaped me into who I am today.

Perhaps who you are is a reflection of where you come from more than any other factor. Perhaps where you come from is even the most significant factor. Then again, sometimes I think that the overriding factor in my own formative years was not the environment but the family I was born into. No soul can choose the people who will be its parents or grandparents any more than it can choose to be born in a tropical location off of Florida or the wilds of Minnesota.

None of us chooses who we are. We arrive in this world to people we are genetically related to and with whom we have a history which we did not get to preview beforehand. Thus, how many of us would accept the choice we have no voice in deciding? Is who we are at birth by chance, or is it by some other higher design? I do not know. This is a question that I cannot answer. I only know that we must make the best with what we are given until we cross back over into the unknown void of heaven or what is after this life to see if there was an awareness of why we individually matter and how we fit in to some plan. Until we cross that bar, we must simply continue to improve what we have here.

Some are lucky to be born into wealth, others lucky to be born into a faith-believing family. No matter the circumstances, the character of human dignity must be vigilantly earned, and we must find our place among those forlorn souls of mortals separate from whatever our origins are. If people have the capacity to think and to know right from wrong and come from something more than a collection of cells, then we are lost from our origin, for otherwise we should always do what is morally right. And surely there is a moral right that does not change. In the beginning, unborn souls are encased in the fragility of human flesh and extraordinary origins. We are born to travel many paths, make many friends, love, live, and just as a vapor, pass back to the sources we have forgotten.

Some wander and fall, never to rise, and others take bitter defeats and do what they were taught to move forward. This is the story of one of those souls who accepted what life had given him and made the best of his circumstances. The most prominent carrier of the flag of defeat was my granddaddy, Gordon Davis Page.

CHAPTER 3
The Deacon and the Preacher:
Gordon Davis Page and Vernon Williamson

I last saw Granddaddy Gordon in what we knew as the fullest of his health in February of 1981. My family unexpectedly relocated to Mississippi that year from Columbus County, North Carolina. I had lived beside my grandparents since I was born. First, in a small trailer adjacent to the house they rented from Monroe Powell and then in a Farmers Home Administration home that cost ten thousand dollars to build in 1968. As I recall, the mortgage was a whopping fifty-three dollars a month. The trailer my parents purchased was adjacent to a sharecropper's house Grandpa lived in from 1952 until 1968 on Mr. Monroe Powell's ten-acre farm. I was three when we moved from the trailer to the small brick house. I have one memory of the house Gordon and Hazel lived in until they moved: I entered the bathroom, and the eye-and-hook latch on the door fell and locked me in. I recall screaming and then hearing the glass window shatter just before Granddaddy reached in and pulled me through the window.

I have photos of the home, which often ended up in the background of pictures, given to me by my Aunt Bobbie. And in them, I can see the green-and-white trailer, which was my home for the first three years of my life. The earlier photos are black and white and are predominately all taken outside. Then later there are color photos that one of my aunts must have taken because in these you can tell it is a family gathering since everyone is there and had to have traveled from Georgia or Delaware. The yard is neat and clean, and everything is in its proper place. Today, the same front yard is not visible for the briars and weeds which have engulfed the house that once stood there. The only remnant of the house is a brick chimney. Where the trailer sat is in a similar state of overgrowth. Later, in 1968, Grandpa built a tiny house on a quarter-acre patch of briars and pines he purchased from Mr. Monroe Powell. Grandpa built his home from surplus lumber from military shipping containers obtained from the military's port in Wilmington, North Carolina. My image of Grandpa is either in overalls during the week or a suit on Sunday. There was no in-between. He was working, or he was at church.

Grandpa, having been reared in the "only true" belief of the Baptists by his mother, Anna Elizabeth, set the nature of most of his descendants: Calvinistic in outlook intertwined with threads of Arminianism. The major distinction is the perseverance of the saints or eternal salvation for those saved. The Baptists are rooted in the South in the same manner a pine tree has a central taproot anchoring it to the ground. The Baptist of my memory insists on a personal public confession of faith in Jesus Christ and immersion in water. Most everyone in western Columbus County had been reared under the roof of a Baptist church. While many have not been practicing Christians, they had been exposed to the sermons of a Baptist preacher and thus shared a common kinship of the faith between them. I am sure there were many among those who were as mean as snakes and did underhanded things, but they knew better.

Granddaddy Gordon reflected the Calvinist traits of discipleship: committed to high standards of artistry and a willingness to witness to anyone interested in listening to the Gospel. I recall my immersion as if it were indeed John the Baptist himself who dunked me under the water. My baptism was held at Cedar Grove Baptist Church when I was in the ninth grade. I sat through many Baptist sermons and witnessed many a soul who walked down the aisle to stand and converse with the preacher on the subject of salvation. My calling or my acceptance of Jesus took place during a revival, which my great-uncle Vernon "Burn" Williamson preached in my ninth-grade year of high school.

Uncle Burn bore a classical resemblance to Reverend Billy Graham in many ways. His philosophical outlook was that the price for sin was death, and without the sacrifice of Jesus, who left His lofty kingdom in heaven and died an inglorious death on the cross, hell was our fate. Uncle Burn preached a sermon on tolerance of sin and the impossibility of man overcoming sin without Jesus's sacrifice.

Uncle Burn's message was, as I remember, centered upon Matthew 6:24, which states, "No man can serve two masters: for he shall hate the one, and love the other, or else he shall lean to the one, and despise the other. Ye cannot serve God and riches."[5]

Uncle Burn was clear in his message that as Christians, we must adhere to the Bible, and to be tolerant of sin was to try to straddle the fence, which cannot be done.

Tolerance is a trickster, leading to the acceptance of behavior that a community of people should not accept. A proud American, Uncle Burn held the rule that tolerance of others' beliefs should be respected. People should not be hounded and vilified for being different, but rather their beliefs that created immoral actions should not be accepted. Burn preached that there are righteous actions and unrighteous actions. I can debate the concept of morality until I am blue in the face, but the "Do unto others, as you would have them do unto you" is a good foundational basis to a community I would desire to live in.

At this juncture in my life, I remain in the pews looking up at Uncle Burn, standing tall in the pulpit, towering with his six-foot frame, sun-toned skin, Bible in one hand and the other raised in the air, telling the congregation the truth anyone desires rests in the pages of the Bible and there is no other truth.

I last saw Uncle Burn at my Grandmother Ara Mae and Granddaddy Pa Joe's funeral. By then, it had been many years since he led me to the front of the church to my confession of faith in Jesus. The fire was still there in his lungs, the Bible in his right hand. He was a bit frailer, and what struck me the most was that the fingers on his right hand were pointed straight down—he had rheumatoid arthritis. When I asked him about what had caused such a condition, he said, "I have shaken many hands in my ministry, and I think that may have contributed to this." I think he actually believed the thousands of hands he shook had worsened his arthritis.

There is one other noteworthy memory I have of Uncle Burn and the subject of religion. The common belief, which bound poor Whites, privileged Whites, and African Americans, was the certainty of a shared belief in the sinfulness of humans and the centrality of death at some point. Death on a farm is ever present—livestock dies, crops die, family members die, etc. We are chased by death because, in reality, life is but a vapor. Most of the people I knew when I was a child accepted that the only way to escape the clutch of death was the acceptance of Jesus Christ.

Reverend Billy Graham had been a saint in my community. If anyone desired to add credibility to what was stated in the Bible, they simply stated, "Billy Graham says" this or that. Uncle Burn, while he stood in the pulpit holding the Bible, would often say, "I agree with

Billy Graham. The central focus of our life should be the cross." Jesus's death on the cross at Calvary made life possible beyond this earthly realm. I eventually moved away from the people of Columbus County, but the centrality of the cross in my life remains. Now in my fifties, the significance of the cross is even more relevant.

I am asked, "What is the common purpose and the mission of this nation? Is there such a thing as a national mission?" Indeed, there is. America's mission is to make a better future for the next generations. What institution do we give our grandchildren? What quality of life improvements do we give our grandchildren? Do we leave them a legacy of indebtedness to a foreign power or the security of financial independence? Perhaps there should be a discussion on the mission, but all I am stating right now is that a person, an institution, or a nation needs to know what they want to accomplish. Granddaddy would state the mission is a well-educated populace, one that thinks independently and critically and has an ample dose of skepticism. Education brings forth knowledge, and knowledge is the fertilizer for making the best decisions that can be made.

Uncle Burn would state the mission is to be in the protection of God. In his second inaugural address, President Abraham Lincoln states:

> With malice toward none with charity for all with firmness in the right as God gives us to see the right let us strive on to finish the work we are in to bind up the nation's wounds, to care for him who shall have borne the battle and for his widow and his orphan ~ to do all which may achieve and cherish a just and lasting peace among ourselves and with all nations.[6]

Uncle Burn and Lincoln share this sentiment of "firmness in the right as God gives us to see the right." We, as a people and individuals, cannot make an appointment with God as we would a doctor, but we can pray for His guidance in the decisions we must make. Uncle Burn and Granddaddy would maintain that seeking God's guidance begins with the Bible, and I agree. President Ronald W. Reagan summarizes our position when he stated: "Can we resolve to read, learn and try to heed the greatest message ever written—God's word and the Holy Bible? Inside its pages lie all the answers to all the problems that man has ever known."[7]

CHAPTER 4
Moving to Wiggins, Mississippi

We moved to Mississippi from Columbus County, North Carolina, when I was fifteen and did not desire to move; I also did not know this was the last time I would see Granddaddy Gordon healthy. I liked being near my grandparents, and I wanted to finish my sophomore year in high school with my friends, who were just getting their driver's licenses, and my girlfriend.

Grandpa was deeply saddened to see us leave. Before this day, his clothes were always worn and faded, even though his vigor and stature—six foot three—usually portrayed an image of strength and vitality. However, on that winter day in February, the opposite was the case. He stood there in the corner of his yard in front of what we called the pea patch, because there was always a garden Granddaddy planted, and each year, there was a well-trodden path across the center of it I had worn by going to and from his house. The last years I was home, there were forget-me-not flowers planted on the last row of the garden, and I recall trying to pull the seedpods off the bush only to have it explode open in my hands. Granddaddy constantly admonished me to walk around the end of the garden, but I did not. Instead, I'd go right across the middle, trying to jump across the plants and wearing down a path. I never got in trouble for this though. In fact, I do not recall ever being yelled at or spanked by my grandparents.

On the day we moved to Mississippi, Granddaddy stood at the end of the pea patch, dressed in a brand-new pair of overalls with his best hat on his head. I will forever recall how the new overalls, instead of making him look youthful, made him look all frail. Granddaddy was a six-foot-five muscular man who tossed one-hundred-pound sacks of fertilizer across his shoulders as if they were pillows. But on this day, his normal erect posture was hunched at the shoulders, and his face had an expression as if someone had just told him some truly devastating news. The smile that was almost always present on his face was missing.

I asked Dad, "May I say goodbye one more time?"

He allowed me to, and I ran to Grandpa and hugged him one last time. I had clung to his pants leg many times in the past, and he always seemed the sturdy post you sought out to lean against in times of trouble. This time his strength seemed that of a sapling. I did not want to move, but he said, "Your dad is waiting on you. You best not keep him waiting."

I turned and walked back to the car, and just like that, we pulled off down the road in a 1980 Camaro headed to Mississippi, the state that then ranked about last in every category of success in the United States. As Dad drove away, I looked back, and there was Granddaddy still standing, not waving, not moving, simply standing like the lighthouse he had always been during my fifteen years of childhood. That was forty-one years ago, and the lighthouse still stands as a beacon warning me of danger as I navigate through life. Even if I ignore those warnings, they still are there.

It tears deeply at my soul to wonder how long he stood there. He'd had cancer once before and had beaten it, but within four months of our departure, the cancer returned and ravaged his body relentlessly until it ended his life. I wonder still if he'd had a feeling something was wrong with his health that day we left.

I saw Granddaddy once more before he passed, but he did not remember my name. The light that had withstood every hardship in his life was only a flicker and would be extinguished within three weeks. We moved to Mississippi in February of 1981, and in the summer of 1981, I returned home. Upon entering the house, I found Grandpa in the living room on the sofa. I walked over to him and looked into his deep-blue eyes. I knew he recognized me because I could see it in his eyes and his smile, but he could not say my name. Not hearing "Jeffrey" from his lips was terribly heartbreaking—to my family, I am Jeffrey, not Jeff. When I hear the voice of my relatives say "Jeffrey," I feel the same comfort I feel when I wear an old flannel shirt in winter. It is as if "Jeffrey" is encased in love and reserved for only those who love me unconditionally.

During those last days, Grandpa was only able to acknowledge Grandma Hazel and Aunt Pattie. I came home that summer because I had promised my Uncle Eddie I would return home and help him in the tobacco fields. Because Granddaddy was sick and I was working with my uncle, I stayed either at my maternal aunt's home or with my other grandparents. It was a Sunday morning, I think, when my Aunt Priscilla woke me, saying, "Jeffrey, Mr. Gordon passed away." People will tell you that those who pass are better off, that they are not suffering any longer. All this may be true, but knowing you will never see or speak to them again takes a bit of you away. It is as if your connection to them, especially those you love, becomes weaker in their absence. You depend on that connection to navigate you through life. It is irreplaceable. But you eventually find a way to cope and hopefully replace the loss with another positive, not a negative.

In the days that followed, I thought that moment had truly been the time I had lost him forever, but he has been with me since he left this earthly realm. I cannot turn around today without feeling him standing near me or hearing him whispering to me. According to the Bible, Jesus sits at the Father's right hand, interceding for sinners like me. Indeed, Grandpa may sit at the right hand of Jesus, interceding for his children and grandchildren.

We lived in Mississippi for only a year before relocating to South Carolina. Fortunately, the distance from where I grew up was now only three hours, and we were able to visit Grandma and the other relatives more often.

As time eases like a slow, meandering river, the story that weaves to its destination will be lost with my passing. What is a life lived? What are the memories that form the quilt of our lives? What was the story of this man, who shadows me like a constant vigil in my life? What began as an attempt to understand who Granddaddy was opened a flood of questions surrounding not only him but the community, the people, and the places that have all receded into memory. A past locked in the minds of those who lived it. Unfortunately, with each day, these memories drip, drip into oblivion. There's a part from William Butler Yeats's poem "An Irish Airman Foresees His Death" that comes to my mind repeatedly when I think about Granddaddy: "A waste of breath the years behind in balance with this life, this death."[8] Granddaddy was here for a little over seven decades, but death did not erase his legacy. His life transcends his death, and its reach is still here, reaching out to great-grandchildren he'll never meet. This book is my attempt to remember and honor the memories of another era and other people and other places.

CHAPTER 5
Gordon and Hazel

Gordon Davis Page and Hazel Turbeville were married in September of 1929. He was nineteen, and she was fifteen. Neither one had very much. However, everyone who remembers them would state that Gordon loved Hazel and won her heart away from another suitor, who interestingly became good friends with Gordon and would come by and take pictures of the family they would then give to my grandparents. I have one of those photos. It's of Grandma Hazel on the back porch, clutching her apron with both hands and slightly leaning forward and grinning. My father is standing in the corner of the photo; he's about two years old. Thus, the picture would have been taken in 1947.

Before Gordon and Hazel celebrated their one-month wedding anniversary in 1929, the New York Stock Exchange crashed, setting the tone of their marriage for many decades to come. My grandparents are considered to be among the generation of Americans called the Greatest Generation. Their children would be called the Silent Generation since they matured during the Great Depression, World War II, and then the realism of the Atomic Age. But I think my grandparents are occupying a gray area between these two generations. They lived, as many did in the South, on someone else's land and were fed by the hope they would one day have a more prosperous life for them and their children. Granddaddy did not fight in World War II. Unlike many of the young men of Columbus County, he did not leave for the Pacific or the European theaters of war. He stayed on the Strickland farm and reared his family.

When my grandparents married, they settled near Proctorville, North Carolina, and lived on someone's farm for about a year until they relocated to the Cherry Grove community of Columbus County, North Carolina. Proctorville is in Robeson County, and Hazel's mother, Bertha Hayes, and her mother's people, the Spiveys, lived in Robeson. Thus, I speculate the Turbevilles were in Robeson because of family. Gordon is listed in the household of Shep Turbeville in the 1930 Census. Therefore, the Turbevilles must have been, once again, sharecropping at someone's farm because they are from South Carolina (Marion County family).

Gordon and Hazel relocated, but the Baptist church cemetery will always be home for their infant son who died during childbirth. I visited once when I was older, perhaps ten years old, and found the tombstone. It reads, "Infant Son of Gordon and Hazel Page." That child was never named, but for this book, he will be called Gordon Jr.

On our way to the grave site, Aunt Bobbie, my mother, and I had driven from Fair Bluff through the swamps, which divide Columbus County and Robeson County. Back then, in mid-1970s North Carolina, Highway 905—now Swamp Fox Highway—was a ring of asphalt surrounding cypress trees and hardwoods standing in knee-high brackish black water. This was a surreal place to travel through, and I could not imagine the courage and perseverance of the men who had hacked a path out of this swamp. The effort it took to pave a road through this black-water swamp must've been unreal. As in many things in my life, the work that had preceded my life is not to be taken for granted. William Tecumseh Sherman, during his march through South Carolina and North Carolina, was guided by Lumbee Indians through the swamps of Robeson County and remarked it was the damnedest marching he ever saw.[9]

I have seen these swamps from a canoe on the Lumber River and can attest that back in 1865, crossing them must have been a herculean task. But as General Joe Johnston of the Confederacy remarked upon hearing Sherman was marching at a rate of one dozen miles a day on corduroy roads through the Salkehatchie swamps, there had been "no such army since the days of Julius Caesar."[10]

There still may be many a log laid by Sherman's army, lying encapsulated in the water and mud of those swamps in Robeson County, for they surely must have felled and laid them in order to traverse and bring cannons through this bog. My grandparents' time in Robeson County was not long in duration. They, unlike Sherman, crossed these swamps in a southern direction and moved to the Cherry Grove community outside of Fair Bluff in Columbus County.

During the editing of this story, my dear Aunt Pattie Page Powell was diagnosed with cancer. She had beaten cancer once before, and now it came out of the shadows again with the determination of a bull to take her. She put up a Spartan fight and remained optimistic in her faith, but in the end the cancer took her, thinking it had won. Aunt Pattie said, "Jesus had whipped their cancer at the cross." My wife and I saw her on a Sunday about twelve days before she passed peacefully in her sleep. I had colorized a picture of Gordon and Vanuel and Minnie Edwards Strickland and saw it on the bookshelf. I stated, "Oh, there is that picture." She told me the story once again about that picture. "Vanuel promised Daddy the farm if he stayed and helped him and Minnie, but Uncle Guilford would not have it." From about 1931 until 1952, Gordon and Hazel lived on the Strickland farm in the Cherry Grove community of Columbus County, North Carolina. It was on this farm that my aunts and father were born. My understanding was the Stricklands were childless and had diabetes. In exchange for helping tend to the farm and them, they made a verbal deal with Granddaddy concerning their farm. Sometime before their death in the 1950s, Minnie's relative Guilford Edwards persuaded Vanuel to go to an attorney's office in Tabor City and alter this understanding with written instrument that gave the farm to Guilford. Having no hope of ever acquiring any land, when Granddaddy found out what had taken place, he moved off the farm. Aunt Bobbie stated, "Minnie begged him to stay, but he said, 'I can't,' turned, and walked away as she cried and begged."

Returning to Nathaniel Strickland's farm, the house is no longer there, but I can quickly identify its location by locating Edwards' cemetery and look off to the right-hand side. This farm was the same spot where the Ku Klux Klan once attempted to recruit Granddaddy as a member of their group. According to my Aunt Bobbie Jean, Granddaddy knew who they were under their white hoods and kindly reminded them he "knew them from the Baptist church and wanted no part of their shenanigans."

The South is supposed to be a monolithic block of one culture and one thought. This assumption is false. The only thing Southerners share in common is sweet tea and religion—though that, too, has changed in my lifetime. Those people who showed up at my Granddaddy's house dressed in white had thoughts and actions found not just in the South. Many in the South are wise enough to see such "requirements" are yet another form of oppression. A person should be free to make up their own mind, not be forced into a uniformity of action that impedes the freedom of another person.

When I was very young, no more than ten, Granddaddy Gordon was working on a house near where the Strickland farm was located. If I am not mistaken, it was going to be for some of the Strickland or Edwards family. Granddaddy Gordon was a skilled carpenter, and had he lived in an area where housing was in demand, he could have made a better wage off his carpentry skills as opposed to farming. I recall turning off a paved road onto a dirt one and passing an old farmhouse on the left side of the road, and then traveling down the road though a heavily wooded area until we came to this house under construction. When I later asked Aunt Bobbie about this house, she said it was the Duffy Farm. Apparently, there was a Mr. Duffy, his wife, Narcissi, and Granny Alice who lived in this house. Granny Alice was from Horry County, South Carolina, and her mother was a Strickland. She was the second wife of Guilford Edwards, who was the father of Minnie Edwards Strickland and would have been a grandfather to Guilford Edwards, who was married to my Aunt Clara. It was Guilford who reported the death of Granny Alice in February of 1952. The more I learned about the people and their relations in this community, the more I realized my Granddaddy's hopes to one day own any land there were doomed from the beginning. Anyway, Narcissi called Grandpa Gordon "Harley" instead of "Gordon" and Grandma "Grandma Hesty" instead of "Hazel." Aunt Pattie states Narcissi called her "Becky Mae" and had a name for Aunt Marjorie and Bobbie, which no one can remember. My dad often called Grandma "Hesty" many times before I moved away from Cerro Gordo. So once my aunts moved away, those names were forever forgotten. I did not want "Hesty" to be forgotten, and when I learned of "Harley" and "Becky Mae," I decided to include them all in this book.

CHAPTER 6
Aunt Bobbie, Aunt Marjorie, and Aunt Pattie

Before departing from the community around the Strickland farm, I need to share the story of my aunts: Bobbie, Marjorie, and Pattie. At the least, this is what I know about them.

I have always been very close to Aunt Bobbie and loved her dearly—all my aunts reminded me of my grandparents, and I loved them all. Aunt Bobbie was charming and very smart with numbers, and perhaps, had she not made a rash decision, she could have avoided much heartache. But then again, she would not have had her two boys. What justice is there in a decision when one must weigh the gift of a child with the pain of an abusive husband? Life is not always just or fair, and sometimes, it feels as though our fate was decided on dice being tossed against a wall.

There was a man named Al Jacobs, also known as "Punk," who worked for a laundry service operating from Tabor City. He was a naval veteran and met Aunt Bobbie while he was delivering laundry in the community. He proposed to Aunt Bobbie, and though she was hesitant, she accepted his proposal through the persuasion of a friend who thought this was an opportunity for her to "get off the farm."

I do not believe Aunt Bobbie and Al actually dated in the sense they went on dates as one assumes. Al drove the laundry truck through the community, delivering and picking up laundry, and I think he simply took an interest in Aunt Bobbie and suggested they marry. I am confident Granddaddy would not have allowed her to go on dates since he would not know where she was. She was still in high school in Fair Bluff but rationalized her decision by assuming she would get off the farm, move to the "city," and go to Tabor City High School, which turned out to be right across the street from where she would live.

Hope is just like that, a whispered desire of a future that may or may not grow in fertile ground. Unfortunately, her hope fell on a barren, rocky plain of despair. She told me, "The most significant regret is that I broke Mama and Daddy's hearts when I came home and told them what I had done." Aunt Bobbie had acted without speaking to my grandparents, who now had to accept what she had done as undoable. Their hope had been for her to complete high school, and now here she was, married in the eleventh grade. Some things are better left for Aunt Bobbie to speak of, but I know the marriage ended up not being a good one. She told me she was devastated she did not speak to her parents before she ran off with Al.

I remember Aunt Bobbie coming to visit Granddaddy and Grandma sometime in 1972. Of course, since I lived next door to my grandparents, I always knew who was visiting. My dad had bought a green Chevy van with orange-and-brown shag carpeting, and I recall Aunt Bobbie rode with us to Fair Bluff and was speaking to Dad about the person she had met in Savannah. His name was Herman, and he was an air force retiree from Brooklet, Georgia. Thankfully, he was the polar opposite of Al.

Herman and I have always had fascinating conversations, no matter my age, and I love and respect him. Shortly after graduating from Brooklet High School in Georgia, he volunteered for the army on the closing days of World War II, served occupation duty in Japan, and transferred to the air force when it became an independent military branch in 1947. Herman was a flight engineer and was in one of the first planes to land at Suwon, Korea, after MacArthur's Inchon landing. He was, indeed, a great man and a hero. But he also had two brothers who served in the military, and one of those had participated in the Berlin airlift.

I was fifty before I found all this out and am proud to know the service to America and humanity is associated with my family, because I consider Uncle Herman a blood uncle for the kindness he has shown my dear Aunt Bobbie, or "Bobbie Jean," as he called her. As of this writing, Herman is ninety-five and plays golf on a weekly basis. Bobbie Jean has always been special to me. She would bring me books to read when I was young, which was terrific, as I loved to read. I recall stopping in Atlanta on the way to the basic training and calling her from a pay phone, letting her know I was doing well. She has always been there when I have needed her, and for that, she has been a true gem.

I did not know Aunt Marjorie, but from what I've heard, she was more reserved like the Turbevilles than outgoing like Aunt Pattie, Aunt Bobbie, and Granddaddy. Aunt Marjorie graduated from Fair Bluff High School and was lucky to move to Delaware with Grandma's sister Marie Scott. While there, she met a man named Stephen "Speed" Sapp. I have been told Marjorie worked for AT&T, and when she was transferred back to Lumberton, North Carolina, Speed pursued her. Speed's persistence ultimately reaped success, and he and Aunt Marjorie were married, and she relocated to Delaware until the 1970s when they moved to Charlotte. My memories of Marjorie are of her coming to visit and always driving a Volkswagen Beetle. She had two daughters, Susie and Robbie, who would come at either Christmas or

Thanksgiving. Eventually, at the death of Uncle Speed, Aunt Marjorie moved back to Delaware with Susie and Susie's common-law husband to be near her daughter Robbie and her family.

Aunt Pattie graduated from Cerro Gordo High School and married her school sweetheart Charles Mitchell Powell Sr., and she remained in Cerro Gordo her entire life. During the editing of this story, she sadly passed. My wife and I stopped by to see her one Sunday, and the memory of her I will hold on to happened as I was walking out the door of the house. Her family had placed a bed in the living room of the house, looking out over the windows and into the front yard and the road. Lying from that bed, she shouted out, "I love you, Jeffrey Page." My Aunt Bobbie was on the way home from the hospital herself on the day Aunt Pattie passed. At the funeral, as photos of Aunt Pattie and Aunt Bobbie played across the screen of the church's audiovisual system, I saw them from young girls to high school girls, and then mothers and wives. In James 4:14, the Bible compares life to a vapor. How true. But my hope rests in Jesus that when my time comes, she and the others will meet me and take me to see Jesus. When I was young, Cerro Gordo was what I knew of a town, and I thought it always impressive to ride by the Baptist and Methodist churches on the way to Williamson's Cross Roads, where my mother's people lived. Uncle Mitchell and Aunt Pattie lived at Powell's Crossing, just across from West Columbus High School. She reminds me of Grandpa Gordon in many ways. She has been a very dear person to me and treated me as one of her children. She would always include me in things she would do with her sons.

Once, when I was in the eighth grade, there was a dance at the Cerro Gordo Elementary School gym, and I met a girl there. She had asked me to come, and I wanted to go until the moment Aunt Pattie tried to drop me off. I clung to the car door and would not let go despite Aunt Pattie's pleas and that young girl waiting for me inside. Eventually, I was allowed back inside the car, and Aunt Pattie said something like, "I do declare, I don't know what I am going to do with you."

At that same gym, she had dropped me off with my cousins Mark and Kale so we could try out for the church basketball team. After several rounds of running up and down the court, I ran right out the gym door and walked the short distance to Aunt Pattie's house. As incredible as it seems, the Cerro Gordo team wore green-and-yellow socks, which resembled the Green Bay Packers' colors. All I had were white socks, and I did not want to ask for the money from my parents to buy the colored socks. Moreover, there was the cost of tennis shoes, uniforms, and getting to and from the games. When the coach had us running up and down the gym to the point of exhaustion, I thought to myself, *I am not getting paid to do this, and I will have to spend money I do not have. Plus, I will never be any good at basketball.* All these conclusions led me right out the gym door and on my way back to Aunt Pattie's house. When I walked in the house, Aunt Pattie said, "I don't know what to do with you." I never did play high school sports, but I don't feel as if I missed out on anything.

CHAPTER 7
Moving to Cedar Grove

In 1952, Gordon and Hazel packed up their belongings in a wagon, moved to the Cedar Grove community, and lived on Monroe Powell's farm. Cedar Grove is about six miles from where they had lived in the Cherry Grove community. This place, now called Blackwell Road, is where I was conceived. My parents moved into the front bedroom of the old house since it was the largest room. Fifty years later, I visited the house where I was conceived, and the roof had caved in on the house, but the front bedroom was somewhat intact. I took a chain saw and cut through the debris until I was able to get to the door of the room. I then pulled out the door and took the doorknob off, taking it back home with me to keep as a memento. I am in possession of several photos, both black and white and color, from when my grandparents stayed at this house from 1952 to 1968. At the time, the road along the house was known by a number, but today, it is called Blackwell Road, most likely because Mr. Monroe's wife was a Blackwell, and I think the farm may have come from her family, though I don't know for sure. Many Blackwells lived on the road, and the Powells and Blackwells married into each other, producing many double cousins.

Mom married while in the eleventh grade when she was seventeen and Dad was nineteen. They married at Macedonia Baptist Church, and the witnesses were my Grandma Ara Mae and my mom's sister Iris and friend Evelyn McCloskey. Mom moved to Cerro Gordo, drove the distance to the high school in Evergreen, and graduated. I am very proud of her for not dropping out of school and for making an effort to complete high school. Mr. Monroe was, perhaps, one of the most generous of the men Granddaddy worked for during his life. He only wanted 50 percent of the profits of the tobacco sale, and Granddaddy could keep the money off the peanuts and the corn. Most landowners at that time in Columbus County took what Vanuel Strickland had taken, which was 50 percent of all the crops. They lived on this farm until 1968 when Mr. Monroe sold Granddaddy an acre of land. He, in turn, gave Dad half an acre to build a house on, and these are where most of the memories I have as a young boy, until I started working in the tobacco fields during the summer, take place. Most of the lumber used to construct Granddaddy's house was obtained from the Military Ocean Terminal Sunny Point (MOTSU) on the Cape Fear River in Wilmington, North Carolina. The MOTSU is one of the largest military terminals in the world, serving as a transfer point for trucks, rail, and ships importing and exporting army ammunition, equipment, and explosives.

Cape Fear kindles thoughts of dangerous swamps among black water and cypress trees canopied in Spanish moss. However, when Englishman William Hilton arrived in the area in 1662, initially, the Cape Fear River was called the Charles River, then the Cape Fear River, and subsequently corrupted to Cape Fear. Hilton was not the first European to have arrived in the area, as both the French under

Giovanni da Verrazano (1524) and Spanish (1526) had prospected the site for a settlement. Upon Hilton's return to the Cape Fear River in 1663 and since that time, the English maintained a presence in the area sporadically until defeating the pirates and natives. It was to the same banks of Cape Fear where Granddaddy and my father traveled with a trailer to haul off lumber from shipping containers, then disassemble and stack them neatly in rows.

During the Vietnam War, six ships were loaded with supplies and ammunition every day. The rule was you bought the stack of lumber that had been set aside by the workers at the facility. Once the stacks of lumber were complete, you were not allowed to purloin selected pieces of wood from other stacks, nor could you add anything from any lumber lying around. If you did this, it resulted in unloading the lumber you may have had on your trailer and leaving as you had arrived: empty. Granddaddy was keen to observe the rules, as it had taken him fifty-eight years to own a house. He passed this lesson of rules on to me. He would say, "The Man makes the rules because he is in a position to do so. If you follow them, you will stay out of trouble. You should only break the rules knowing there may be severe consequences and be ready to face them."

In my fifty-three years of life, I have been fortunate to have owned five homes. I have a brief memory of building Granddaddy's house, but I was only three, and that memory consists of a small hammer Granddaddy gave me to pound on some wood. The house he built eventually became a refuge I retreated to when things did not go as I thought they would. Anytime there was an argument between my mother and father, I told Mom I was running away from home and would do so by going to Granddaddy Gordon's house. If I was hungry, I would go to Grandma Hazel's, and she would prepare something to eat for me. She liked to hide chewing gum and put it where I could not reach it in an upper cabinet. I knew where it was, as she would always catch me pulling a chair over to the counter to stand on in an attempt to get the gum. She would scold me and say, "You cannot chew the whole pack at one time." Then she would hand me one piece. The other thing that lingers in my memory is when she baked homemade biscuits, which was often since Granddaddy Gordon had to have them with every meal. She would let me eat the small balls of dough that remained in the biscuit pan. Something that was interesting about Grandma was she caught rainwater and used it to put in her iron. The few times it snowed back home, she would make snow cream but said since the Atomic Age, she was afraid to eat it because they had blown up so many bombs in the atmosphere, and eating snow would kill us. Thus, the knowledge of the Atomic Age was impressed upon me because I knew it had made snow polluted to the point where it could not be eaten.

Granddaddy's house was the place I returned to as I witnessed Grandma slowly recede beneath the square glass window as she seemed to shrink in height as she aged. I spent many a night there and would sleep in the red bedroom, as it was called due to the carpet being red. This house was where Grandma taught me the Lord's Prayer as she stood over the bed and recited it to me before I fell asleep. In the backyard, there were two pecan trees Granddaddy had planted in the hopes of one day having pecans. Unfortunately, the trees did not anticipate his death thirteen years later, and he left them still reaching for the sky and maturity.

Grandma Hazel's brother Lee Berry Turbeville and his wife, Aunt Ethel, lived next door to my grandparents. Our three houses were lined up, one next to the other. Uncle Lee had several outbuildings, two tobacco barns, and often, a new car under the carport. Dad always said Uncle Lee found some money in an abandoned house and was able to buy the farm he owned. Of course, there may not be any truth to this story, but the reality is Lee and Ethel moved from, I think, South Carolina and bought a farm. This seems incredulous, but it needs to be understood that the South lost the Civil War, and there were marauding Union troops and Confederate deserters throughout the South in the waning months of the war in 1865. It is very plausible that some farmer or a person of means may have hidden away their gold or silver to be discovered by a fortunate person at some point in the future. My Uncle Eddie rented land from an elderly woman in the 1970s, and she told him her mother told her stories of the trains passing through Cerro Gordo on the way to Wilmington, carrying cannons, food, ammunition, and other supplies during the war. Thus, the area of Columbus County, while not seeing battles during the war, did contribute and saw activity as a result of the war.

From what I remember, Ethel and Lee seemed to have been better off financially than we were. They had a rather large family, and many would visit during the holidays or summer on their way to Myrtle Beach, South Carolina. Once, their daughter, Peggy, stopped by during one of these visits and brought her three daughters with her—two were older than me, and one younger. This was over fifty years ago, but I recall walking around the house with the youngest daughter, and I seemingly made the error of picking some of Aunt Ethel's flowers, resulting in an angry phone call to Grandma Hazel, and I never again played with anyone who visited Aunt Ethel's. According to my mother, she also received a call from Grandma Hazel, which was why she made sure I did not go to Aunt Ethel's house again. The visits to Aunt Ethel's house continued for other family members, and when the children would play in the yard, I would just stand in Grandma Hazel's yard and watch the visitors come and go from Aunt Ethel's house but never dared to venture over there. I am not sure what was said to me to make this place some verboten hell, but it must have been a powerful mojo. I never returned to their house unless I was with Grandma or Grandpa Gordon until after I had moved away from Columbus County.

When I returned to visit Grandma, I would see them sitting in a swing beneath the shade of pine trees. Uncle Lee had this yellow cat that seemed to be as old as the mountains and would always be there. When I would venture over to speak to them for a few moments, the cat would rub against my pants leg, and I thought, *Boy, this is the same thing this cat did, or one like him, back when I was a small boy.*

I wanted them to know I was no longer afraid to cross the no-man's-land that was marked by their pine trees on the edge of the yard. I realize this seems trivial, but let me tell you a quick story to illustrate this point. When my dad began to play golf years ago, I borrowed his clubs one day and was practicing out in the front yard. When I hit the ball with one of the woods, it literally sailed past Granddaddy's house and landed in Uncle Lee's yard. I was so fearful to go over there, the golf ball ended up remaining exactly where it had fallen. I never retrieved it, nor did I hit any more of Dad's golf balls since I would have to explain why all of them were in Uncle Lee's yard. I cannot gather the words to describe what it was like to know there is a place where you are so unwelcome—especially a relative's home. Perhaps I was a hellion … I do not know the reasons why, but the memories of this have not diminished over five decades.

As Uncle Lee progressed in age and then became ill, Aunt Ethel realized she did not know how to drive. This presented some harsh realities. In the event there was an emergency, who would drive them to the hospital? If Uncle Lee died, then how would Aunt Ethel get around? Grandma Hazel lived next door, but she did not know how to drive either. When I was young and growing up in Cerro Gordo, there were many women in the community who did not know how to drive. For a man, the finances of owning a car was the chief obstacle to knowing how to drive. My grandfather did not own his first car until the 1950s, and even then, it was a used one. Thus, Grandma Hazel never had the finances nor the car to learn such a skill. When the husbands passed, many women were left to their own fate if they did not have any family living nearby to drive them places. Thankfully, Aunt Pattie was always there to help Grandma Hazel, and eventually, she mastered driving a small truck and obtained her driver's license. I think that was a huge accomplishment for someone her age.

Of all the children Uncle Lee and Aunt Ethel had, none of them stayed near home. Dad once stated that the only one who may have was Michael. I never knew Michael, though, since I was three when he passed. I first became aware of Michael Turbeville when my brother Patrick passed away, because Michael's tombstone was adjacent to Patrick's at Powell's Cemetery. I later learned that one day in 1968, Uncle Lee came to Dad's house and asked him to help Michael. Dad was a little perplexed but went with Uncle Lee. As they walked down the field, Dad saw Michael lying on the ground with a pail of milk spilled out around him. Apparently, a thunderstorm had come and gone in a minute, and the one time lightning flashed during the storm, it had sadly struck and killed Michael.

Grandpa kept his Farmall tractor under Uncle Lee's barn, and it was with Grandpa that I ever again found myself over there. Thus, my first fifteen years of life were spent on a dirt road named Blackwell, roaming the distance of an acre of land between my house, Grandpa's house, and very rarely, Uncle Lee's home. Occasionally, I may have ventured a bit farther on my bicycle but never far from the eyesight of one of these houses. The two towns that occupied most of my youth were Cerro Gordo and Fair Bluff. Thus, it is there I shall begin.

CHAPTER 8
Where Are We from, Granddaddy?

Both Granddaddy and Grandma were circumspect concerning any family history. They rarely spoke of anything about the past. Their reluctance to share anything with me was very disappointing, as I had developed a keen interest in history during the sixth grade. I did persuade Grandma to sew me a family flag out of some red, blue, and white cloth, with three red stars in the middle of the white field. This was shortly after I read the biography on Napoleon, and the French flag was easy to replicate. Grandma said I needed to make it my own, and she suggested adding three red stars to the center. She had plenty of red cloth, and had there been an abundance of any other color, the stars could have been blue. Any information concerning my ancestry was shrouded in mystery. I could not progress any further in the past beyond the town of Boardman on the Lumber River or some vague mentions of Virginia. Granddaddy confessed his family lived a short time in Boardman when his father, Daniel Return, worked at the lumber mill there. I have a photo of the family standing in front of a three-room house in about 1913 that is evidence of their stay there. But the fact is both his parents had deep roots in Tabor City, North Carolina, and Loris, South Carolina, though both Daniel Return's mother and Anna Elizabeth's parents' identities were something that would lie undiscovered until I was in my fifties.

Later, through genetic testing, I discovered I am 50 percent English, 19 percent Scottish, 19 percent Welsh, 10 percent Irish, and 2 percent Norwegian. This assessment was seemingly confirmed when I had a much more expensive test performed by the Levine Cancer Center. The Levine test showed I was a carrier for a gene responsible for hereditary hemochromatosis. The C282Y gene is located on the short arm of the sixth chromosome at 6p21.3, which regulates iron retention. The mutation typically occurs in northern European descent and affects one out of four hundred individuals and was only discovered in 1996. The modification of the gene usually does not manifest itself in men until their fifties and in women until their sixties, as menstruation acts as a natural removal of excessive iron.

According to an article I found in *Irish America*, this condition has been referred to as the Celtic Curse, Irish Illness, Scottish Sickness, and the British Gene. Researchers conclude the mutation took place among Gaelic people to conserve iron because they lacked iron in their diet. The C282Y gene mutation is linked to either a Viking or an Irish individual seventy to ninety generations ago.[11] Thankfully, only 1 percent of individuals will develop clinical features of hemochromatosis. My research into the origins of the C282Y gene mutation is supported by the Ancestry DNA test results, which report Irish, Scottish, and Swedish ancestry. I found a study in the *Daily Mail* which cites a report carried out by Britain's DNA. This article discussed a study that analyzed the Y chromosome passed from father to son, which led to the discovery that a substantial percentage of Scotland and northern England still carry the blood of Viking raiders, who first set ashore on the British Isles around AD 970. For instance, the Shetland Islands are as high as 29.2 percent, North West Scotland at 9.9 percent, and Wales as little as 1 percent.[12] Furthering the results of both DNA tests I have done, this also confirms that since 85 percent of mine is British, there is a large percentage of the Germanic Anglo-Saxons in my lineage. An article in *New Scientist* confirms that 10–40 percent of their DNA is present in half of modern Britons.[13] Another study in *Nature* confirms there is not a single Gaelic group but instead genetically differentiated subgroups.[14]

On Grandma Hazel's family line, the Turbeville family may be part of the Norman invasion that conquered England in 1066. Payn "the Demon" de Turbeville was one of the Twelve Knights of Glamorgan, who built Coity Castle and assisted Robert Fitz Harmon in the conquest of Wales. The legend of the Twelve Knights was built upon an actual person who lived during the Norman conquest of Wales. Still, English historians, most notably Sir Edward Stradling (1529–1609), question the credibility of such an organization. Nonetheless, the possibility of such a connection is intriguing and seems to be validated by the DNA test.

One of the more exciting stories of the Turbevilles is a ghostly coach that crosses a bridge to Woolbridge Manor, Dorset, and only those with the Turbeville name can see it. The coach contains the spirits of John Turbeville of Woolbridge and his fiancée, Ann, daughter of Thomas Howard, Viscount of Howard of Binden, on their elopement. Perhaps a trip to Woolbridge is needed to reveal if I retain enough Turbeville blood to see the spirits of John and Ann sprinting across the bridge. The Viscount of Howard's eldest sons, Henry Howard and Thomas, were the second and third Viscounts, respectively, but both died childless and without a male heir, and the line became extinct in 1611. Honestly, this story may all be fanciful conjecture.

As far as I know, the Turbevilles showed up in Boston and Somerset, Massachusetts. Somerset was settled in 1677 on the Shawomet lands and was officially incorporated in 1790. The town was named for Somerset Square in Boston, which was named for the county of Somerset in England. However, from what I have gathered, both William John and Sarah Pinney Turbeville appear to be from Worcestershire, England, in the West Midlands. I have no record of their voyage across the Atlantic, but apparently, the family migrated to Virginia and then wound up in the coastal part of South Carolina. Concerning the Turbevilles, it may be worth noting that Absolam Benjamin "A. B." Turbeville was a private in Hatch's Coastal Regiment and was at Appomattox when Robert E. Lee surrendered to Ulysses Grant. Absolam survived the war and returned to farming in Horry County, South Carolina, and Columbus County, North Carolina. Absolam Benjamin Turbeville and his wife, Sarah Jane Arnette, reared eleven children: James Richard, Asa, George, Neal B., Sarah Elizabeth Alice Rebecca, John Walter, Adella Della, my great-grandfather Sheppard, David E., David Devon, and Fred.

The only visit I have made to Fort Fisher was over a decade ago in 2005. I sat on the rocks on the shore in perfect tranquility with the sea splashing against my feet. I had no thoughts that two of my ancestors had been here attempting to keep the Port of Wilmington open to blockade runners critical in supplying the Army of Northern Virginia. Sarah Jane Arnette Turbeville's father, Cade Arnette, was at Wilmington, North Carolina, during the war and died during the second battle of Fort Fisher. Fort Fisher was referred to as the Gibraltar of the South and the last major coastal stronghold of the Confederacy in the waning days of the Civil War.[15] The Union bombardment by Rear Admiral David D. Porter must have indeed seemed like hell had opened and poured its fury out on the earthen fort made of dirt and sand. In the end, the Union army and navy carried the assault.

The fall of Fort Fisher was the nail in the coffin of the Confederacy and for Nathaniel Strickland. Nathaniel served with the Confederate navy from 1861 to 1864. While home on leave, he heard his son Alston had suffered a leg wound in the first battle of Fort Fisher. Confederate commanders determined Nathaniel was a nondisabled man and impressed him into service in defense of the fort. When the fort fell in January of 1865, both were captured by the Union army. Initially, both were sent to Point Lookout, but Nathaniel was later moved to Elmira, New York. Nathaniel Strickland eventually died of pneumonia at the Union prisoner-of-war camp in Elmira, New York. This camp equaled the squalor and death rate of the notorious Confederate prisoner-of-war camp at Andersonville, Georgia. Originally known as Camp Rathbun and Designated Camp No. 3 during its existence from summer 1864 until the end of the war, this camp housed approximately twelve thousand Confederate enlisted men. About three thousand men died here. Nathaniel Strickland, some Williamson cousins, and many of the men captured at Fort Fisher are buried at Woodlawn Cemetery in Elmira.

Another relative who served in Wilmington and Fort Fisher was Return Strong Worley. At age forty-one, he volunteered for duty and was enlisted as a private in Company D of the Second Artillery, Thirty-Sixth North Carolina Troops on March 13, 1862. Return Strong Worley appears on a list of sick prisoners at Point Lookout, Maryland, and he was paroled after signing an oath of allegiance to the United States on June 3, 1965. Interestingly, he is described as being five foot nine inches tall and having hazel eyes, which is my exact height and eye color. Grandma Ara Mae's eyes were the same color too.

The conditions at the prisoner-of-war camp in Elmira were hell. While the weather was mild during summer and fall, in its first year, approximately nine hundred prisoners were without housing until early January. Prison records show that men died from typhoid fever, dysentery, and pneumonia, as well as malnutrition. The Confederates lacked adequate rations and medical care thanks to insufficient medical supplies. Prisoners infected with smallpox were often moved to a remote location and forgotten. It was not uncommon to see a frozen body lying outside a tent, waiting to be loaded for transportation to the cemetery. Another contributing factor to the problem of disease was a stagnant pool known as Foster's Pond. This pond stood between the camp and the river.[16]

According to the book *Fort Fisher to Elmira: The Fatal Journey of 518 Confederate Soldiers* by Richard H. Triebe, about 1,154 men were sent to Elmira Prison in Elmira, New York. Other Union prison camps received prisoners from Fort Fisher. Of those, 639 were sent to Point Lookout Prison, Maryland, 97 were sent to Fort Columbus Prison in New York Harbor, 61 were sent to Fort Delaware Prison, Delaware, and 22 were sent to Fort Morgan Prison, Virginia. The Union navy ships used to transport the prisoners were *California*, *DeMolay*, *General Lyon*, and *North Point*. There were 1,121 Confederate soldiers sent to Elmira from Fort Fisher. Of those, 761 or 68 percent of the men were "Tar Heel" North Carolina soldiers, 357 were from South Carolina, and 4 were Confederate marines. Out of the 1,121 Confederate soldiers sent to Elmira, 518 or 46 percent would die within five months. The major causes of death at Elmira were pneumonia, diarrhea, and smallpox.[17] The youngest Fort Fisher man to be sent to Elmira was seventeen-year-old Private William H. Faulk of Company E, Thirty-Sixth Regiment, Second North Carolina Artillery. He was fifteen years old when he enlisted at Columbus County, North Carolina, on February

9, 1863. He was exchanged on the James River in Virginia on March 2, 1865. There were also many Williamsons captured at Fort Fisher, among them was Joshua Robert Williamson, who died there. More than likely, William H. Faulk was also a distant relative, first cousin five times removed.[18]

Another ancestor, Cade Arnette, possibly became a casualty of the Yellow Fever epidemic—not a Union bullet—which swept Wilmington during this time. I have been unable to pin down exactly how he died. He is buried at Oakdale Cemetery in Wilmington, North Carolina. His son Benjamin, who was sixteen at the time of his father's death, also died in 1864. Cade's wife, Elizabeth Barfield, had roughly sixteen children, and among them was Sarah "Sallie" Jane Arnette, who married Absolam Benjamin "A.B." Turbeville, my great-great-grandfather. Alston Strickland went to Camp Lookout, Maryland, and after taking the Oath of Allegiance, was released on July 25, 1865. He died many years after the war, alone in the woods, when the wound he received at Fort Fisher opened up, and he bled to death.[19] Family lore holds that a neighbor heard him hollering in the woods for help as he bled out.

One of the females who married into the Turbeville line was Susannah Saunders, who married Charles Turbeville. In *A History of Marion County, South Carolina, from Its Earliest Times to the Present, 1901*, William Sellers notes the Saunders name but states that in 1900, it had become extinct in Marion County. He further notes that the family came from England. He relates a story many in America today seem to have all but forgotten in the seven-days-a-week retail sales and business as usual, even on Sunday.[20] One of the Saunders was cutting a cypress tree in the swamp on a Sunday, and when it fell, it hit an ash tree. The collision resulted in the ash violently falling and hitting Mr. Saunders in the head, killing him instantly. Afterward, an ash sprouted beside his tombstone. The family took it as a sign of the fate of anyone who violates the commandment to rest on Sunday, as it is reserved for God. Susannah and Charles Turbeville's son, named either Absolam or Solomon, was listed as killed during the Revolutionary War. His wife, named either Lucy White or Lucy Windham, when she filed a widow's pension claim after the war, stated he was killed by the British in 1782. Absolam, or Solomon, is listed in Bobby G. Moss's *Roster of South Carolina Patriots in the American Revolution*.

The Turbevilles seemed to have large families, but the two I know best were Uncle Lee Berry Turbeville and Aunt Clara Turbeville Edwards. Uncle Lee is discussed late in the story, as I saw him most often since he lived only a few hundred feet from where I grew up. Aunt Clara, as I was taught to call her, married Guilford Edwards Sr. They lived in the Cherry Grove community, not far from the South Carolina state line. I made several visits to her house with Grandma and Granddaddy when I was young, and I remember these trips well because she had a long driveway we could enter on either side of the yard. The way it was always lined with trees and a patch of lush green grass seemed to make a statement of order and maintenance, as if it were a mini castle. When we would reach the house, sitting under the carport was a 1963 Corvette that belonged to one of Aunt Clara's sons—she had an extensive family, and I cannot recall the name of the son; however, that car was a shining jewel I certainly took a liking to. She had a screen porch you entered before going into the main house. Aunt Clara would always be sitting in her chair ... seriously, I do not recall her moving about very much. Grandma and Aunt Clara seemed to be best friends as well as sisters when they spoke to one another. Their closeness was clearly evident because Grandma Hazel rarely laughed, but when she was with Aunt Clara, she seemed to be less reserved than she was by nature and instinct. Before Grandma passed away in 2000, I asked her about Aunt Clara, and she said, "I love Clara, but she could always pick more cotton than I could." I found this remark interesting since Grandma married at age fifteen, and it was many decades since she and Clara had picked any cotton.

The other intriguing aspect of Aunt Clara is the tone of her skin. There has been much speculation concerning any other blood in the Turbevilles other than English. The only instance of this I have discovered is photos of Uncle Asa's wife, Fannie Jane Israel, and her mother, Amanda Taylor. Amanda was from Robeson County, North Carolina, which has a large population of Lumbee Indians. Amanda is listed as "Indian" on the 1900 Census of White House Township, Union City Town. However, in 1880, she was listed as the spouse of Allen Jones, age 23, with Fannie Israel (15), Monroe Israel (10), Catherine Jones (2), and Vance Jones (1), who are all listed as "Black." In the death certificates of Catherine and Vance, it again states "Indian." Such is the multiculturalism and ethnic diversity of Robeson County, with 38 percent of the population identifying as Lumbee Indian in the 2010 Census.[21]

Of the Turbevilles, my dear Aunt Bobbie states Clara was like a mother to her, and she and the other two Page daughters grew up with her children as if they were siblings. Perhaps this is the source of much speculation, but it does not put to rest the questions, as Aunt Clara would not have been affected by her uncle's marriage. My dad, on the other hand, states, "They never liked me." Such are the branches of a tree. The most interesting aspect of Asa Turbeville, brother of Shep, is he was related to a dear person I spent a year dating named Donise. In researching this, I learned Donise was the third great-granddaughter of Asa, which would have made us distant cousins.

At this juncture, considering the Turbeville association with the Lumbee Indians, I feel it is appropriate to share the story of Henry

Berry Lowry. He and Nathaniel Strickland, my ancestor, share an unexpected connection that unites them for a moment in time like two grapes on a vine. Both were victims of the unintended consequences of the Civil War—Nathaniel screened who was simply seeking to rescue his sick son, and Henry and his people, who were suffering from the class system in Robeson County, which imposed dictates on the Lumbee they did not want. In my eyes, both were asked to take part in a war started by a small percentage of Southerners at the ultimate expense of the entire population. Much like any war, those who run headlong into the conflict often tend to drag everyone else down with them. Henry, moreover, escaped from the jail in Columbus County in 1866. Thus, his exploits are worthy of inclusion in my story since he traveled the same area. Nathaniel was impressed into service while visiting his son at Fort Fisher. Similarly, Henry's kin and fellow Lumbee Indians were being rounded up and impressed into service for labor gangs in the lower Cape Fear River region. Henry claimed to be Tuscarora, but Fannie Jane Israel and Amanda Taylor may have been a mix of White and Native American.[22]

During the Civil War, impressment gangs roamed Robeson County, seizing Lumbee Indians and forcing them into service for the Confederacy, building earthen works at Fort Fisher and other construction works. In response to the impressment, the Lumbee did as they knew best and retreated into the swamps. Since the European settlement in Robeson County, the natives had been pushed into the swamps, and the swamps became a refuge, similar to how Sherwood Forest was to Robin Hood's band in England. In the face of legislation which banned Lumbee from owning firearms, the Lumbee squirreled them away and prepared for a fight. Henry was only eighteen at the time and, perhaps encouraged by the success of General Sherman, formed the Lowry Gang and fought back. The Confederate Home

Guard was charged with keeping the Lumbee under control. Henry's father, Allen, was accused of stealing hogs by James P. Barnes. Allen's son Henry killed Barnes on December 21, 1864, and subsequently a conscription officer, James Brantley Harris, on January 15, 1865, for abusing female Lowry family members. In March 1865, the Confederate Home Guard searched Allen Lowry's home and found firearms, which free people of color had been forbidden to own since after 1831. After convening a kangaroo court and finding Allen and his son, William, guilty, they were executed in March 1865. Eighteen-year-old Henry is alleged to have watched this hidden in some bushes. Henry swore revenge as a result of this sham justice.

Moreover, it seemed the Lowry family had an ongoing dispute with Harris. Harris had ambushed and killed Henry's first cousin Jarman Lowry and never was charged with his murder. He also was instrumental in the efforts to seize Jarman's brothers, Allen and Wesley, on a charge of evading service. Both, subsequently, turned up missing and then dead. After the killing of Harris on January 15, 1865, the Lowry Gang robbed guns and cash from the Robeson County Courthouse, and then Henry simply vanished.[23]

Henry represents sectionalism, which was, in my opinion, the Civil War *within* the Civil War. This sectionalism, or division of loyalty, may be as much responsible for the Confederate defeat as Grant's or Sherman's armies. When President Lincoln transformed the rebellion to the question of slavery, and with only 3 percent of the South owning any significant number of slaves, he sowed the seeds of division that existed before and during the war. In West Virginia, the mountains of North Carolina and Tennessee were repeated in areas populated by poor Whites and people like the Lowrys. Both, to varying degrees, were abused and used by the plantation aristocracy. Yet today, the South and its people are routinely lumped together like a behemoth of like-minded giants. In researching this book, I came across a book written by *New York Herald* correspondent George Alfred Townsend. His work is titled *The Swamp Outlaws, or, The North Carolina Bandits: Being a Complete History of the Modern Rob Roys and Robin Hoods*. It was written in 1872, in which Townsend describes Henry in the following way:

> Henry Berry Lowry, the leader of the most formidable band of outlaws, considering the smallness of its numbers that has been known in this country is of mixed Tuscarora, mulatto, and white blood, twenty-six years of age, five feet nine inches high and weighing about one hundred fifty pounds.
>
> He has straight black hair, like an Indian, a dark goatee, and a beard graceful in shape but too thin to look very black. His face slopes from the cheekbones to the tip of his goatee to give him the Southern American contour of physiognomy, but it is lighted with eyes of a different color—eyes of a grayish hazel—at times appearing light blue with a drop of brown in them, but in agitation dilating, darkening, and, although never quite losing the appearance of a smile, yet in action, it is a smile of devilish nature. His forehead is good, and his face and expression refined—remarkably so, considering his mixed-race, want of education, and long career of lawlessness.
>
> A scar of crescent shape and black color lies in the skin below his left eye, said to have been made by an iron pot falling upon him when a child. His voice is sweet and pleasant, and in his manner, there is nothing self-important or swaggering. He is not talkative, listens quietly, and searches out whoever is speaking to him like a

man illiterate in all books save the two great books of nature and human nature above all. The color of his skin is of a whitish-yellow sort, with a mixture of copper—such skin as, for the nature of its components, is in color indescribable, there being no negro blood in it except that of a far remote generation of mulatto, and the Indian still apparent. It is enough to say of this skin that it seems to suffer little change by heat or cold, exposure or sickness, suitable housing, or wild weather. The very relatives of the white men who were killed by Henry Berry Lowry admitted to me that "he is one of the most handsome mulattoes you ever saw."[24]

Before I began my research, I was unaware of the family connections I had in Robeson County. Through the swamp that straddles the Robeson and Columbus County line in North Carolina, there was a rich history of family connections in the Marietta community and across the state line in South Carolina. On a journey through this area, I came across Page Circle Road, Bear Swamp Baptist Church, which was filled with many tombstones with the Page name, and other family connections in cemeteries with unmarked graves, such as Jesse Spivey (a grandfather). Thus, many of my ancestors would have lived contemporarily with Henry Berry Lowry and his exploits.

CHAPTER 9
Worley and Williamson

Of course, the Pages were not the only grandparents I left behind in Columbus County when I moved to Mississippi. My mom's parents, Joseph "Pa Joe" Williamson and Ara Mae Worley of Princess Ann Road in Tatum Township, were still living, and my summers had been spent at their house working in the tobacco fields.

Pa Joe used to keep hogs at Mr. Ed Hammond's farm. I recall going there with him many times when I was young. Back then, it was as if stepping through a portal to another world. The hogs were kept fenced in near a swampy area, but during their delivery of piglets, they were moved and kept in a hog house. Pa Joe did not have the standard white hogs commercial farms raise today. Rather, he had heritage breeds like the Berkshire, Duroc, Hampshire, and Tamworth. Every November, there would be six to eight of these hogs stretched out on a pole, hanging from a crossbar. Sometimes, it is better not to have the image of where bacon comes from to continue to enjoy eating it. I was traumatized by the razor sliding against the male piglets' gonads and the casual way they were tossed into a bucket to be delivered to the older man down the road who fired and ate them.

Ara Mae Worley Williamson
While I still find my thoughts lingering on Williamson's Cross Roads, I should pay a visit to my relatives who lived in the Cherry Grove community that borders the state line between South Carolina and North Carolina. Most are buried at Cherry Grove Baptist Church, located on Swamp Fox Road. I begin first with my grandmother, Ara Mae Worley Williamson. Ara Mae was born on October 26, 1921, to Bruce Eddie Worley, "Poppi," and Dalmas Cotas Strickland Worley, whom Mom and everyone called "Goggama." Grandma Ara Mae would state Decoutapeg as a name too, but this was Ara Mae being Ara Mae. Dalmas's father was Moody Strickland, and her mother was Arabella Grainger, a descendant of John Grainger. Moody Strickland's father was Brazil—or maybe Braswell—Strickland, and his mother was Latitia Strickland. The Worleys were descendants of Nicholas Worley, who originated in Duplin County, North Carolina. As is the case with many of the other families in Columbus County, the origins of the Worleys prior to their arrival in North Carolina are in Virginia. In my research, I have found they, too, migrated first to Alabama, then to Mississippi, and then to Texas.

Brazil, or Braswell, entered Confederate service with the Eighteenth Infantry Regiment Company C on April 24, 1861, in Whiteville, North Carolina. He is listed as being six foot, three inches tall, with light hair and blue eyes. He was wounded at the battle of Hanover Courthouse on May 27, 1862, during the Peninsula Campaign. He first appears on a list of injured in the Gaines's Hospital at Gaines' Mill, Virginia, on June 5, 1862, and then, later, was admitted to a Union hospital at Chesapeake on June 18, 1862, and later sent to Fort

Delaware. Subsequently, he appears on a list of Confederate prisoners on the steamer *Katskill*. On August 5, 1862, he was exchanged by a detachment of New York Volunteers at Aiken's Landing, Virginia.

The Worleys may be traced back to England and Edward and Mary Worley. Their son, Nicolas Sr., was born about 1711, and his wife was Ann Gray, whom he married in about 1750. Nicholas Worley Sr. of York County, Virginia, moved into Edgecombe County, North Carolina, about 1739. He purchased land from Joseph Sims, which had previously been patented by Barnaby McKinnie Jr. He sold the land to Alexander McCulloch in 1755. He was a neighbor of Lodwick Alford. Ann Gray Worley's will was probated in Duplin County, North Carolina, in 1795. Nicolas Worley Jr. was born about 1755. He is listed on the tax list of Duplin County in 1783, along with his mother, Ann. He moved to Bladen County about 1800 and found himself in Columbus County when it was created in 1808. Some list his wife as Patience McKinnie, but the Worley family holds his wife was Patience Strong. Geological researcher Jason Bordeaux has shown that she was not a McKinnie, so perhaps the Worley family is correct in that it was Patience Strong.[25] Her father was perhaps Return Strong, who was granted a land grant in Gapway Swamp between Tabor City and the Cherry Grove Community. Nicholas Worley Jr. and Patience's child was Elijah, who married Charity Ann Coleman. One of their children was Return Strong Worley, who married Helen Amanda Coleman, who had Bruce Eddie Worley. Bruce Eddie Worley married Dalmas Cotas Strickland, who had Ara Mae Worley, twin of William Gray Worley. Ara Mae is my mother, Dollie's, mother. Interestingly, Return Strong leaves few male descendants to be traced in Columbus County, but his other daughter, Elizabeth Mary Strong, sister of Patience Strong, married David Page Jr. of either Lake View, South Carolina, or the Marietta Community in Robeson County,

North Carolina. Interesting enough, both sisters Elizabeth Mary Strong and Patience Strong would reconnect six generations later with me and my sister, Kimberly, their descendants.

It was said that Ara Mae met my Grandpa Joseph "Pa Joe" Nathan Williamson while he was selling moonshine to her relatives. I do not know if there is any truth to this, as earlier Williamsons had married into the families of the Cherry Grove community. The distance between the Cross Roads and Cherry Grove community, where Ara Mae was born and reared, is about fifteen miles. I can only speculate there may be truth to this claim. Ara Mae's family had a proud history of being descendants of Nicholas Worley; they owned a prosperous farm, and she was, perhaps, one of the few people to graduate from high school—Cerro Gordo High School. In comparison, Pa Joe left school during the fourth grade in order to work, as did my Grandpa Gordon. She was also the only girl with three male siblings, one of whom was her twin. From the photos I have of her and what I've heard, she seemed to have the latest fashion of the day as far as clothes and accessories and was a hilarious and cheerful person. She enjoyed games, humor, and laughing like few people I have known. She was also a very religious woman. I did not realize this until later, but Granddaddy Gordon taught her Sunday school class at Cherry Grove Baptist Church. My general assessment is her social position in life was one of modest privilege and comfort.

Ara Mae took exceptional pride in gathering children around her and playing games, like Chinese checkers, checkers, and naming all the state capitals. She would make a move and then look at her opponent without saying anything. Once they made their move, her face would turn to a grin, and then she would laugh at the mistake they made and the one she was about to capitalize upon. She was also a prankster. She would have a child curl their hand up into a fist as she held one of her hands around their wrist and simultaneously rubbed their knuckles. When they opened their hand, she would take her thumb and index finger and pull a spark of electricity from the palm of their hand. Another thing she seemed to enjoy was taking her thumb and index nails and popping them together while she held her hand behind a child's ear, telling them lice were eating at their head. However, the one that topped all this was the mysterious Bloody Bones and Raw Hide who lived under the bed. When she put a child to bed, she told them that if they thought they could sneak out of bed, either the Bloody Bones or Raw Hide was sure to grab them by the ankles and pull them under the bed, never to be heard from again. For those who consistently violated her admonishments to go to sleep, the fate of having either Bloody Bones or Raw Hide pull them to hell through a hole in the floor awaited. Now this fate seems unrealistic, but for me, having grown up in a Baptist church and been fed weekly sermons of hell being real and waiting for all those who violated the commandments—of which honoring your elders was one—this was as much a reality to me as school buses.

Another character she made up was called Tanky Tanky. I am not exactly sure what relationship Tanky Tanky had to Bloody Bones or Raw Hide, but it indeed had to be the superior beast, as the jingle went, "Tanky Tanky, why, why did you kill the baby?" It was because the baby refused to be quiet, and Bloody Bones or Raw Hide could not silence it. Thus, Tanky Tanky was the hit man called in to solve the dilemma of a noisy child. This seems frightening, but to listen to Grandma Ara Mae's threats, it all seemed quite funny … and a little life damaging.

There was one time I had to pee and refused to get out of bed because I was afraid of being pulled to hell through the hole under my bed. When Grandma Ara Mae discovered a wet mattress the next morning and asked why I had not gone to the bathroom, I whispered, "Bloody Bones."

She said, "He pees too. So he will understand if I tell him."

The other thing I recall about Ara Mae were her good friends Mrs. Rosada Hammonds and Mrs. Roberta Brown. These three women were as jovial as three monkeys in the jungle. They also *had* to have the finest gardens in the community. Ara Mae's gardens were overflowing with beans, peas, corn, okra, squash, cucumbers, and other vegetables, in which she took immense pleasure and pride. Much of the summer was spent shelling and canning. Both Mrs. Rosada and Mrs. Roberta would come to my mind as kindred Bible-loving gospel music fans. They certainly loved to talk, and parting from any of these three ladies required an ample dosage of repeated, "I have to go now."

Mrs. Roberta was actually the mother of my Aunt Priscilla's husband, Charles Brown. She lived in a very old house just down from the Crossroads and was very much proud of her Scottish heritage. She was also one of the many widows who lived in the community. It seemed all the husbands died some thirty years before their wives, as there were usually many widows within a mile of the Crossroads. I recall her homeplace because my uncle had a tobacco patch there. The one issue that was a bit prohibitive to a person of my age back then was I could not go around barefoot at Mrs. Roberta's home. The entire area around her house was littered like a minefield with these sharp, spiky sandspurs that, if stepped on, would dig into your foot like a razor. If the Vietcong could have had a supply of these, they would have proven most useful as a deterrent against reconnoitering an area. Back then, it was common practice to run around everywhere barefoot, especially for the younger ones. Mrs. Roberta said she used to have to pull sandspurs from her children's clothes and toss them back in the yard. She had a huge oak tree in her backyard that shaded her pump house. After a few hours in the hot July sun, it was constantly refreshing to brave the sandspurs, make a path to the pump house, sit underneath that tree, and drink cold water out of the garden hose. She was a lovely woman who consistently offered you something to eat if you happened to be there. If you had sufficient time, she would also pull a harmonica from her apron and play you a church song. Given a day or more, you could venture to the very back of the cultivated land and search for Indian arrowheads. Each time the fields were plowed, there seemed to be a new cache of arrowheads unearthed. To my knowledge, there was no other place around the community where this was the case. Perhaps, at some time in the past, this was a settlement, and this is why there ended up being a crossroad at this location. Sadly, the house she lived in is no longer there. Nor is the tobacco barn or the pump house. What stands in its place is a giant white water tower, which could be considered a monument of sorts but is lacking the words, "Here lived Roberta Brown, Scotswoman, Christian, harmonica player, and sower of sandspurs." Each time I ride by there, I see the old dirt road underneath the oak tree with the weathered wood-clad home just beyond the oak. There stood Mrs. Roberta's castle surrounded by a formidable tangle of sandspurs awaiting anyone who dared run barefoot across the yard.

Joseph Nathan Williamson

The Williamsons also seemed to originate in Wales and may have possibly migrated to the Scottish border area. They brought to America a familiarity to wield defiance with a gun or sword, and many of them would serve and perish in the American Civil War. Their journey to America brought them to Virginia into the area of the Isle of Wight. My distant cousin John Hybert Williamson speculates they may have been Welsh and come down from Pennsylvania or Delaware. The English officially called it the Isle of Wight Plantation Area in 1634, but the region continued under its old Indian name, *Warraskoyak*, for many years. Researching facts concerning the Isle of Wight, I discovered that a Puritan and noted English merchant Christopher Lawne led fifteen to twenty other Puritan colonists to the Isle of Wight and started a colony of Puritans in 1618 before he died in 1619.

Additionally, several members of the Puritan Bennett family also settled there, including Richard Bennett, who led the Puritans to Nansemond, Virginia, in 1635, and was later appointed as governor of the Virginia Colony. Both men are from the general area of southwestern England—Lawne from Dorset and Bennett from Somerset. Both seem to confirm the trend of people migrating from a shared site, as many of my ancestors did.[26]

At some point, Grandma Ara Mae met Pa Joe, and they were married just before he was drafted and shipped to the Pacific theater (New Guinea) to fight the Japanese in World War II. Until I was about fourteen, I knew nothing of Pa Joe and Ara Mae's meeting. However, in the summer of 1980, Denise Lawson, granddaughter of Roscoe Lawson of Orrum in Robeson County, showed up at Pa Joe's house. I am not sure how she ended up there, but she and Uncle Eddie started dating. (The Lumber River divides Robeson from Columbus County, and for many generations, men and women have made the journey across the river in search of a spouse.)

Denise knew something about the Williamsons I did not and had heard no one speak about before. Pa Joe had a son back in 1936 when he was twenty-one. I am unsure how the family kept an uncle a secret, but I had never heard anyone allow this fact to pass their lips into the public domain. The son was named Joe Edward Williamson, and in 1980, he would have been forty-four years old. It was another twenty-eight years before I ever saw Joe Jr. and another ten on top of that before I learned more about this.

The mother of Joe Jr. was Lucille Williamson, a descendant of a common ancestor four generations from Lucille and Pa Joe, Elias Williamson, who was the son of Joshua and grandson of Lewis Williamson. Lucille's ancestry goes back to Lewis Williamson and Mary Tatum, as does Pa Joe's. Both Lucille and Pa Joe would have been twenty-one or twenty-two when Joe Jr. was conceived. Denise enters the picture in this story because her Grandfather Roscoe's brother, Leo, later married Lucille, and they had four children. I was able to locate a photo of Lucille, which appears to be from the 1940s. She was beautiful, and somehow, I feel a connection to her. Maybe it's because she is a Williamson and I would be kin to her regardless of the circumstances of Joe Jr. But, perhaps because given the events in 1936, she gave birth to Joe Jr. and seemed to move forward with her life. From what I gathered, Dock Richard and Annie Haywood Williamson, Lucille's parents, reared Joe Jr., putting the puzzle together further. On the 1940 Census, Annie is a widow of Dock, and Joe Jr. is six years old, living with her. My Uncle Eddie remarked that Annie had told Joe Jr. that the most important thing he could do was make sure he obtained an education. (Annie's education obtainment level on the 1940 Census is listed as the second grade.) Joe Jr. went on to have a successful career in banking, and to my knowledge, Annie lived to see this. I am sure the Lumber River holds many secrets within its black water, or its banks act as a barrier between the counties, keeping those secrets on one side or the other. However, I am happy the knowledge finally found the light of day and became known to me.

Interestingly, I have two female cousins, the daughters of Joe Williamson Jr., I have never seen. All those years of Thanksgiving and Christmas gatherings, they were not there. That is sad, and I hope this book becomes known to them because I want them to know they are my people and welcome at my house.

One last note on Joe Jr. ... Uncle Joe spent his youth with his mother's family, and I do not recall ever knowing of him until I was a teenage boy. It seems odd that Pa Joe would have never mentioned him, but after speaking to my Uncle Eddie on the subject, his perspective is interesting. Uncle Eddie remarked, "Back then, Joe Jr. may have thought he had it hard not being around his daddy, but had he been with Daddy, he would be where I am, broke and physically broken from all this farmwork. All Daddy ever taught me was hard work and how to work. Joe was able to get an education and did well. Life sometimes gives you obstacles, but you have to deal with those circumstances. Joe Jr.'s appearance leaves no doubt as to the fact his father is Pa Joe. They look just like one another in the way the Williamsons carry themselves and their facial features."

Pa Joe was the eldest of seven children. Pa Joe's name came about because, as a young boy, I was calling him Joe, and Grandma Hazel suggested I call him Pa Joe. Regardless of its origins, by the time he passed, everyone knew him as Pa Joe. He was the son of James Carlie Williamson, who died October 10, 1974, and was called Carlie, and Jessie Lee Williamson, whose maiden name was also Williamson. Carlie's parents were Emery Lorenzo Williamson and Absilla Nance; Absilla's parents were Daniel Faulk Nance and Zylphia Walters (daughter of William Walters Jr. of Robeson County). Emery's parents were Elias Williamson and Dorothy Nance. Elias's parents were Joshua B. Williamson and Nancy Godwin. Joshua's parents were Lewis Williamson Sr. and Mary Tatum. Lewis Williamson was the progenitor of all the Williamsons on the western end of Columbus County.

A third cousin of mine and a descendant of Lewis Williamson, John Hybert Williamson of Davidson, North Carolina, has done extensive research on the Williamsons, which he shared with me. Based on DNA testing he has done on multiple Williamson descendants, his hypothesis is Lewis may have been encouraged to move to North Carolina to work in the naval stores industry. John's research has conclusively shown two sets of Williamsons came to southeastern North Carolina and are not related to the other Williamsons in the area. "The Cerro Gordo/Evergreen Williamsons originated with the arrival of Lewis and Mary Tatum after February 13, 1788."[27] The Bug Hill Williamsons originated with John and Nancy Williamson, who moved from Sampson County to Brunswick before 1800.[28] John has verified this by Y700 DNA test. The two original Williamsons settled at opposite ends of the county but must have been related. John's research also indicates that these Williamsons are Welsh.

The Welsh Roots of the Williamsons

The Welsh connection is intriguing, as a Welsh colony was located in the New Hanover District in 1733. There was also a Welsh colony in South Carolina along the Great Pee Dee River. The first colonial settler in the Pee Dee region of South Carolina was a Welsh lawyer named James James Jr., who led the first group of immigrants into the area in 1736 by way of a ferry down the Great Pee Dee River. The Darlington County Historical Society has one of the first Bibles in the state, which documents the Welsh presence in South Carolina. The Bible was ninety years old before it arrived in the Mars Bluff area in 1736.[29] "The first wave of settlers who came into the Pee Dee spread throughout the 'Welsh Tract' of colonial South Carolina, in what is present-day Marion, Darlington, Marlboro, and Chesterfield counties along the Great Pee Dee, at the behest of Royal Governor Robert Johnson."[30] In the *Records of the Welsh Tract Baptist Meeting, Pencader Hundred, New Castle County, Delaware 1701 to 1828*, published by the Delaware Historical Society in 1904, some members were removed from the rolls and transferred to Pee Dee in South Carolina.[31] However, I have not discovered any being transferred to North Carolina.

The Pencader Church in Delaware sent a letter of introduction to the Church of Christ in Charles Towne or elsewhere in South Carolina for the immigrants to constitute themselves into a church.[32] My seventh great-grandfather Nathaniel Evans, 1717–1774, and nineteen other Welsh men left Delaware for the Church on the Pee Dee. His wife, Ruth Ann Jones, followed him there. I do not know if they were married before departing Delaware of if they wed in South Carolina. The Evans family was part of the migration from Wales to Delaware (Pennsylvania). Nathaniel and Ann's daughter Mary Catherine married William Baker, whose granddaughter, Sarah "Sallie" Baker, married Jesse James Spivey Sr.

The early Welsh who settled along the upper Pee Dee River in South Carolina were Calvinists who believed in predestination and became disillusioned by the Arminian practices that included the belief in universal salvation. More than thirty families migrated from Pencader Hundred Baptist Church in Delaware to South Carolina between 1736 and 1746. Some families, particularly the Harry, James, and Jones families, were slaveholders and imported their slaves from Delaware to South Carolina. In addition, a distinct Welsh cultural identity prevailed in the upper Pee Dee River area of South Carolina, at least to 1760.[33]

Judging from the number of Baptists in Columbus County, it is not a farfetched assumption that the Welsh in North Carolina shared the Baptist Calvinist beliefs.

In the early eighteenth century, the Welsh settlement of the Cape Fear region extended eighty to ninety miles inland along the creeks flowing into the Cape Fear and the Northeast Cape Fear. These bodies of water included Rockfish, James's, Swift's, and Smith's Creeks; Black

Mingo and Goshen Swamps; and the Black River near Elizabethtown. Today, this region covers parts of Bladen, Columbus, Duplin, Onslow, Jones, Brunswick, and Sampson Counties. The Welsh settlement was spread out because of the naval stores industry; when the British Parliament granted a bounty on naval stores in North Carolina, this encouraged Welsh settlers to migrate from Pennsylvania—later New Castle County, Delaware—to the colony in the 1720s. The Welsh settlement in North Carolina preceded the Welsh settlement that began in South Carolina in 1736 on the upper Pee Dee River near the present town of Society Hill.[34] Indeed, John H. Williamson's hypothesis has good credibility, as both Lewis and John Williamson signed a petition in 1779 to divide Bladen, Duplin, and New Hanover Counties to form a new one, Sampson.[35]

James Carlie Williamson, Pa Joe's father, died when I was relatively young, but I have memories of meeting his mother, "Jessie Lee" Williamson. I say "memories," but in actuality, there are only two occasions where I recall meeting my great-grandmother. The most vivid memory was when Mom and I went to her house. At that time, I do not remember going any farther than the kitchen, which was located at the back of the house. We also did not stay for a duration of time that would be considered a visit. From what I can gather, Grandma Ara Mae said something hurtful to Jessie Lee many years back, and Jessie Lee, her memory being as sharp as a tack, never forgot what was said to her. I believe the anger she harbored toward Ara Mae was reflected upon Ara Mae's daughters since she didn't spend much time with any of them. Nonetheless, I do wish I had been able to visit more often and listen to the stories she could have told me. For one thing, in the middle of a field just before Haynes Lennon Road goes through Dunn Swamp on the way to Cerro Gordo, Jessie Lee's parents, Andrew Morgan Williamson and Dollie Wade Williamson, their daughter

Lizzie, and granddaughter Waive, who was Lizzie's daughter, are buried there. Lizzie died in her twenties. It's said that when Waive died at a young age, Lizzie grieved herself to death. However, based on my research, I suspect both Andrew and Lizzie may have died of tuberculosis. These are the sort of things Jessie Lee could have confirmed. My Uncle Eddie knows many of these stories because he seemed to be close to Jessie Lee. When he goes, much of the history that has been passed down to him from Jessie Lee will also disappear.

One of Jessie Lee's sisters, Rose Elma Williamson Day, was listed on Pa Joe's World War II draft card. I had difficulty reading the name and took the print out of the registration card to Uncle Eddie to read. He took one look at it and said, "That is his aunt. Your Pa Joe sure loved her, he spoke of her more than his mother, Jessie Lee." I had never known of Elma. Lizzie I knew because she is buried in the cemetery. I knew their brother Walter Pearson Williamson because as a young boy, my mother stopped at his house a few times. They lived on the left in an old white house just before you entered the darkness of Dunn Swamp on the way to Cerro Gordo. Walt and Hazel Callahan Williamson was what my mother called them. But Elma was a surprise to me. Elma died at a young age of forty-two in 1954. Uncle Eddie stated the last three months of his life, Pa Joe would holler out loud, "Elma, where are you." He would constantly call her name. Yet I knew not anything about her nor had ever heard her name. What other secrets or important matters have I failed to uncover that will remain lost to time? Rose Elma Day is buried at Macedonia Church Cemetery alone. Elma's husband was Woodrow Day, and he lived until 1987, but I have not found where he was buried. I have not uncovered any children they may have had either.

The other son of Andrew Morgan and Dollie Wade was Enoch Bernard Williamson, whose first wife was Kate Elizabeth Benton (son

Neal Morgan Williamson) and second wife was Lucille Gregg (son Enoch Gregg Williamson). Kate's mother was Marietta Williamson, who was a descendant of Lewis Williamson. Another reminder of the tangled web of roots akin to the bald cypress knees in Dunn Swamp.

It was said that Jessie Lee was a woman who ruled the roost, and everyone was expected to follow her direction. My great-aunts, Elgie and Emily, perhaps reflect Jessie Lee's belief that women should work as hard as men. For example, when Elgie married her husband, there was one morning when they both got up early. Elgie's husband had planned on cutting the underbrush along the ditch banks that day. This is of paramount importance in eastern North Carolina because if a hurricane or much rain comes, the ditches will back up with water and flood the fields. As he was walking out the door, Elgie came out of the bedroom, wearing her overalls. He asked her, "Where are you going?"

She replied, "To cut the ditch banks with you."

I never saw either Elgie or Emily when they were not wearing pants and a cap on their head; most of the time, they were in overalls, jeans, or work pants. When I was given a photo of them by my great-aunt Sue Williamson, I was shocked to actually see them in dresses. Emily seemed to be the more relaxed of the two, always smiling, with the curls of her hair poking out from under a cap. Elgie was tall and lean and wore jeans and a Western shirt. I had known them best because we put in tobacco together. The families would get together and exchange labor to get the crop from the field to the barn.

I am told that when Jessie Lee spoke of Ara Mae, she would say, "Ara Mae and those girls." I think this is because Ara Mae was so unlike Jessie Lee in regards to her attitude toward work. Similarly, from the conversations I have had with my mom and Uncle Eddie, I think Ara Mae was put off by the harsh attitudes toward femininity Jessie Lee manifested. Ara Mae was the only daughter of a moderately well-off farmer, and I think she expected a woman to exhibit the attributes of a duchess. Jessie Lee was more like the Iceni Queen Boadicea, ready to lead her (female) people to war against Rome, whereas Ara Mae expected the men to lead such an attack. I never recall Ara Mae being in the fields, but Jessie Lee's daughters Emily and Elgie had been reared to work the same as any man. But even Jessie Lee had a soft spot for her youngest daughter, Virginia, who my mother says did not work as Elgie and Emily had.

Uncle Eddie confirmed this when he said Ara Mae had told him on numerous occasions that he did not need the help her daughters would need. "Eddie, you are a man, and you can look after yourself," she told him. "But those girls may marry a bad man and will need my help." Thus, I definitely think there were some differences concerning the roles a woman and man must play, according to Grandma Ara Mae. What is interesting is this assistance her daughters would supposedly need seemed not to apply to my mom. When she was married to my father, instead of living on a piece of land owned by Ara Mae and Pa Joe, they moved into the farmhouse where my paternal grandparents lived on Monroe Powell's land. The dynamics of this situation reflect the individual circumstances of both women.

Another story that has been related to me by my third cousin, Cindy, Emily Lee's granddaughter, is how Jessie Lee ran both Emily's and Elgie's husbands off—I'm not sure why; I just know she ran a strict household and refused to let the men take control. She would stand at the Cow Branch Bridge up from Macedonia Baptist Church and guard it with her shotgun on Sunday to keep the husbands away from her daughters. To my knowledge, they never returned to the house. Uncle Eddie stated the basis for the dislike of one of the husbands was he sometimes forgot he was married. He had a son by Elgie, who lived in Columbus County, but simultaneously had a daughter born the same time by a woman in Bladen County. Of course, Jessie Lee was not one to mitigate her opinions about any subject, and certainly her son-in-law's infidelity entailed her confronting him head-on, like a ram charging.

Of course, I did not know Jessie Lee, but the picture I have is one of a hardworking, feisty woman. My Uncle Eddie stated that Carl Meares, the Sage of Fair Bluff, said Jessie Lee and Elgie could outthink and out negotiate any attorney in Columbus County.[36] For better or worse, that is my impression of her. She was born in the 1800s when the expectation of a woman was to be a mother and wife, but Jessie Lee could hold her own against any man. Moreover, she was the bastion of sound judgment and risk-taking, which was what kept the family afloat through the Great Depression, crop failures, and natural disasters, like hurricanes that often came sweeping inland from the coast, bringing torrential rain. Given her birth's historical circumstances, had she been born a male and more accepted for her masculine tact and aggressiveness in negotiation and business, she would have probably owned Tatum Township.

Back to Pa Joe ... He was drafted in the summer of 1941, and when the United States entered the war, he was mobilized with a Connecticut Army National Guard unit and sent to New Guinea. It must have been a unit filled out with men from the South because there were very few people in this unit other than Yankees. During this time, Pa Joe's best friend was a man named Wittenberg from Rome, Georgia. Any time he spoke of the army, Wittenberg was sure to come up too. Pa Joe never talked about his experience in New Guinea other than how he was in an artillery unit, and the natives of New Guinea would often bring the heads of Japanese soldiers to the base to be paid for killing them. But after Pa Joe died, I was given photos Wittenberg had taken in New Guinea and sent to Pa Joe before he passed away—or

Wittenberg's son had forwarded them to him after Wittenberg died. In these pictures, there are several men, but they are marked with two words: "Joe" and "Me." The other men in the photos are unidentified. Instead of showing any details about the war—those may have been confiscated by the government—the photos are of Pa Joe washing clothes in a barrel, standing with a man in a grass skirt, and sitting on a log while eating out of a can of rations with a spoon raised to his mouth. Such things are typical of the camp life I experienced as an air force veteran deployed to Afghanistan. The moments away from the fighting are just living and passing the days until the day comes when you finally get to go home. Pa Joe spent three years, three months, and six days in New Guinea and then was sent home. He was one of six people who got to come home in 1944. According to Pa Joe, the unit drew names, and his name was the last name drawn. Discharged from military service at Camp Blanding, Florida, Pa Joe returned to Williamson's Cross Roads.

    I do not have many memories of visiting Pa Joe and Ara Mae until I was about six years old. If I had to characterize Pa Joe, I would say he was a practical and serious man. Anyone who was reared in Jessie Lee's household would have been instilled with a seriousness about them, even if they had resisted it for years. The slow assault of a glacier wears down the resistance of rock, and that had been Jessie Lee's persistence. The other reason I think I am correct in this assessment is that Uncle Eddie always said, "My daddy taught me to do it the right way. If you think there is an easy way to do something, you are wrong, and the easy way will be more expensive in the long run." This independence is also manifested in Uncle Eddie's sentiment, "Daddy said if you have to take the short end of the stick in a transaction and are in doubt, let the other man get the benefit, lest he say you are a crook." In the end, people will know who the real crook is.

As Pa Joe grew older, he became much more capable of laughter. But in those early years of my life, he was distant and scary. Unlike with Granddaddy Gordon, who laughed and played hide-and-seek with me, I do not recall ever playing any games with Pa Joe. He was not the person to ask to throw a football with. It is difficult to express. I had more interactions with Pa Joe as I matured, but as a young boy, there were very little. I remember riding home in the truck with him and my mother one time. As we drove though Dunn Swamp, I only remember him telling Mother not to trust such-and-such person and to be on guard when interacting with people.

When Mom and Dad were married, they asked Pa Joe for a small piece of land to put a trailer on. However, for some reason, Pa Joe did not give it to them. That particular piece of land was first given to his brother Emmet to put a trailer on, and today, it is the place where my cousin has built a house. I tell this story because it is central to the outcome of where I am in life. At the time, it seemed like devastating news because my parents would have to move in and live with my paternal grandparents, but because Mom and Dad did not build on land given to them by Pa Joe, I think it actually made it easier for us to leave Columbus County in 1981. There was no emotional attachment or a connection to the land. My parents did not have anything other than a quarter acre of land and a Farmers Home Administration house. Thus, there was not that much to leave behind. That move slowly began to change the economic prospects for my family for the better. Because of this decision by Pa Joe, Gordon asked Mr. Monroe Powell if my parents could put a trailer on his farm. Mr. Monroe Powell agreed, and the trailer was placed adjacent to the sharecropper's house where Gordon and Hazel lived. That house has collapsed, but I have several pieces of wood from the structure hanging in my home and that I used to make a frame to put paintings in.

CHAPTER 10
Aunts and Uncles

In many regards, I had many interactions with my mother's siblings. I have been close to all of them and remain so until this day. There are two of whom I would like to include in this as illustrating the many lessons one can learn in life from family: her younger brother and youngest sister.

Eddie Leekota Williamson
In his essay "Calvin and the Christian Calling," Alister McGrath suggests that for John Calvin, "work was thus seen as an activity by which Christians could deepen their faith, leading it on to new qualities of commitment to God. Activity within the world, motivated, informed, and sanctioned by Christian faith, was the supreme means by which the believer could demonstrate their commitment and thankfulness to God. To do anything for God and do it well was the fundamental hallmark of the authentic Christian faith. To work and to work well and do something well is a benchmark of being a good person. Diligence and dedication in one's everyday life are, Calvin thought, a proper response to God."[37]

The worst adjective a person could be labeled with is "lazy." Laziness does not discriminate and will establish sovereignty over anyone who yields to its pressure. Back home, when I was young, saying someone was smart did not equate to being bright from formal education but rather that they could grasp the problem at hand and quickly resolve the situation. This concept seemed to permeate the air my family breathed. Hell is undoubtedly full of sinners, but there were the lazy people who are sure to be wallowing among the charcoals too. The one person who first molded my thoughts on a work ethic was my mother's uncle. His name is Eddie Leekota Williamson. He was named after his mother's father, Bruce Eddie Worley, and her mother, Dalmas Cotas Strickland. He is ten years older than me, and it seems as soon as he could walk, his father, my Pa Joe, thrust something in his hands to do. He is the only male among five girls and started helping my Pa Joe out on the farm from an early age. Pa Joe's time spent in New Guinea fighting the Japanese resulted in health conditions that prevented him from doing many things. Primarily, his eyesight was a considerable obstacle to overcome. Uncle Eddie said his nerves were "no good" either. This was why he needed so much help on the farm.

When I was about six years old, Uncle Eddie took me to the dirt road that led to the swamp and sat me down in the seat of the tractor. I recall two things about this more than any other memory. First, the tractor was orange. Second, I had to slide down in the seat to press the clutch. Uncle Eddie took the tractor to a road that ran between the fields and spent time showing me how to drive it. He also backed up to the disc and told me how to hook it up to the tractor. From then on, until the age of fifteen, I would spend my summers helping him put in the tobacco. Even today, forty years later, he takes the time to explain how things should operate and the best approach to work smart.

I would do various other things later on the farm, from cropping tobacco, hanging tobacco in the barn, suckering tobacco, and then emptying the tobacco from the barn and taking it to the packhouse. For each one of these, there was a correct way to do it and a way not to do it. What I learned was the correct way was a perfect way, and the incorrect way was just the sloppy way to do it. Not reflecting pride in your work was, dare I say, the lazy, half-ass way to do something. As I recall, I was paid ten dollars a day to drive a tractor and twenty dollars for cropping tobacco. Uncle Eddie was sure to make a lasting impact on me as far as work ethic, but I cannot hold a candle to the work ethic of the people in my family during those times. I saw women work as hard as men if it was needed in order to harvest the crop. My mom once told me that when her first cousin Pat got engaged, her father remarked to his fiancée, "If you are marrying Jessie Lee Williamson's grandson, get ready for endless work because that is all the Williamsons know." There is not as much work going on as there once was. I ride through the community now, and it seems quiet along the roads. There is no rustling in the fields, tractors going to and fro, or expectations of a six-year-old to know how to drive a tractor. When Uncle Eddie was a boy, he had to wake up early in the morning to do his chores and then be at school on time. He still tells of how he would have to assist in delivering piglets by reaching in and extracting out those that were having difficulty being born.

This seems a strange concept to younger people today, but it really was not that long ago. The idea of privilege was not seen as it is today. The privilege one had back then was the belief that they had been blessed by God to have a good year on the farm and were able to feed their family. They were doing even better if they had enough money remaining to buy clothes for the school year. In my case, the first pair of jeans I bought was from money earned in the tobacco patch. It was not seen as a particular advantage one person had over another because most were in the same boat in making ends meet. Yes, there were the few who had more, but most families just survived from one year to the next.

One summer, on the last day I was home before I went back to Mississippi, something happened where I had to crop tobacco that day. Since I was leaving the next day, I wanted to take care of my bill at Tom's service station, which he had bought from "Shorty" Martin, and do other things. Thus, I was not looking forward to cropping tobacco. This was also reinforced by the fact that the tobacco field was at Ms. Sue McCloskey's, which was the barn we were attempting to fill. Now the fields at Ms. Sue's seemed to go on forever, and the rows seemed as if they were the length of a football field. Her barn had to be the largest one in the area, and the only comfort it offered was a colossal pecan tree that stood at the front of it. Her barn was a behemoth that sometimes took two days to fill.

In 2016, the barn was one of the few remaining flue-cured tobacco barns standing in the community that was not a new buck barn. Most of the old tobacco barns and the more recent buck barns are falling apart and returning to a natural state of vegetation. I had many memories of the McCloskey barn and was glad to see it was weathering the storm of time. At the end of the tobacco season one year, we had a fish fry at Ms. Sue's barn. This barn was also where my Uncle Charles delivered the bicycle my mom had bought with money she earned from tobacco. It cost $65, which is $212 now. The saddest memory attached to that barn is when Ms. Sue's grandson William went out there one morning with his shotgun, sat under the overhang, and ended his life. I had not seen William since I was thirteen, and I remembered him as a simple county boy who had a John Deere tractor and was as proud of it as if it had been a new Mustang. William once remarked to me that he would rather dig a ditch with a shovel than sit in school. It is strange the things you recall about a person. The family tore down the barn after William's passing in about 2020 or 2021, and today, the field runs uninterrupted from Princess Ann Road to the very back of the property. That barn stood as a sentry guarding those tobacco fields for at least five decades, but I understand why it was taken down.

Anyway, when Uncle Eddie came to pick me and my cousin Shawn up that morning, I just simply did not go. I had no way of knowing then, but that was the moment I broke from my rural roots. I would never again walk down a row of tobacco fields, nor work on a farm. What remains now are memories of the smell of a barn full of tobacco when the doors are opened, the smell of a cigarette lit just before dawn, the laughter, and the detailed instructions from Uncle Eddie on how certain things are done.

The one aspect that remains consistent with my Uncle Eddie is his ability to tell a good story. One of these is about an older man named Griffin, who had a considerable amount of land in the area. While he was endowed with many acres of land, he came up short on sons to help him manage his acreage. He had only one son, who somewhat lacked the motivation necessary to meet the demands of farming. One day, Old Man Griffin rose early to take care of business in town. He instructed his son to take one of the mules and start plowing one of the fields. That way, when the father returned home, the other mule would be ready to go, and Old Man Griffin could speedily join his son in the fields rather than waste time addressing the need for plowing.

Upon his return to the farm, the mules stood there in the barn unharnessed and idling, looking back at the old man as if saying, "Well, we knew the field needed plowing, but we could not harness ourselves." In the house sat the younger Griffin, not doing anything. Old

Man Griffin looked at his son and said, "If this is what you plan on doing, then you will not need all this land I have."

When telling this story, Uncle Eddie then says, "The older man went to see my great-grandmother Jessie Lee and offered to sell her nine hundred acres of land, which back up to Porter Swamp and her property. I am not sure if this had been Williamson's land at some point in the past, but I know that a Williamson daughter married a Griffin in the 1800s. Thus, perhaps Old Man Griffin was giving the family first opportunity at what had been theirs in the past. Jessie Lee then went to see a Cox man in Tabor City and borrowed the money to buy the land." Eddie does not reveal how much money this was.

That summer was a long and dry one, and then a hailstorm came through and destroyed the corn and tobacco crops. Jessie Lee was fraught with anxiety about how she would make the payments back to the man from Tabor City. After considerable hand twisting and thinking, Jessie Lee stated, "Well, I guess I will have to go see Carl Meares in Fair Bluff."

When she saw Carl, he remarked, "Jessie, if you had come seen me in the first place, you would not be in this mess." Mr. Meares went to Tabor City and paid off the Cox man that same day.

Jessie made good on the payments and gained ownership of the land because it was passed to her children and grandchildren. What intrigues me concerning this story is that Jessie Lee's husband, James, seemed to have played no role. The stories Uncle Eddie tells always feature Jessie Lee as the decision maker and the person doing all the work. As a history teacher, I am bombarded with the assumption women have played no active role in making America great and strong, yet, insofar as Jessie Lee Williamson, that is not the case. My Pa Joe's place was near this property, and I do not know if the field behind the "Big Canal" he farmed was part of this purchase, but instead of giving this field to Pa

Joe, Jessie Lee gave him a lifetime right on it. When Pa Joe died, the property went to her daughter Emily's grandson.

To my knowledge, none of the properties, which were owned by Jessie Lee, went to Pa Joe as an inheritance upon her death. Did Jessie Lee not give Pa Joe any of this land because of his wife? Uncle Eddie further states that Ara Mae refused to give the entire small farm my Pa Joe owned to Eddie because he was a man and knew how to work. If their daughters married "sorry" men, they would need a place to go. Thus, tying this together, Jessie Lee did not give anything that would end up with "those girls"—my mom and her four sisters. Yet today, three of Mom's sisters live on that farm along with three of their grandsons. Thus, to consider myself part Williamson, I have to look past this injustice.

The grandson of Jessie Lee borrowed money for two hundred acres of what was Old Man Griffin's property and could not repay the money and lost the farm as a result. Some of it is owned by a great-grandson, and the widow of a son owns some. Old Man Griffin eventually sold the land and retained a lifetime right to the house. In the end, his lazy son did not inherit the farm or even the house.

Glenda Gray

My first memories of Glenda Gray Williamson were of Elvis and a guy she dated who drove a blue Corvette. My Aunt Teresa Rose had been married to Tommy Horton before he shipped off to Germany with the army. In anticipation of this event, Grandma Ara Mae had installed an orange shag carpet. I know this because I can recall Aunt Glenda and her date laughing at me being unable to twist my hips and mimic Elvis's moves as I danced on the carpet.

I do not remember the guy's name, but I detest him with every fiber of my being due to that one night they came to my house. I was delighted to show him the comic books my Aunt Pattie Powell had given me, which had belonged to her son Chris. He proposed swapping my comic books for the ones he had, and like a fool down the primrose path, I agreed. Well, that was the last time I ever saw those comics. Aunt Glenda should have chastised him to the point of death and made sure I had my comic books returned. Alas, the true nature of humans revealed itself as a slithering snake, and I will never forget the thieving bastard.

Sometime after Glenda graduated from high school and left the Comic Book Thief with the blue Corvette, she met an ex-marine from Bladen County, North Carolina, named Ricky Armstrong at a bar in Chadbourn called the Zodiac Lounge. During this time, in the early 1970s, the Zodiac Lounge was most appropriate for the age. Armstrong was probably a descendant of those many Highland Scots who migrated up the Cape Fear River and settled in Bladen County. He told me stories about the marines and driving back from California to North Carolina. Ricky would attempt to persuade me to do crunches and "get in shape." I did not see the need to do so at age ten or twelve. The physical rigor demanded of a marine was not, and still is not, one of my pursuits. Nonetheless, I enjoyed him coming over. On his visits to the house, he often took the time to shoot basketball with me. He also seemed to be a traveled adventurer who had seen places outside of southeastern North Carolina.

He told me about how during basic training at Parris Island, there had been another Armstrong in his platoon who always caused trouble but would never own up to what he had done. Consequently, when someone would say it was Armstrong who had committed an offense, both Ricky and the other Armstrong were punished since the guilty one never admitted his guilt. Ricky said, "I solved that problem by catching him in the toilet and giving him a good whipping." Never again did the other Armstrong cause any trouble. Ricky was also the first person I ever saw with a tattoo. In my youth, only veterans and drunks had tattoos ... well, the fact that they were drunks was told to me by others. I was too young to distinguish between causation and result, and I thought a tattoo caused a person to be a drunk, yet Ricky had one and was not a drunk. Any twenty-year-old who took the time to speak to a ten-year-old about the military and then shoot basketball was a good man. He was one of the best men I have ever met, and sadly, he died in his fifties.

The Williamsons are hell on wheels and have been for some time. Perhaps one day, the Welsh gene will be identified as what makes these people so ornery. Glenda and Armstrong moved to Oklahoma, where he worked as a welder at a nuclear power plant. As far as I can recall, they lived in Lawton, Oklahoma, or somewhere nearby, for about a year. Ricky would often follow the money and take a job at the highest-paying company to earn top dollar. In rural Bladen and Columbus Counties, the demand for industrial welders could not support someone of Ricky's talents. My dad said, "He is a top-notch welder and did not have any difficulty getting a job paying good money." They had initially moved into a trailer across from Armstrong's parents in Bladen County. When that did not work, they went to Oklahoma. Oklahoma did not suit Aunt Glenda either. When Glenda came back to Columbus County, she brought pictures of bison and other animals I had never seen before. It was as if Oklahoma was another world. And in many respects, I think it was for Aunt Glenda. I imagine that with Ricky working and her staying at home, the environment and culture of Oklahoma was too different from southeastern North Carolina.

In the 1820s, many residents of Columbus, Bladen, and Horry Counties had packed up and moved west. Our ancestors stayed in Columbus County, and Glenda must have been true to the people who found it too difficult to move to another state. Thus, Ricky and Glenda moved back home. By this time, I was about thirteen or fourteen. I recall waiting up at Pa Joe's house, waiting for them to arrive. Aunt Glenda showed me those photos of bison, and I imagined Oklahoma being the far-off Western world I saw in the movies. I never imagined I would make the same trip along I-40 to Oklahoma to attend the C-17 Loadmaster School in Altus. After returning from Oklahoma, my aunt and Armstrong moved across the road from Pa Joe, and that is where Glenda remains today, back on the land that has been with the Williamsons since before the Revolutionary War. If only this land could tell the stories it has seen.

Armstrong attempted to make things work with Aunt Glenda. In my opinion, I am sure Glenda and Ricky loved one another, but oil and water do not mix. Glenda—again, in my opinion—comes from a long line of women who are independent and assertive in the lead of decision-making. They do not particularly like sharing the role of decision maker with anyone. It is their way or the highway. I think with a like-minded person, which I perceived Ricky to be, there may have been a crack in the relationship that grew into an uncrossable gulf. Of course, in fairness, this is only my opinion, and I have not interviewed the living partner. However, when we moved to Mississippi, Armstrong and Glenda moved there too, and he secured a job at the navy yard in Bay St. Louis, Mississippi. I recall a piece of metal he had welded and brought home that the company then bent to check for proper welding. The weld looked like it had always been one solid piece of forged steel with no air bubbles. "Smooth as a baby's ass," he said.

When I returned to work in the tobacco fields that summer, Glenda was back at Williamson's Cross Roads, and Ricky was gone. I never knew what happened, but those secrets will probably come out one day. Insofar as Armstrong, I only saw him occasionally after he and Glenda separated, perhaps maybe four times. I always wanted to speak to him and have a long discussion, but it was not to be. Then, twenty-some years later at their son's house, I saw Ricky shortly before he died. He was still the same person I remembered as a young boy. Shortly after, I learned he died while lying on the couch.

Sometime after Ricky and Glenda had ended their marriage, Glenda dated a person named Stanley Wayne Nance from the Crossroads, and I went out with them once. I had one too many beers that night and only remember almost peeing in my pants. It did not work with Stanley, though, and she started dating a man with the last name Long. They were married and had one son. Over the years, I stayed in touch and would go by and see them. She was only seven years older than I was and was sort of an older sister, not an aunt.

My grandparents eventually passed, and the family farm was left to the six children. I had many a good summer on that farm. As I saw it, that place was a part of my grandparents and, in a way, a part of me. My mom had not been given a place to put a trailer, but I was sure I would be different. I only wanted an acre to connect to something in Columbus County other than the graves, which contain all my family members. I begged Mom to deed me her portion of the property, but she did not. I have no idea why she never did. The only reason I can imagine is she perhaps knew the den of vipers I would be involving myself with if I had to deal with the others who had inherited a portion of the land. In retrospect, she probably did me a favor by signing her portion over, but it would have been a welcome gesture had she discussed her move with me beforehand. Likewise, Glenda should have had the decency, as she proclaims herself a good Christian, to speak to me before she acted rather than after the fact.

I moved away and joined the air force, and as time went by, first one grandchild and then another were given a piece of land to build a house on the old farm place. Glenda and I remained close all this time, and then my mom became ill with several different issues. To my surprise and dismay, Glenda convinced Mom to sign over her portion to her. Glenda took Mom to Tabor City, and in the same manner Vanuel Strickland was taken to Tabor City in 1952 and signed over his farm to Guilford Edwards, Mom signed her interest over to Glenda.

After the fact, Glenda swapped her part of the land with her sister Teresa and husband, Horton, and they gave her his part of Great-Uncle Earl's land they had bought together. Glenda called me and was sincerely apologetic, saying, "There is nothing I can do now. Do you want a piece of Earl's land?"

Uncle Earl's land is landlocked and part of a vast area that has only dirt roads leading to the Kingdom of Rattlesnakes, where some snakes are as large as my leg. It is bordered on the west by Buck Slash Bay and the east by Paget Bay, which means standing water during some part of the year. There is no way I would ever venture into that kingdom of snakes and critters. I would not even desire to step out of the vehicle for a moment to pee. So I replied, "No, thank you."

From my perspective, the first lesson is there are not any new exploits of a treacherous relative to be discovered. There are fallen angels who chose to be demons. It sometimes seems as though life is a circular repeat of the same story of backstabbing relatives who waste no effort in securing their fortune over those they claim to love. If kings and queens are guilty of coveting a crown, then even yeoman farmers are susceptible to the greed of a few acres of bay land in Buck Slash Bay. The second lesson in this is to realize that no matter how close a person may seem to someone, when it comes to a tangible asset, there are no angels. Sometimes, the same people who sit in church praising the life of Jesus as an example to follow should be the ones hanging next to Judas for their deceit and betrayal. It was not as if I ever planned on moving back and homesteading in the community. The people connected to my memories have all died and gone. I return to that day in the summer of 1980, when Pa Joe, Shawn, and I walked through the freshly cut survey line, nailing hog food sacks to pine trees and wondering why people lie to their kin.

Is it not like chopping off one's arm? Like a case with other family members, what is the motivation for saying something negative about a relative without cause? In the end, the Lord had other plans for me, and the betrayal, while not forgiven, has been rectified by my being blessed to purchase part of a farm near Cerro Gordo of my own right, not inheriting it or having it be given to me by anyone.

CHAPTER 11
Williamson's Cross Roads

Located up the Lumber River and about four miles from Cerro Gordo through the swamp lies a place called Williamson's Cross Roads. It lies at the intersection of Princess Ann Road and Cerro Gordo Highway, also known as Haynes Lennon Road or State 242. The swamp between Cerro Gordo and the Cross was actually a substantial ditch the Army Corp of Engineers dug to drain the land around the area where Dunn Swamp from the east joins with Porter Swamp, and then the latter joins Cow Branch before meandering into the Lumber River. The result was a straight waterway that resembled a neat gash in the land continuously filled with dark water.

When I was young, on each side of the canal, there was a ribbon of hardwood trees that, in the summer, provided a mysterious atmosphere because it was a very dark place to pass through. I always approached this passage with trepidation and feared the car would break down and I would have to walk alone through to the other side. It is difficult to convey the feeling when I would enter the swamp. The temperature seemed to drop substantially even in the dog days of August; it was many degrees cooler, as if opening an ice chest. The trees shaded the road considerably, and it was difficult for light to penetrate through and shine down on the asphalt. I recall the few times I rode my bicycle through the swamp, and it seemed as if I could not pedal quickly enough to get through to the other side, where I knew it would be warm and sunny. Today, most of the cypress trees and other hardwoods have been harvested, and the allure of the swamp is nothing but a memory. Cypress stumps, as if the remains of monuments, are all that emerge from the tapestry that still ribbons the waterway as motorists from Yankee states zip through the swamp with recreation vehicles in tow, heading to Myrtle Beach. Those cars are easily spotted, as they have license plates on the front and back of the vehicle. Little can they imagine the frightening spectacle that stretch of the swamp was in the 1970s.

Traveling north out of the swamp on Haynes Lennon, the next prominent feature of the land was Williamson's Cross Roads. On the west side of the crossroads sits Williamson's Cross Roads Baptist Church. One of Lewis Williamson's Scottish ancestors was one of the founders of the original church that sits at the junction of Princess Ann and Haynes Lennon Road. I am confident there are many Williamsons scattered along all sides of the crossroads, and those who do not have the last name Williamson are most assuredly related to the Williamsons in some way. It is said that the other family names in the community are a result of Williamsons tending to have daughters, and the only new blood that entered the area was when one of them married and brought her husband to the community. Then the families more or less cross-pollinated from the same trees among the Iveys, Nances, Browns, or Floyds. Occasionally, some did not have the required number of children to maintain a presence in the community, or children abandoned the community for economic reasons, like those who headed to Alabama in the 1820s.

In my youth, the economic mainstay was tobacco, and activity centered around a local gas station. There was one on both ends of Princess Ann Road—one at the junction of Homer Nance and Princess Ann, and one at Haynes Lennon Road and Princess Ann. Floyds Gas Station at the west end of Princess Ann is now in the hands of the next generation of a Floyd daughter. Haynes Lennon Road's service station, first known as Shorty Martin's and then Tom Williamson's, has vanished and is now a grassy lot owned by Williamson's Cross Roads Baptist Church. On the opposite side of the road sits a store that was not there when I was young.

The Service Stations of Williamson's Cross Roads

The community roads which lead to Williamson's Cross Roads are not as busy as they were during my youth. At one time, adjacent to the Baptist church, there stood a large watering hole, gas station, and local gathering place. I first knew it as Shorty's, then Tom's, and then lastly Greene's. The last owner, Greene, sold the property to the Baptist church, and now the lot sits empty.

Shorty, as I recall, was a Martin, and kept a somewhat disorganized parking lot. The right side of the building facing the Baptist church was littered with soda bottles and crates. It looked as though a bull had run rampant and tossed bottles and containers all over the place. This scene was somewhat challenging to understand since, back then, the crates and bottles had a deposit on them and could be returned to the manufacturer for credit. That everything has value was something I also learned to appreciate at an early age because the bottles were five cents apiece. I quickly developed an affection for bottles and collected them behind the storage shed from as early as I can recall until I had a truckload, which I would then take to Lumberton and sell. Because of Shorty's untidy parking lot, I would occasionally purloin a few that seemed to be out of the periphery, like lost sheep that needed to be returned to the fold. I am not sure what happened to Shorty, but Tom Williamson and his wife, Paulette, eventually purchased the store and orchestrated a remarkable change to the outside and inside of the building. As I recall, Paulette had the place ready for even a military inspection. The crates and soda bottles were neatly stacked and arranged for the delivery truck, and the inside of the store was tidy and organized.

When the Williamsons took over the store, I was probably about twelve years old, and Shorty's became Tom's. I recall the time because I started to keep a tab at the store and paid it weekly. I even allowed my sister to purchase things and charge them to my account. When we moved away to Mississippi in 1981, I returned one last season to work in tobacco with Uncle Eddie. That summer was the last time I had my hands on tobacco and the last time I had any dealings with Tom's. I ended my career in the tobacco patch by driving to Tom's and paying my bill.

Over the years, I occasionally stopped there when I visited my grandparents. On one of these occasions, I saw a distant relative pumping gas into his car with a cigarette dangling between his teeth. Some things remain the same, but each time I returned there, the parking lot seemed less busy, and the bench seemed missing many of the older men who would sit there for hours, swapping stories. Death and the decline of the tobacco market forever ended what a robust and entertaining place of meeting that station was. Tom's is no more, but the memories of a few of its patrons still resonate in my mind.

During the summer months, it was challenging to find a place to park there. Summer was tobacco season, and there would be many people stopping to get gas, cola, and a pack of peanut butter crackers. Others would occupy the benches outside the store and sit there for a significant part of the day, discussing the local news, weather, or continual subject of tobacco. The older men of the community conducted most of these discussions. The one I recall best was Mr. Rory Griffin. He had a biting candor that was reflected in his observations of everything from politics to the fact that the potato chip bag was larger but with more air and fewer chips in the bag. When the price of a cola increased to thirty-five cents, the world had changed so much, it was no longer recognizable to him. Thankfully, a pack of cigarettes was still fifty cents, and chewing tobacco was holding its own against inflation.

There were two others who were sure to be sitting at the bench: Ray Brown and Bear. I do not recall Bear's last name, but everyone called him "Bear" because he resembled one. He actually had an old white Chevrolet that was big enough to have room for a coffin in the back. Bear would drive Ray around, and when they arrived at Tom's, Ray would exit the car, complaining about how the springs in the seats were picking his polyester pants. The reason for this was rather apparent, as the cushion and material that once covered the seats were missing. Bear would step out of the car barefoot, with his bare chest and belly prominent like a well-lit full moon, and state, "Well, if you don't like the car, get someone else to drive you around." Ray was as skinny as Bear was round. Ray had a severe demeanor, while Bear's grin, partially hidden beneath a full beard and mustache, could charm a snake. Once, while putting in tobacco at the McCloskey barn, we all loaded up in the pickup truck and drove to the gas station for a drink and pack of crackers. While Bear was sitting on the tailgate of my uncle's pickup, I saw him hold his bare foot down to the asphalt as the truck sped to Tom's.

It was a customary practice for most people who were putting in tobacco to load everyone up in the pickup and drive to the station in the morning for breakfast. Usually, the barn help went separately from those who picked the tobacco in the field. In the case of the field help, an order was usually given, and their food was brought to the field. I said "breakfast," but if one ever ate anything other than a can of sausage or potted meat, they would probably be as sick as a dog when the sun rose to its most total position in the sky later that same day. The dew on the tobacco and the gum from the tobacco would turn one's arms and clothes as black as coal. When the sun dried the tobacco gum and you made the mistake of eating a heavy meal, you could guarantee you would lose your lunch. Whatever the chemical reaction was, the smell of the tobacco gum and the hot food seemed to trigger an immediate reaction from your stomach, which was quite unpleasant.

Many other people came and went from this store and many others, which were just like Tom's and Shorty's. Each family in the community had a store they would patronize regularly. On Princess Ann Road, I recall four on a stretch of road no more than five miles before it dead-ended into the Lumber River. This remembrance of the river leads to two other unique features of Princess Ann Road: the blues bar, or honky-tonk, called the Red Barn, and the Sandbox.

CHAPTER 12
The Red Barn

Sometime after Williamson's Cross Roads Baptist Church was organized, the church hired a new preacher. Part of the congregation was pleased with the new preacher, but the other was not. I do not know for sure, but generally, in a Baptist church, the major reason for a split congregation is the preacher usually steps on the toes of sinners by calling them out, not by name but by deed, from the pulpit. This may have been what caused part of the congregation to start another church. The acceptance by a portion of the church resulted in those who did not accept the new pastor leaving the church and starting a new Baptist church about five miles down the road, which they named Macedonia Baptist. My mother's family was actually attending that church. Its members built the church on the curve of the road where Boardman meets Princess Ann. The rear of the church property was a swamp, and the cemetery occupied the land opposite it. This is where many a generation of the Williamsons, Nances, and Browns lie today. About three miles down from the cemetery was first the Red Barn and later, on the same stretch of road, the Sandbox.

The Red Barn was a red barn perched over part of the Lumber River and the happening place to be on a Friday or Saturday night. I was too young to have been there, but my mother's mother and many others portrayed it as a den of sin. When I was young, even driving your car past the turnoff was similar to crossing the Rubicon River. My grandmother would actually tell us to roll the windows up. This was before air-conditioning, so it was not pleasant to be locked in a hot car while we passed by. It was located on the right side of a dead-end road. On the left-hand side of the road were several houses that all belonged to the Williamsons. It was odd that my very conservative and religious grandmother would even ride down this road since there was no way out. It was either drive straight into the river, turn into the Red Barn, or turn around on the left side of the road at the Williamsons'. Here we found ourselves, windows up and holding our breaths in order to prevent sin from infecting our lungs and possibly spreading to others, as Grandma attempted to turn the car around without getting too close to even the pavement that marked the periphery of the Red Barn. I guess she was afraid the sin that had been committed in that building would act as a giant vortex and suck the car and all of us into the black water beneath the Red Barn, never to be seen again.

I would like to relate three instances concerning the Red Barn and Sandbox I recall with vivid detail. The first concerns a time just before I moved to Mississippi. I was staying at my aunt's house because her husband worked shift work. It was shortly after midnight when I heard a knock on the window of the bedroom. My other aunt's husband was frantically beating on the window, saying he needed help.

This was what had happened. There was a slight curve in front of my granddaddy's house that proved difficult to maneuver if one were slightly intoxicated or driving too fast. Many a weekend, my grandparents would wake up on Saturday or Sunday to find one of their trees damaged, their mailbox in the field, or worse, or a car in the ditch or over in the hogpen. This was the first time I saw the results of the aftermath of the den of sin. Two men on a motorcycle failed to make the turn at the curve, then drove off the road and hit a concrete culvert in the drive, causing the bike to flip over my great-uncle's chicken coop and land in the woods where it remained unseen by us until the following day. That night, all I saw was one man lying in the road. I still recall seeing he had the remains of a red shirt on because the following day, for some fifty feet down the road, there was a small trail of red cloth on the black asphalt. The other person was not found until we traced the origins of the moans coming from the woods. Not seeing the motorcycle, we were not able to piece together the story until Sunday morning. To illustrate the closeness of kinship in Columbus County, one of the victims was a Turbeville and related to Grandmother Hazel. At the time, when Ricky and I were searching for the riders that night, I did not know I was related to one of them.

The second instance occurred that same summer. I had just gotten out of the shower when I walked through the kitchen to see a rather attractive brunette woman speaking to someone on the phone. She was crying hysterically, and her makeup was pooling all over her face. My grandparents had a phone cord that was about twenty feet long, and she had somehow wrapped herself in it. It appeared she had just escaped from kidnappers. I was fifteen, and to have such a nice-looking yet strange woman in the house was surprising. My Pa Joe had been known as a flirt, and I imagine when she walked up to the door, distraught and crying, he readily let her use the phone.

As I stood there, a North Carolina state trooper walked into the house and right over to the girl and asked her to come out of the house. He told her an ambulance was on the way to check her for injuries. After coaxing her off the phone, she started talking about hitting the biggest cow she had ever seen. The trooper asked my Pa Joe, who had remained silent this whole time, if he knew anyone who had cows in the area. He replied, "No, there are some just down the road a bit further but not here." I found this rather odd since he had several Black Angus cows in the pasture. Apparently, the woman was on her way to the Red Barn when one of my Pa Joe's jumping cows made it out of the fence, was hit by her car, and then miraculously made it back into the pasture some one hundred feet from the road and fell over dead. Of course, we did not know this when the trooper was walking the wailing woman out of the house. However, within thirty minutes, Pa Joe, my cousin Shawn, and I were scanning the pasture with flashlights to see if anything was amiss. Thankfully, the cows usually stayed under a group of trees at the back of the pasture during the night, and there we found her. Without haste, I was told to get the tractor, and then we hauled that heifer to the very back fields where we spent the next Sunday morning digging a hole large enough to bury a full-grown Black Angus heifer. The den of sin—the Red Barn—had struck again. One day, some scientist will discover her bones in the sandy soil and perhaps attribute her death to some ritualistic sacrifice. Still, Pa Joe would call it lucky the trooper did not pry too deep since he was overly concerned with assisting an attractive twentysomething girl in distress.

The last incident I recall concerning the Red Barn was in 1975 or 1976. There was a shootout there, which resulted in the death of a man. I am not too familiar with today's record of events, but I recall that the Williamsons had blocked the road off at the Red Barn and then had a Western-style shootout with a man. As I recall, the name of the man who was killed was Tart Nance. I heard he did not have enough buckshot in his gun to kill a bird. Such gunfights were common around the river on the weekends.

As stated in the record for the State v. Owens:

> Evidence for the State tended to show the following events. About midnight on 9 January 1982, defendant, Nance, Williamson and others were in the parking lot of the Red Barn nightclub. Defendant threw a cigarette butt at Nance and Nance threw it back. Defendant verbally threatened Nance and Williamson and then shot both of them. Nance was hit in the chest and died of his injuries. Williamson was shot in the right forearm and received medical treatment at a nearby hospital.[38]

Those times Grandma Ara Mae would make us hold our breath in a hot, stifling car with the windows sealed taught me a lesson. I still shy away from bars or clubs.

CHAPTER 13
Fair Bluff

The town of Fair Bluff appears on nineteenth-century maps and is one of the oldest settlements in Columbus County. The people who founded Fair Bluff laid it out along the bend of Drowning Creek—known today as the Lumber River—in western Columbus County. I remember the town as one of the most picturesque towns I have ever seen. The main street was lined with small businesses, and the Fair Bluff Baptist Church was situated in the fork on the road, which crosses the river and heads into Robeson County. Andrew Jackson Highway runs along the banks of the river for a few thousand feet at this spot, and the black water of the river has often reached the banks and crossed the road. Spanish moss hangs from cypress trees that stand sentry over the place where countless people have drowned attempting to swim in the river, hence the name Drowning Creek. The name was probably meant to be a warning many chose to ignore or did not understand.

The town revolved around farming and the farmers who lived in the area. One of the men the businesses and communities depended on was Carl Whiten Meares Sr. His name resonates in my memories because I heard my granddaddy repeat it many times. Uncle Eddie and my father both stated that the farmers around Fair Bluff and Cerro Gordo would not have made it had it not been for Carl. To illustrate this, Uncle Eddie said that Carl's son had once gone through the account books of farmers who were delinquent on their payments or had not made any payments at all to Ellis Meares and Sons. Eddie said Carl told his son to put the accounting book back on the shelf and never take it down again, which he did and never brought the subject up again.

Even today, thirty-two years after I left home, Uncle Eddie still swears by the honesty, integrity, and benevolence of Carl Meares. He often tells the story of how Carl gave his father the money to buy him a pony. When Uncle Eddie had visited Bladenboro with Aunt Elgie, he saw a pony called Goldie and fell in love. He pestered his dad about that pony until his dad said, "If you want it, you will have to ask Carl Meares if you can borrow the money to buy it." That pony was $150, which was a lot of money in the 1960s. Nonetheless, when Uncle Eddie made it to the Ellis Meares and Sons store in Fair Bluff and asked Carl Meares if he could have a loan, Mr. Meares gave him the money to buy the pony. His daddy said later, "Son, you will have to raise a heap of pigs to pay that loan back." After Eddie had saved up fifty dollars, he asked Pa Joe to pay Carl for him, and his daddy said, "You borrowed that money, you pay it back to him."

But when Eddie went to pay Carl, Carl told him, "Since you came to make a payment on that pony, I tell you what I am going to do. I am buying that pony for you, and you do not owe me another penny."

Carl continued to help Uncle Eddie later in life when he needed some money to buy a few barns to cure tobacco. Carl told his secretary, Clara B. Waddell, to write out a check and give it to Eddie whenever he needed one. Uncle Eddie also tells how Carl asked Eddie to come work for him, and he would show him how to make real money because he would never be able to do that just by farming. Carl was growing older and started having difficulty seeing, so he said to Uncle Eddie, "Eddie, I can't see any longer, but my mind is solid, and I can talk and tell you what to do if you will just come and work for me. My children don't need anything, and I can help you have anything you want, but you have to work for me." Uncle Eddie thought about leaving the farm, but the needs of his dad and mom and the counsel of a family relative persuaded him not to leave. Plus, his daddy was depressed. His eyes were bothering him terribly, and he could not work as he used to.

I asked Uncle Eddie if this was a result of Pa Joe's service in WWII in Papua New Guinea, and Uncle Eddie answered, "Affirmative. Daddy made many trips to the veterans' hospital in Durham during this time. One day, we were at the hogpen down in the woods, the one that backed up to the Count's place. You remember that place?" I did. "Daddy sat down on the fence and started crying and said he thought Ara Mae would get some help if he were dead." That frightened Eddie, and he said he hugged his daddy and told him not to talk like that. This exchange is something I never could have imagined if Uncle Eddie had not told me about it. I remember Pa Joe being tough as iron nails and having a callous indifference to things. This emotional moment indeed reveals more than the briary personality I recall. "Daddy would go to Carl Meares and borrow a hundred dollars at a time to give Iris, Teresa, Glenda, and me money to buy clothes and lunch at school," Uncle Eddie says. "There were three people I loved at that age: my daddy, Carl Meares, and Newbert Williamson." Newbert was a distant relative who loaned his truck to my Uncle Eddie and Pa Joe to take the hogs to the market in Chadbourn and helped the family in other ways.

Uncle Eddie also relates that Ara Mae's father, Bruce Eddie Worley, had always done business with Carl Meares. However, one year, "Old Man Eddie," as Pa Joe called him, was persuaded to buy his fertilizer from a store in Tabor City at a lesser price. The next year, there was a shortage of fertilizer, and no one had any but Carl Meares in Fair Bluff. Uncle Eddie said, "Grandpa Eddie just had to tuck his tail between his legs and go to Fair Bluff, but he was too prideful to ask Carl for fertilizer. Thus he just walked around the pallets of fertilizer, looking at the quantity Carl had in stock. Carl eventually saw Eddie and said, 'I know why you are here. Go get your truck and take what you need, but next time, keep your business at Ellis Meares and Sons and not Tabor City.'"

Another time Carl Meares came to the assistance of Uncle Eddie was when Eddie started farming on his own when he was around sixteen years old. He went to the Waccamaw Bank in Chadbourn and asked for a loan of twenty thousand dollars to begin farming. The bank manager asked him if he had any collateral or if his parents would sign for him. Eddie answered both questions with a resounding "No" and filled out the reference section, listing Carl Meares as his first reference. The manager stated he did not think he could make a loan but would present it to the board and answer in two weeks. The next day, the bank manager called and said the loan was ready. This prompt action shocked Eddie until he went to the bank. The manager informed him, "We only had to make one phone call, and that was to Carl Meares. He came down here and cosigned the loan for you."

Growing up, the name Carl Meares seemed like an institution rather than a person. On a recent trip, I rode through Powell Cemetery in Fair Bluff to see if I could locate the grave of Carl. I reasoned that he would surely be there among all the farmers he had assisted during his lifetime. Sure enough, I found the tombstone he shares with his wife. It is impressive but not flashy. It reminds me of a great oak stump embedded in the soil with deep roots.

Uncle Eddie stated that Carl Jr. did not have any interest in operating the store in Fair Bluff, but Carl Sr. had made him promise he would keep it open as long as the last employee he had hired was working. Carl kept his promise, and when the last employee, Mr. Cribb, was the only remaining person working that Carl Sr. had hired, Carl Jr. told his father that when Mr. Cribb was ready to retire, Carl Jr. would lock the door when he walked out and that would be the end of the business and the promise. Ultimately, when the second floodwaters of a hurricane ravaged Fair Bluff, the store finally closed. Nature had intervened on behalf of Carl Jr. and relieved him of his promise to his father.

There is one last piece of advice Mr. Carl told Uncle Eddie that is relevant for all ages.

Eddie stated that Carl told him in dealings with family and strangers, "Money, time, and greed will alter the way people feel about things." Uncle Eddie stated, "When I was a young boy and Mr. Carl said this, I did not believe him. Especially when I considered the implications of this concerning family, but now that six decades have passed since he stated this, I see he was right, as he always was." Eddie further added that anything to do with business and land or dealings with people needed to be in writing, signed, and recorded at the courthouse in Whiteville; otherwise they were promises vanished into the air moments after they were spoken.

The Fair Bluff in my memories is one of expensive-looking homes backing up to Drowning Creek. I remember when I would drive through Fair Bluff, I would see the tennis court that looked like something out of a luxury magazine. Mostly, I remember seeing the funeral home where I said goodbye to my granddaddy and baby brother. When I used to pass the Veterans of Foreign Wars post perched on the banks of the Lumber River next to US Highway 76 or Andrew Jackson Highway, I would see the rope that always hung from the moss-covered tree. Occasionally, there would be people swinging out over the dark-black water, and as they reached the apex, they would let go and drop beneath the dark water in a splash. My mom would always remark, "Don't ever let me see you do that. Those people are lucky they come back up." Perhaps the river should have kept its original name of Drowning Creek as a precaution.

In 2016, the river and Hurricane Matthew declared war on Fair Bluff and put the town's future in jeopardy. As Jess Bidgood and Alan Blinder stated in the *New York Times*, "Fair Bluff was incorporated in 1873, with the Lumber River—currently inundating the town—and a railroad as its lifeblood, supporting logging and trade. By the 1970s, it was small but thriving, sustained by tobacco farms and warehouses, said Ken Elliot, 48, who, like many people here, grew up in a tobacco farming family. When those tobacco farms began to go under, people found new work. Mr. Elliot became a firefighter and paramedic, and he spent last weekend rescuing his friends and neighbors from the encroaching floodwaters. Others found jobs in a new plant that makes vinyl building materials."[39]

I recently drove through Fair Bluff on the way to Powell Cemetery, and an article I read in the *News & Observer* by Martha Quillin best described the scene I witnessed. She wrote, "A few of the century-old buildings have been emptied out, but dried river mud coats the warped floors, and black mold laces the walls. Ruined paint cans and brushes sit on the shelves at Ellis Meares & Son True Value, and in a shop where former mayor Randy Britt once sold women's Sunday dresses, the chrome racks stand empty. With power still out to most of downtown, even the clock on the post outside what used to be Elvington Pharmacy is frozen in time. From my perspective, it looks like a movie set in a Hollywood backdrop to a *Walking Dead* episode. A far cry from the bicentennial parade I witnessed there in 1976. The floats seemed endless and stretched the entire length of Main Street from the Baptist Church to the Ford dealership a distance of over a mile."[40]

Then, the town's downtown area that is now abandoned had the largest fireworks show I had witnessed up until that time. From my perspective, I am sad to see the town slowly crumble into the streets and witness the bricks being carried off to someone's backyard at the beach. But the reality is Carl Meares is in the cemetery, and there is no one to replace him because there are no industries to bring people into towns such as Fair Bluff. In my youth, there were three tobacco warehouses in Fair Bluff, and they had long ago been abandoned to be swallowed by time and nature. The vibrancy of these towns was the hardworking people, and now, the people who remain standing have to find a living in other places.

Turning right in front of the Baptist church was the bridge that led you to Robeson County. Once you crossed that bridge, you were in the swamp, and in the end, the swamp and river will reclaim what was once floodplain when the first Europeans ventured into this area and claimed a fair bluff to build a town.

As I was completing this manuscript, the town of Fair Bluff was to begin removing the flood-damaged stores in downtown and has plans to begin a new town. My hope is there will always be a town and community on the fair bluff of the Lumber River (Drowning Creek) in western Columbus County.

CHAPTER 14
Cerro Gordo and Cerro Gordo School

I have always thought the school building is situated on Highway 76 or Andrew Jackson Highway in Cerro Gordo like an impressive Roman- or Greek-like structure. This building would not have been out of place on one of the Seven Hills of Rome or the acropolis in Athens. Other than the crumbling buildings that once composed the downtown area, the school was the largest brick building in the town. Those brick structures that consisted of a once-vibrant street lay on one side of the railroad tracks.

Sometime in either the fifth or the sixth grade, I thought for sure I could forever capture the school's magnificence on paper. I attempted to draw it to bring home and place on the refrigerator since that was the spot all the family's art went, for it was the spot most often visited by anyone, so there was a higher chance of being bragged on by those who saw the artwork. I soon found out my talent for drawing was almost like my talent for singing, speaking, or dancing—about what could be poured into a thimble belonging to a Lilliputian.

Across from the railroad tracks stood an old train depot, which was built of wood, and on the other side of the depot was perhaps the best-kept building in the town: Wallace Oil and Gas. The windows in this building were clear, and the inside was lit up, as if it were repainted every day before opening. The older buildings on what was once the area where several storefronts faced the railroad tracks were in various stages of distress. The one on the left was still intact but empty, and someone routinely seemed to pile it with stuff that was no longer worthy of being thrown away but not good enough to keep nearby. Thus, over the years, it continued to fill with various castoffs from people's lives.

The store across from it was vacant for many years until someone attempted to open a ceramic shop. This perhaps lasted no more than a year, and then it was boarded up again. The store next to the abandoned building was home to Anderson's. Today, it would be called an "emporium of various everything at some trendy, affluent neighborhood off Park Road in Charlotte" because it was a place to get just about anything you needed from fishing bait, hammers, household items, and sugar. Despite the fact it was the busiest place in town when I was young, I never ventured in there much with my family, primarily because we lacked the money to buy anything in there other than a soda.

There was one time I explicitly recall going in there and being simply amazed. I had stayed with my cousins, and they were friends with two of the more affluent boys in the community. Their dad was taking us fishing, and he stopped in Anderson's to buy some crickets and worms. I remember standing in front of a wall of candy Milton Hershey would have been proud to put in a museum. I have never seen such a variety of candy in one place. From gummies to chocolate bars, it was all there and more. It was candy heaven in Cerro Gordo, and all I had ever done was ride by it on my way to Cedar Grove.

Anderson's holds another special memory: that of my cousin Charles Mitchell Powel Jr., or "Chris" as we called him. In my eyes, Chris personified the best traits in a man. He was always smiling, was respectful, was friendly—he always called my dad "Page" rather than "Uncle Mitchell"—and had the prettiest girlfriend and old muscle cars. One day, he took me to play basketball at Porter Swamp Baptist Church, and on the way back home, he played a Richard Pryor eight-track tape. (Interestingly, I never imagined I would own property only a few hundred yards from this church.) As we crossed the railroad that divided the town, he sped up his 1968 Z-28 Camaro, then slammed on the brakes to circle in front of Anderson's store, stopped right in front of the vending machine, hopped out, bought two bottles, got back in the car, and handed me one. It was as if I was living in the cola commercial when L.C. Greenwood gives the kid his jersey. Most of my life, I only witnessed people taking things from others. Thus, seeing someone of immense talent and position freely give his jersey to a child made an impression on me. I would rather be that type of person than one who basks in glory without giving back to those who are less fortunate.

I do not know what the building next door to Anderson's and what used to be a bank was back in the early 1900s, but my memories are that of a tire store. My father knew the person who owned it because I recall stopping by there one day. I stood there surrounded by black rubber tires and men asking me to say "shit" until they were rolling-on-the-floor laughing. Apparently, they thought it was hilarious to hear me say that word. I had a difficulty pronouncing my words correctly, and it came out sounding like "sit." This difficulty became an embarrassment, especially when the speech pathologist would come to the school and pull me out of class to take lessons in the back of the auditorium. At least the school made an effort to improve my speech, whereas my dad encouraged me to say things wrong because it was funny.

As mentioned, the building to the right of the tire store had perhaps once been a functionally designed brick building housing a bank. The story is that once the Brown and Williamson Lumber Company that operated in Cerro Gordo burned and closed, the employment base in the community slowly disappeared and with that, the deposits. The final nail in the coffin to the future of the bank was the Great Depression. The front of the building was still there, and the door was boarded up. However, if you walked around to the right of the building, it looked as if it had been left from some forgotten part of a battle General Sherman waged during the Civil War. The facade was still standing, and the wall adjoining the other building was still there, but it was mainly piles of brick and rubble. That is, except for the metal safe that crowned a pile of rubble and brick in the back. At the time, I imagined there were all kinds of treasures and valuables sitting in that safe. It was as large as a modern stove. Seated in all that rubble, overlooked by everyone, was the key to happiness, no matter what may have been inside. Of course, the Depression had taken any money in that safe back in the 1930s, but seeing it lying on top of the rubble kindled thoughts of Blackbeard's treasure for a young boy like me. I do not know what happened to that safe, but I still wonder what was inside it.

During the Bicentennial of the United States in 1976, the community's women attempted to revitalize the old train depot. It received a new coat of fresh white paint, the area around it was planted with flowers, and a few concrete statues were placed next to it. It would have been a pretty sight to see if the train from Wilmington still stopped there. However, by 1976, the passenger train was exclusively a freight train, and it merely slowed to a gallop as it passed through Cerro Gordo. The only time anyone even noticed the depot was perhaps when the railroad's arms descended across the tracks, stopping traffic as the trains rocked and swayed as they moved by and into Fair Bluff and then South Carolina. I recall sitting there one day, watching and growing numb from the monotonous click of metal against the track as one dull reddish-brown car after another clanked and thudded against the metal rails and swayed left and right. Sitting there on those tracks, I momentarily glanced over and admired the efforts of the civic-minded onlookers trying to see history but was inevitably rocked to sleep by the long parade of one railcar after another, as if the train's tail stretched to Wilmington. In the end, many like me would be just like those reddish-brown railcars heading off toward Charlotte or Wilmington only to come through Cerro Gordo on the way to the beach. Today, as I sit recalling this, there is not much of the old Cerro Gordo remaining.

The old depot is a patch of sandy soil now; you could never imagine one having been there. The buildings on the opposite side of the tracks are gone too. In their place lies a nice square patch of green grass that looks like it belongs on a football field. The only thing that remains on that side of the road is the stop sign at the corner, where my mom stopped on many occasions before making that right turn onto Cedar Grove Road. I knew that spot well, for from that point on, it felt as though you left civilization and traveled to some different place separate from Cerro Gordo. The only connection the two areas seemed to have was their shared zip code. I never enjoyed making that right turn, and I still do not today because each time I turn there, I am reminded of where I was born. However, it is a turn I will continue to make for as long as I can because it reminds me that there is always a way out. I was loved and have never gone hungry, but to do something and improve one's self really *means* something. It is just another problematic turn that must be made like any other turn in life. How could it be so bad if what lies beyond that turn was home and memories of people and events?

But I digress and need to return to Cerro Gordo School.

As I have stated, the school was one of the most classical places in the area. In her beauty lies my fondness for columns, quoin corners, and brick. Long before I saw a Roman or Greek building in a history book, I had Cerro Gordo School for inspiration. The building was built with federal assistance in either the late 1920s or the 1930s, and it brought grace to the community and is still in use today. Currently, the school is in the process of being replaced, and although I have not seen the plans, my inclination is the classical architecture will be modernized and only be a memory.

My father graduated from there, and when I attended, I sat in the same rooms as he had. My mother's mother, Ara Mae, walked its corridors and attended every high school reunion until she died. She was actually the only one of my grandparents to graduate high school. Back then, to have a high school diploma said much about you and even more about the status of your family in the community. Anyone who had money graduated from high school, and those who did not indicated their families did not have much.

During the late 1960s or early 1970s, the county added a wing onto the building for kindergarten through fifth grade. Thankfully, they had the decency to connect the two parts with an extended covered walkway. Thus, the old school, built in the 1920s, still stood there with its red brick facade capped with white columns, its annex with the flat roof, its tiny windows looking like a garden shed, a flat tail on a magnificent kite. The addition that was added onto the schools did not bear any resemblance to the original Federal-style building. The original school could have been placed in any community, and anyone would have stated it was dressed as a federal public building. I think public buildings should speak to the part of "public." They should be edifices as the Romans and Greeks made them and convey the sense of community and standards of who we are. The old school did that; the annex was a single hallway with classrooms off the hall. The roof was a three pitch at the most, and the windows rose from halfway up the floor to the ceiling. There was no "entrance" graced with columns of plaques with quotes from great leaders. Just two steel doors leading to an open hallway. It resembled a stable more than a school.

My first memories of the school are not ones I recall with any degree of fondness. I have never learned why this is the case, but my birth month prevented me from attending kindergarten with other students who were born in 1965. However, when it came time to be in the first grade, I was labeled old and qualified enough to be in the same class as those who had a year's head start on me. It was as if the runt piglet had been given a chance to prove himself and then was randomly tossed in the litter with those who had front-row seats to the teat for over a year. Whatever the reason behind the decision, I was among a hostile tribe.

I have two distinct memories of first grade.

One is of the most beautiful creature I had ever seen up until that time. Her name was Angie, and I thought she was a porcelain doll someone had made in a factory. I recall Angie had curly brown hair and was the prettiest girl in first grade. I will forever remember the day we had our school pictures made, and she sat in the front row of the auditorium, waiting her turn to get her picture taken. She was wearing a blue dress and her blonde hair was styled, and I just thought she was the prettiest thing in the world. However, she was also the most intimidating person. After mustering enough courage to speak to her that day, I did not talk to her again for many years to come. She and others were placed in a different class, separated from us until the fourth grade. The next time I would ever say two words to her would be in the seventh grade, when she sat across from me in Ms. Powell's class. She had long since given up dresses and was wearing jeans and a Bee Gees T-shirt—that was the year the Bee Gees were a smash hit because of *Saturday Night Fever*. Angie was maturing into a young woman, rolling her tongue across her upper lip while staring at me. It was as if the snake were dangling from the tree, holding ripe red apple in front of my eyes. It scared the dickens out of me ... it really did. I asked Ms. Powell if I could move my seat, and luckily, she changed the whole layout of the room. This time, Angie was two seats in front of me, and I was safe. From a distance, I overheard her and some others talk about how they had managed to gain access to a club called the Gator in South Carolina. It was as if they were five years older than me. I was still imitating an aircraft and flying it to the bus in the afternoon. Pretty accurate to state I was still a child.

My other memory of this time in school is of a boy who would be an on-and-off-again friend until I moved. His name was Dion. After lunch, we usually had recess, and everyone would save their milk cartons and dig in the school ground for worms. I remember coming home with a carton of dirt and worms. It seems a bit disgusting now, but back then, it seemed normal enough to catch as many as possible and stuff them into a milk carton. I had no idea what to do with them when I came home, and usually, Mom would simply dump the worms in the yard. We had fertile dirt because every day after school that I came home with a pint of worms, Mom would have to dispose of them in the yard. I think back now and think how disgusting this was.

Anyway, there was an altercation between Dion and me when I was in the first grade, and he ended it by throwing sand in my face. I cannot recall what the disagreement was about, but as I noted, I was a newcomer to a class that had already had a year of school behind them. Well, I threw my fist into *his* face and hit him squarely on the nose. That seemed to prevent any further aggression on his part, and I remember standing over the water fountain at the end of the hall washing sand out of my eyes and face. He and I would eventually become somewhat friends, and he would go on trips with my family to the beach or amusement parks in the future.

I'll be frank. As my memory serves me, I loathed school and found it difficult to make friends. The entire click had been set, and I was like a cow left out of the roundup and then discovered but left outside the fence to fend for itself while the others circled inside. Mom must have felt obligated to come to my rescue, as she always did, and gave me a birthday party in the sixth grade. I just hid in the woods as she begged me to come out and entertain the guests who had come to celebrate my birthday. From my perspective, they were all enemies who would not play with me at school, who threw sand in my face, or who broke my tender young heart. Of course, I received two obligatory invitations to two birthday parties in return: Monica's, who had been a relative of my Uncle Mitchell and best friends with Angie, and even Angie's, but it may as well have been a trip to the principal's office. Many years later, I learned not only were they friends, but they were related to one another. I did not desire to go to the birthday parties, but I did and was never again asked to attend any birthday party after that.

The only good memories I have of school are of the first grade teacher, Ms. Church. Perhaps her grace came from her name, but I do not know if she could have been any sweeter if her name was Ms. Sugar. I truly believe I only made it through first grade because of her. One time, while under Ms. Church's teaching, I recall wanting a pair of scissors in order to make the paper dolls Grandma Hazel used to show me how to make. Since I did not have a pair of scissors, I took the ones from the classroom and slid them into my pants pocket. Unbeknownst to me, I had slid them into the pocket with a hole, and as I stood up, they slid down my leg and onto my shoe. I stood there frozen, as if I were Lot's wife. Ms. Church immediately saw the scissors and said, "Jeffrey, you must have dropped those. Please give them to me." She did not say another word, nor to my knowledge, did she say anything to my parents.

At some point, someone recommended to my parents that I repeat the first grade, but neither of them could fathom the possibility of me being any less than my classmates and insisted I be promoted just like the rest to the second grade. The following year, I found myself back with the same classmates I did not fit in with and who seemed not to like me too much. I am not sure if Mom and Dad were aware of my exceptional circumstance or not, but the fact was I lost my one chance to escape.

Once, one of my new peers told me I was famous because if one spelled my last name, Page, backward, it was "Egypt." I guess he meant it *sounded* like "Egypt" because it was actually "Egap." I took the bait—hook, line, and sinker—and felt a bit proud for being famous.

I remember struggling so much that a teacher, Ms. Gerald, allowed me to come over and be tutored by one of her students, Ward Cribb. Usually, Ward helped me by having me count straws. He would hold up two in one hand and then three or four in the other hand and have me add and subtract them. After a few minutes of this, I was sent back to my classroom to be the king of Egap. That was what my tutoring consisted of … plastic straws. The unique arrangement continued through the third grade but changed when I started the fourth grade.

That summer, I had worked in tobacco or "backer," and as August ended, I dreaded having to return to school. My anguish was extreme. Standing outside the door of Ms. Renfrow's class with Mom, I was begging to go home, but Mom said I had to be in school. Ms. Renfrow was a short lady with white hair balled up in a military-style bun on the back of her head. She would have made an excellent drill sergeant with her demeanor and military-like bearing. She simply told Mom to leave and then grabbed me by the arm and told me to "go inside that class at once and sit down." Well, I had no other choice at that point. Mom was leaving me, and Ms. Renfrow had a death grip on my arm. The only way I could get free was to walk through the door and take my seat in the second row. At the end of the year, with a C in all my subjects, I progressed to the fifth grade and Ms. Willis's class where I was the king of Egap again. There I reigned until the sixth grade.

During my sixth grade year, I had a fairly older teacher named Ms. Hayes. As I recall, she was not nice and not very empathetic. My perception today is she should have been enjoying retirement and not teaching children. I thought she probably had taught my Grandma Ara Mae when she was a young girl. Sometime between September and November, Ms. Hayes's age caught up with her ambition, and she did not come back to work. We had a substitute until Christmas break, and when we returned in January, our new teacher was Ms. Debbie Strickland. She told us to call her "Ms. Debbie." She was in her twenties and, thus, very different from the older teachers. I did not know it at the time, but we were kin on Grandma Ara Mae's side because Ara Mae's mother was a Strickland. To this day, I am not sure why Ms. Debbie took an interest in my education. Maybe she was just doing her job as a teacher, or perhaps she knew Strickland blood coursed through my veins as it did hers. Nonetheless, she sent me to speech class with a tutor, who came once or twice a week to the school. We would meet in the back of the gym/auditorium with about three other students. Again, I found myself with a select few separated from the herd. I realize this was beneficial to my future, but at the time, it was only another sign of me not quite measuring up. Being conscious of the difference in my speech still continues to nag at my self-esteem, but I have found it better to embrace and laugh at myself rather than stand silently as others laugh.

Ms. Debbie did one other thing that changed my life. She would take us to the library, and Mr. Faulk, the librarian, would take us on tour around the small library, showing us how to find things. It was there on the bookshelf against the long wall toward the back where I found a book on Napoleon. Of course, I did not know who he was. The only stories of history I knew or had heard of were about the Civil War and the war Pa Joe had fought against the Japanese. But inside this book was also a person from Corsica who had made himself master of Europe and took the crown from the pope. I found him to be incredibly inspirational. This ignited a desire to read every book I could get. Books became objects of desire, and when the book drive came, and you could order books off an ordering form, I collected all the change I could to get one or more. Ms. Debbie gave me an opportunity to prove myself. I did not know at the time that she was a Strickland, but perhaps she knew who my family was and that one of my great-grandmothers was a Strickland. Therefore, maybe she was giving me a chance because I was related to her. Of course, Ms. Debbie was a genuinely kind person who felt the need to reach out to all her students and not cater to those whose parents were in positions of influence in the community.

When my Uncle Charles was dying of cancer in the hospital, I saw Ms. Debbie when she visited him. I thanked her then for everything she did for me in school. Later, thirty-eight years after the sixth grade, I saw her again while she was mowing her grass. She had retired from the North Carolina school system but was working in South Carolina at Loris. I thanked her once again, but I am not sure she even knew who I was then. As a teacher who sees hundreds of students each year, she probably just simply forgot about me, which was fine with me since I consider her to be a good teacher. She was one who made a difference in my education, but perhaps she just did not understand what she had done for me. The point is that I knew and shall always be grateful, if she remembers me or not. I stayed with my 1965 class from that point on. I was no longer separated from the smarter ones but was placed with them instead. I had crossed over because of a book and a teacher. I am sure the prayers of my parents and all my dad's effort helped too. I used to pray to "get it" and even slept with a book to hopefully absorb the knowledge by osmosis, and somehow, it came to me as naturally as if my missing shadow finally caught up to me. In the seventh grade, I made the Junior Beta Club.

"What Did You Say?" Speech Back Home

There are many people in Columbus, Bladen, Robeson, Marion, and Horry Counties who originated from Virginia, and the Carolina Pages, my ancestors, migrated from Virginia and Craven County, North Carolina, which were crisscrossed and laced with impassable swamps and contained very few easily traveled roads. Further, from what I have gathered, most of "my people" came into North Carolina and South Carolina through Virginia, not from Charleston. Thus, even though the area lacked the vast slave-based economies of South Carolina and Virginia, many people had slaves.

From 1815 to 1835, North Carolina was called the Rip Van Winkle state for its lack of economic progress. Historian William Powell claims that not much was "going on anywhere" in the early- to mid-1800s, and people seemed satisfied with their state of affairs.[41] Further, a legislative committee report in 1830 observed North Carolina was "a state without foreign commerce, for want of seaports or a staple; without internal communication by rivers, roads, or canals; without a cash market for any article of the agricultural product; without manufactures; in short, without any object to which native industry and active enterprise could be directed."[42]

Most of the settlers who came to the eastern part of the state did not do so by way of Wilmington but rather by way of the interior, down from Virginia. The typical pattern in other states was to land at a port and then migrate into the interior. North Carolina had some people who came to a port city and then ventured into the interior, but many more moved down from Virginia after their ancestors had settled around what became Norfolk, Virginia. William Hilton navigated the waters of the Cape Fear in 1662 and 1663, but New Hanover County, in which Wilmington resided, was not created until 1729. In 1734, Bladen County was carved from New Hanover, and in 1808, Columbus County was formed from parts of New Hanover and Brunswick Counties.

The slow settlement of this part of North Carolina was indicated by the efforts to establish Bladen Precinct—Bladen County. Attempts were made in 1732 in the general assembly to provide two new precincts, Onslow and Bladen, from the more significant precinct of New Hanover. Bladen Precinct was erected on October 31, 1732, but at this time, a controversy arose over constitutional authority to erect new precincts. Further attempts made in 1733 were also unsuccessful. When the matter was brought before the council in Edenton, it was again refused. The council stated, "In Bladen, there are not over three freeholders, Nathaniel Moore, Thomas Jones, and Richard Singletary, and not over thirty families, including these freeholders."[43]

Ironically, because of this isolation and the lack of immigration until the modern era, many places in the South remained, somewhat, distinctively English. For example, the South accounted for less than 5 percent of all foreign-born people in the United States from 1850 until 1985. In 1900, the foreign-born population in North and South Carolina was 0.2 percent and 0.4 percent, respectively. As I have discovered in my family research, many of the families were very closely related to one another. In *The South Old and New: A History 1820–1947* by Francis Butler Simkins and Charles Pierce Roland, the English settlers of the South "suffered grievously at times because of an unimaginativeness that prevented the adaption of English ways to non-English conditions." Moreover, they "still retained more English characteristics than any migration of Anglo-Saxon since the original members of the race colonized Britain."[44]

The information I have gathered on the people of Columbus, Marion, and Horry Counties indicates an origin in England in the southwest and adjacent to the border of Wales. Many of these people came to British America as indentured servants. David Hackett Fischer in *Albion's Seed: Four British Folkways in America* states, "A majority of Virginia's indentured servants hailed from sixteen counties in the south and west of England, the same area that produced Virginia's elite." He further states that Virginia's Isle of Wight, where many of my people had landed, "originated from the counties of Gloucester, Somerset, Devon, Dorset, Wiltshire, and Hampshire." Of course, this is a generality, as the Strickland origins are farther north on the border of Scotland and England. In general, the stomping grounds of these people had been the old kingdom of Wessex. Fischer mentions the "Turbevilles from Bere Regis" as one of the first families of Virginia—the same Turbevilles made famous by Thomas Hardy in his novel *Tess of the D'Urbervilles*.[45]

Today, Bere Regis is still a tiny village with one shop, a post office, and two pubs, the Royal Oak and the Drax Arms.[46] Moreover, southwest England had less than a few thousand people in 1600. In Dorset, the largest town was Dorchester, with only fifteen hundred people.[47] The isolation of the swamps was something these people were accustomed to, and this further developed the independence trait, which multiplied itself by families intermarrying over the generations. In the end, the majority of Columbus, Marion, and Horry Counties were

English but not dictated by the same attitude as the Barbadians, who had settled Charleston, and the Cavaliers of Virginia. The two cultures never seemed to mesh despite their common English origins.

Another aspect of Columbus and Horry Counties I am compelled to include in this is the accents of the people I knew. When I moved to Mississippi in 1981, the people who lived there kept asking me to speak because I had an accent. This was dismaying to me, as I was in the Deep South. To me, they were the ones who had an accent, but for the year I was down there, they kept entertaining people with "onliest zinc" for the kitchen sink, "meiciderzn" for medicine, "dere" for there, "hoo do" to mean doing someone wrong in a deal, "addled" to mean fraying one's nerves by pestering, and many more.

In *Albion's Seed*, Fischer noted the speech pattern developed in early Virginia. Instead of "I am," "you are," "she isn't," "it doesn't," and "I haven't," the Virginians said, "I be," "you be," "she ain't," "it don't," and "I hain't." The words "mess of greens" were for vegetables, "cater-cornered" for crooked, "chomp" for chew, "innards" for insides, "bandanna" for handkerchief, "right good" for very good, and so on. Others are "dis" for this, "dat" for that, "holp" for help, and "puriddy" for pretty. All these words and phrases bombarded my ears as I grew up. They were also identified as "archaic" or "provincial" expressions, but they persisted for three centuries. Fischer stated these expressions were not invented in Virginia but have their origins in the South and West of England during the seventeenth century in Sussex, Hampshire, Dorset, Wiltshire, Somerset, Oxford, Gloucester, Warwick, or Worcester.[48] My research confirms that almost all my people originated in the places mentioned. Fischer also verified that these speech patterns had been established before the importation of African slaves had much impact on the language.[49] While some words of African origin did enter my vocabulary, there were not many.

The English, who had migrated to Virginia and then to Columbus and Horry Counties, were known as "poor Protestants" who did not exhibit reliance on plantation agriculture like the coastal areas did. Horry and Columbus Counties were the frontier in the late 1700s. Consider the following: In Georgetown County in 1820, there were 1,830 Whites, 15,546 slaves, and 227 free Blacks. In the same year in Horry County, there were 3,568 Whites, 1,434 slaves, and 23 free Blacks. While there were slaves in Horry County, the ratios of Whites to Blacks in Horry illustrate individual families and small farms settled the area.[50]

In my lifetime, the language patterns of my childhood were easing their way into extinction. Illustrating this best was the fact that when I moved to Chester County in 1982, the same phenomenon which had taken place in Mississippi took place again in Chester. The statement, "You can sure tell you are from Mississippi," was all I heard for the first six months. I always just laughed and thought, *No, this is eastern North Carolina.*

When I returned home with my New Jersey wife, she was lost and confused and needed an interpreter. She met one of my aunts for the first time then, and this was what she heard: "I holp to die if y'all are not running out of here like a scalding dog."

Translation: "I really wish you would stay longer and not be in such a hurry."

Wherever I go, the accent and words are carried, and so, too, is Columbus County. Incidentally, when I was living at home, there were different accents in Columbus County. My dad's friend Wayne Register sounded much different from anyone I had heard speak before. Wayne was from Crusoe Island in Columbus County. Back then, Crusoe was only a place on one side of Lake Waccamaw, the Waccamaw River, and the Green Swamp. Only later did I learn of the origins of Wayne Register's brogue.

Legend has it, Jean Formy-Duvall, a French army surgeon in the late eighteenth or early nineteenth century, conspired with an execution squad to spare the lives of a small group of royalists. Formy-Duvall and his coconspirators filled the executioners' guns with blanks. As the firearms discharged, the condemned feigned death. Formy-Duvall created fake death certificates, and he and those whose lives he had spared headed for the French countryside. When the conspiracy was discovered, the group fled for Haiti, but their time there was relatively short lived. A slave insurrection arose there in 1791, and many French settlers fled the island. Formy-Duvall and his group supposedly took to the Caribbean in an open boat. Sometime after that, they were picked up at sea by a ship, which eventually dropped them on the North Carolina coast at Smithville—now known as Southport.[51] Another origin of the people of Crusoe was reported upon by Ben Dixon MacNeill of the *New York Herald Tribune* in 1931.[52] Then, about four generations removed from the slave revolt in Haiti in 1804, his research suggests that four to five French families managed to find a boat to flee Haiti during the slave revolt. These people were picked up in the ocean by a ship headed to Wilmington, North Carolina. The captain feared reports of his assisting these French families would be discovered and reported back in Haiti. Therefore, he dropped them off thirty miles south of the Cape Fear River and Wilmington at the mouth of the Waccamaw River in South Carolina. From there the French families migrated up the Waccamaw and toward Lake Waccamaw in Columbus County. There they discovered remnants of a Portuguese colony from the result of a Spanish ship running a Portuguese ship aground in the Carolinas a hundred years earlier. The memories of the slave revolt in Haiti that had killed three thousand to five thousand French families alive in their minds, the people of Crusoe Island slowly became less French and more native Carolinian. For example,

Cluceires became Clewis, De Saucerie became Sasser, and Formy-Duval degenerated into half a dozen variations. Whatever the origins, Crusoe Island is a unique place in the county and North Carolina.

Natives of Crusoe claim they are not French, and descendants/residents of Crusoe Island have long disputed the story of three early English settlers: Cornelis Clewis, Laspeyre Long, and Elias Register. Rochester, Kent, England is perhaps the origin of the name Register. This place has existed since the Romans occupied Britain. Originally called Durobrivis, it was pronounced "Robrivis." The word *cæster*—"castle" from Latin *castrum*—was added to the name, and the city was called Robrivis Cæster. Bede mentions the city in ca. 730 and named it Hrofes cæster, mistaking its meaning as "Hrofi's fortified camp." From this, we get ca. 730 Hrofæscæstre, 811 Hrofescester, 1086 Rovescester, and 1610 Rochester. The Latinized adjective Roffensis refers to Rochester.[53]

From what I have pieced together, these words may have originated in Suffolk, England, as a Suffolk dialect. The word "yesterday," as well as any other words ending in "-day," becomes "-di" as in "Toosdi." Another example is words containing /au/ sounds—as in "ouch"—becoming something resembling "e-oo." This affects words like "now," which becomes "ne-oo." One final example of this, which is familiar to my Columbus County ears, is words such as "picture" and "lecture," which become "pitcher" and "letcher."[54] Today, passing from somewhere in my youth, I exclaim the expression, "Stop hem haw assing around!" which is to say, "Stop dragging your feet or wasting time." Another is "slap ass wide open," which is to express a wide-open situation that can be exploited by an adversary. And somehow, the word "onliest" is to emphasize it is the only one left. Rather amazing that some of the British words survived the journey across the Atlantic and then remained isolated in the rural districts of the Carolinas.

CHAPTER 15
Wiggins, Mississippi

As discussed earlier, when I was in my sophomore year at West Columbus, the family moved to Mississippi. Interestingly enough, it was a trip many of my relatives had made 150 years prior. As opposed to the months it took those earlier relatives to reach Mississippi, our trip took about twelve hours. I cannot imagine crossing all that territory without proper roads and convenience stores along the route. Those relatives who came in the 1800s stayed and became Mississippians, Alabamians, Louisianans, or Texans. When we moved to Mississippi, I did not know what my outcome would be, but in my heart, I would always remain a Carolinian and hoped I would return home or closer to home one day.

Wiggins, Mississippi, is off Highway 49 between Hattiesburg and Gulfport and is the largest city in Stone County. We approached the city from Hattiesburg, traveling south. We had made a left-hand turn onto some road. I do not recall the name of that road, just that it meanders through the center of town and then reconnects itself to Highway 49. It's really no more than a side road off the main path. We came to Wiggins,

Mississippi, after Dad had been fired from his job at Georgia Pacific. We spent the first four days in a double-bed motel adjacent to Highway 49.

During one of these days, Mom took me to Stone High School and enrolled me in the tenth grade. I was not ready for this, and I would spend the next few months not knowing what to do with myself during lunch breaks. The high school had a central courtyard, and during the holidays, all the students who had given me the impression they came from some level of economic security loitered along the walkway between the two buildings. Those who were White and of lesser economic means seemed to gather among the grassy courtyard. African-Americans who attended the school were nowhere to be seen, as they gathered somewhere behind the gym. I did not know where to place myself. From my perspective, the high school needed a Lost and Found, and that was where I needed to be, placed directly under the sign in the forlorn hope someone would find me and put me back where I was supposed to be. This place—my imaginary Lost and Found—is where I have become oddly familiar with ever since that time. I never seemed to know where I belonged in Columbus County, and here in Mississippi, I was even more hopelessly out of place than I was at home. Searching for a place, I have become like most Americans who move and are not tied to any place, but I think of the places where most of my ancestors are buried as "home."

Despite my trepidation, I enrolled in Stone High School while staying in a hotel until permanent housing for the family was found. The realtor who took us by to see some houses evidently did not comprehend that tenant houses should not be on the list of properties to be seen. It was a lesson that would forever taint my opinion of the profession of realtors. I've never felt as poor as I had when we pulled up to a white-clad board house, which looked like something that had survived the Great Depression or could have been some abandoned home on the delta of the Mississippi River. The shingles on the roof were curling up on the ends, like potato chips that've been overbaked. The paint was cracking and peeling off the walls in such a manner, the winds of a hurricane would have probably stripped any remaining paint off within seconds and sent it flying off to Alabama. A peculiar odor seemed to linger in the air and shroud the house, as if a skunk had recently sprayed the front porch or was still lodged somewhere in the walls. I learned later that the smell was from the town's largest employer: a nearby pickle factory. As I recall, Mom did not even get out of the car, which was a delightful decision.

The house we finally found and rented until we found something to purchase was not far from the white board home we first saw. It was a brick home in a long line of about ten or more brick homes on both sides of the street—we did not stay here long, as Dad found an older brick ranch just outside of town. The primary thing I remember about this place was the girl who lived down the street from our home. Her name was Becky, and she had lost the lower part of one of her legs in a motorcycle accident. She had this frenzied auburn hair and was a bit on the chubby side in the face.

One night, a friend of mine was driving me around the neighborhood. On the way back to the house, they gave Becky a ride home—I don't recall where she had been—and I was forced to sit in the back seat with her. She was a truly wonderful person, but I was not romantically interested in her. Thus, when she made her move by leaning into me face-first, I simply opened the car door and jumped out. When my friend spread the story, they said I had been afraid of "one-leg Becky" and jumped out of the car to escape from her. Becky was much more aggressive than I was accustomed to, and besides, I hardly knew her. Well, I am not ashamed to say that was the truth. We soon relocated to our permanent home, and I never saw Becky again.

One day, I was at my new high school named after the county, which I still find hilarious to name a school "Stone," when an argument erupted between a short, stocky guy named Johnny and some other boy whose name I do not recall. I remember Johnny mainly because he always wore cowboy boots, had straight blond hair that he parted down the middle, and could not have been more than five foot six, but he conducted himself with a swagger and assuredness that a wolverine would admire.

There was one sport the boys of Mississippi seemed to love better than hunting, and that was fighting. These two were determined to settle the score, like Ali and Frazier. From my perspective, I saw this as my opportunity to win approval and friends, so when there was a deadlock as to where they could settle their dispute like some old Western television show, I volunteered the pecan orchard behind my new house. My new friends took the suggestion, and after school, I led the duelers and onlookers to my home. When we showed up at the house, I told Mom I would show them the pond where I had caught my first bass fish—it is still hanging on the wall behind me as I write this. We proceeded to climb over the fence, about six to eight of us, and headed to a spot we thought was safe from parental vision, between two large pecan trees. Johnny and his would-be-Aaron-Burr opponent stepped off and stood in front of one another, appraising each other like two rams.

And then fists went flying.

I had never seen a fight before. Rather, I had only heard people make threats, so this was the first fight I had ever seen; the ducking and lunging did not seem too attractive. It certainly could not match the exhilaration I'd had when I landed that bass on my fishing rod. Catching that prize felt amazing. I could not reel him in, so I had to grab the line and run up the hill until I had pulled him out of the water and onto the bank. I am not sure anything could match that desperation.

Johnny and the other guy had landed some pretty solid hits on one another and were still engaged in combat when I heard Mom shouting. I saw her climb the gate, coming our way. It seems a fight can end as quickly as it begins. It was as if Mom's shouting was the whistleblowing at the company factory because everyone scrambled like quail—everyone but me, as I had nowhere to go. That was the end of my Don King promoter experiment.

The other pastime people seemed to enjoy was going to the creek, either Black Creek or Red Creek, which is a tributary of the Pascagoula River. Two tales relate to the creeks. The first one is when I had foolishly decided to go swimming with three of my friends during the summer, which almost resulted in me drowning. I drove us there in my Camaro down this dirt road through a gauntlet of bushes to get to the creek. When we arrived, three of the boys quickly swam to the other side of the creek to swing from a rope attached to a cypress tree. As I started across, I stepped into a hole and went under several times. Panicked, I bobbed up out of the water and shouted for help, gulping water and sinking again, bouncing off the bottom and returning to the top to see Dale Smith had come to my rescue. Dale could not have weighed more than 130 pounds, but somehow, he managed to pull me up and swim to the bank, clutching me in his arms. I do not know where Dale is today, but each moment I have had since that incident is because Dale Smith saved my life.

The other incident involved a sort of going-away party on Black Creek. There was a long bridge, which went over Black Creek at this specific spot, and consequently, there was a lot of open land under the bridge. It was possible to drive several cars down to the creek and park under the bridge to drink. I was only fifteen at the time, but purchasing beer was not an obstacle in Mississippi. Consequently, we had bought a good bit of alcohol for the "creek party." At some point during the night, someone decided to start a fire. Unbeknownst to me now, because of my inebriation, I decided to jump over this fire to prove I could do so to the people there. As I landed on the other side in a rather large puddle of mud, I slowly realized I was covered in mud. A girl named Becky jumped across the fire too and landed right next to me. We were laughing as much as the people around us, covered in mud and drunk. My family and I were relocating to South Carolina the next day, and I cannot recall much after landing in the mud other than finding myself at the door of our hotel room.

One of the first people I met in Wiggins was Billy Ray Bond. Billy Ray was a delightful and friendly person. He reached out to me and tried to include me in things from the first moment he met me. He had a motorcycle and would come by the house and pick me up and take me places just for the heck of it. One day, he picked me up and took me to visit a friend named Brian Scott Hall, who would also become a good friend of mine during my short year in Mississippi. Brian, his girlfriend, Tammy, who resembled Linda Carter from the *Wonder Woman* TV show, and Tammy's cousin, Penny, came with us to my first Alabama concert. I had never been to a concert before, and I enjoyed it, especially when all the lighters were lit simultaneously. The best part of it was spending twenty dollars on an Alabama T-shirt and wearing it to school the next day. It was my way of letting everyone know I'd gone to the concert, even if it was a little pretentious. Despite the kindness Billy Ray showed me, I did something I have grown to regret.

Our neighbor in Wiggins was an air force retiree and owned a large piece of property east of Wiggins. Hunting in Mississippi was as much a way of life as breathing, and I had permission to go hunting on his property. When I received the landowner's permission to go hunting, I only wanted Brian to go with me. I cannot recall the reasons behind my decision, but I lied to Billy Ray since I did not want him to go. I made up a story to him about how I was not able to go so Brian and I could go alone. When Dad found out, he pretty much read me my Miranda rights for lying to Billy Ray. And after I was properly scolded and corrected, I realized that with all that land, it probably wouldn't have made a difference if Billy Ray had gone with us. I'm sure the sting of my lie still bothers Billy Ray. Pa Joe once said that if you want to keep a secret, "you had better not tell anyone, do whatever it is alone, and hope no one sees you do something. Even then, the walls have ears, and the windows will talk." Thus, I am sure someone mentioned something to someone else, and eventually, the truth found its way back to Billy Ray.

I lived in Wiggins from February of 1981 until February of 1982. Twenty-three years later, I traveled to Lackland Air Force Base in Texas and stopped in Wiggins and spent the night. While I was there, I saw Brian and his wife, Tammy, and Brian took me to speak to Billy Ray and Mark Davis. Billy Ray and his family, who are very musically talented, were doing well, and he had become a Baptist preacher. However, I could sense I had ruined our friendship back in 1982, as Billy Ray was not as outgoing and humorous as he was once.

During that visit, I also saw Mark Davis. Mark was "pure country." I remember him for his ability to do the best turkey calls I had ever heard. I had never been raccoon hunting until Mark took us out on his family's land one night. It was hysterical and fun, running through the woods and listening to dogs barking in the distance while trying to tree a raccoon. Treeing a raccoon involves having a pack of dogs get the scent of a raccoon and chasing it until it climbs a tree. The hunter comes along and then dispatches the raccoon. Fortunately for the raccoon, we never did catch up with him. Just as well, as Mark filled me in on how they would climb out onto the limb, and you could shine a light up and see their freaky eyes.

Returning to Billy Ray and his family, his grandma was a character. She had a love for Jerry Lewis and would not tolerate anyone speaking ill about him. The first time I met her, Billy Ray goaded me to ask her about Jerry Lewis and his marriage to his cousin. Well, I got an earful of how love is love. Billy Ray also had a half sister he had helped rear. She was a pretty girl but, perhaps, had gotten involved in a relationship that was not good for her. One day, Billy Ray asked me to go with him and his mom to pick her up from her house in Pearl River County, Mississippi. It sounded like an adventure. I eagerly volunteered. Pearl River County is adjacent to Stone County and lies along the Mississippi River. Therefore, I do not recall the trip being more than an hour. We passed several bridges, which must have been over Black Creek and the Wolf River. Eventually, we turned off Highway 26, made a right, and arrived at the house.

The sister was indeed very attractive, and I was happy I had made the trip. We proceeded to load up the small Toyota pickup truck—one of the very small ones—and the trailer attached to the truck. When we took the last items out of the house, I thought we were done, but the sister opened the door on the room to the right, and to my surprise, it looked like a horticultural lab in there. I had never seen marijuana plants before. I had seen the T-shirts with the characteristic weed plant on it, and looking at the leaves of this horticultural Bob Marley paradise, it was obvious they were marijuana plants. Moreover, why in the world were there so many of them in the front bedroom with artificial light? We loaded them on the trailer and departed. Of course, I did not ask any questions as to why we had loaded the pot plants, but the answer was forthcoming. As the truck approached the bridge over the

Pearl River, Billy Ray's mother slowed to a stop and pulled over halfway on the lane and the curb of the bridge. The sister pulled up behind the trailer and instructed us to grab the plants. One by one, they were summarily tossed over the bridge and into Pearl River. I had just participated in one of the most summarily executed plans I have ever seen.

When I lived in Stone County, the purchase and sale of alcohol were not allowed. Stone and Pearl River Counties were both "dry" counties. My understanding is Stone County is no longer dry as of 2015, but Pearl River County still is. But the abolition of sin does not equate to the absence of sin, and my experience in Wiggins bears this out. The county south of Stone, Harrison, and the county north of Stone, Forrest, were not dry. Thus, the sin, which was outlawed in Stone, was readily available to be imported into the county. I discovered this was also the case for someone fifteen years of age too. There was a place in Harrison County, just past the county line, called the Pines, where I went several times to have a beer or margarita. As I mentioned before, Billy Ray's entire family was gifted musically, and they would often play at different venues, including the Pines. It was the first time I had heard Eric Clapton's "Cocaine" song rendered with a mellow Mississippian accent. The other place of notoriety was a place we called Ms. Monk's, which was located on Highway 49 in Forrest County. Ms. Monk was a 1960s/1970s woman stranded in the early 1980s. Her clothes and persona were stuck in the early 1970s. Her hair was a beehive atop her head, and she had enough makeup on her face to be a stockholder in Max Factor. Each time we would go to Ms. Monk's, she was always sitting on a chair behind the bar. It was as if she were a fixture, and the other accouterments had come off the beer truck.

Now Ms. Monk did not break the law, but she did take donations. What I mean by this is that if you laid the proper amount of money on the bar top, a skinny Black man, who sat on a barstool in the corner, would gingerly get up and mosey to the back room. A few minutes later, he would mosey back and sit right back down on the barstool in the corner. Upon walking out of the bar and going to the car, a mysterious package would be there on the hood or in the trunk. It was as if the tooth fairy had become weighed down and tossed off a case or six-pack of beer that then fell ideally upon your vehicle. It sounds pretty audacious that we could carry on to such an extent without harming ourselves, but we did.

For generations, probably four hundred years by 2023, my family has lived in first Virginia and then Carolina—if not within fifty miles of the Atlantic Ocean. Our sojourn in Mississippi was only for a year, but I shall forever harbor memories of the kind people I met there and the kindness they showed me. There were many others who touched my life in some way:

Buffy Shrewsbury, whom I did not have to ask for her name because it was stamped on her leather belt.

Faye Harrell, whom I owe apologies to. Brian and Tammy had set me up on a date with Faye. We went to the fair together, and I abruptly just left her there. I never explained why I had done so; I just walked off, and that was it.

Heidi Covington, who was well dressed, well spoken, smart, and pretty. Like me, I think she moved to Wiggins. She was in Ms. Shaw's psychology class and had the prettiest blonde curly hair. I was smitten with her from the moment she sat beside me. If I had stayed, maybe I would have found the fortitude to ask her on a date.

My history teacher, Mr. Chambers, who had prosthetic arms and would allow you to ring the "Big Bell" if you made an A on an exam. Another teacher, Ms. Shaw, was kind enough to send me a package from the entire psychology class after I moved to Chester.

Finally, Carol Stringer, a wonderful person who, in the years since I left Mississippi, experienced some hardships and disappointments and is no longer with us. Carol and I would talk endlessly on the phone about nothing at all. When Facebook debuted and I connected with Buffy, who was friends with Carol, she told me that when Carol and her daughter were going through pictures, Carol found one of me. While I lived in Mississippi, I had my wisdom teeth pulled out, all four at one time. When I left the dentist that day, I drove over to Carol's sister's house in Bond, Mississippi, and recall sitting on the couch and visiting with Carol. She was a delightful person, but something told me I was only in Mississippi temporarily, and I did not want to develop many serious connections. I knew that if I stayed and graduated high school from there, I would join the air force or make my way back east. I have fond memories of speaking to Carol and was delighted to have someone as pretty as her express an interest in me. I only lived in Wiggins for a year, but the places and the people will forever live in my memories, and I am happy they do.

PART II
Families

CHAPTER 16
The Pages

As I return to the question I had asked Granddaddy back in the 1970s—"Who are we?"—I am pleased to note I have discovered more than he could have possibly told me back then. Therefore, in the following section of this memoir, I devote time to noting those families who made me possible.

I am indebted to the late William W. Sellers, Esquire, who authored an extensive book entitled *The History of Marion County, South Carolina: From Its Earliest Times to the Present, 1901*. It was published in 1902. Sellers was, according to the preface in the book, eighty years old in 1898. After an exhaustive career as an attorney, Sellers was compelled by friends and citizens of Marion County to pen a history of the county and its inhabitants. In his book, Sellers acknowledges the existence of the Pages living mostly on Bear Swamp and Ashpole Swamp near the North Carolina state line.[55] My discovering Sellers's seminal work and then visiting the Old Zion Methodist Church Cemetery off Swamp Fox Road—about ten minutes from Gallivants Ferry—seemed to confirm the Pages Sellers mentioned in his work were, indeed, my Pages.

I further chanced upon a website on the history of Fairmont, North Carolina, owned by Curtis McGirt. He stated that the vast swamps straddling the state line between South Carolina and North Carolina seemed an impregnable obstacle to White European settlement. Still, they concealed vast tracks of ridges ideal for settlement. Those arable tracts of land were not overlooked by natives, loners, or those armored with the fortitude to traverse the acres of black water, snakes, and cypress trees. McGirt wrote that early surveyors in the 1730s mentioned natives with copper skin and blue eyes inhabiting the area, already Christian and speaking English.[56] McGirt additionally makes light of a fact I can attest to, having grown up near the Lumber River. The tenet of the swamp was hardiness and usefulness, and multiculturalism existed here among Europeans, natives, and African Americans centuries before any civil rights era. Moreover, someone fleeing from authority or war with firsthand knowledge of the area would undoubtedly be able to elude capture, which, from the burial place of most of the Pages at Old Zion, is again confirmation I am on the right track.

There is another kernel of information that ties these families back to the Virginia and North Carolina area around Craven County, North Carolina: the founder of Fairmont, North Carolina, Isham Pittman. "After buying a royal land grant issued by King George III to Daniel Willis, brother of John Willis, founder of Lumberton,"[57] Pittman settled on a branch of the Ashpole Swamp. But during the Revolutionary War, he sent his wife back to Craven County to live with her relatives. After the war, Pittman began purchasing land grants from North Carolina, and eventually, his holdings totaled more than twenty-four thousand acres. This land was near Ashpole Swamp and the area that would become downtown Fairmont, North Carolina. About 1792, Pittman began preaching and organized a meetinghouse, which later became a Baptist church. Around 1820, he recognized he had no children and persuaded a nephew in Horry County, South Carolina, Elias Pittman, to move to his lands and take care of him in exchange for inheriting most of his property. He executed his will on March 31, 1823, and after he died, he was buried a half mile west of the First Baptist Church.[58] Pittman's daughter or adopted daughter is one of my fourth grandmothers. I have seen research that states Absela was adopted and others that state she was an only child. Even if she were adopted, the multiple marriages of the families straddling the banks of the Lumber River (Drowning Creek) still connect me to the Pittmans. Thus, when Granddaddy replied "Virginia" to my earlier question, he was correct, for it seems just as Pittman migrated into the southeastern corner of North Carolina, many others from Virginia had found their way to the southeastern corner of North Carolina and into the northeast corner of South Carolina straddling the border. It was as if the Scots remained adjacent to Cape Fear, and the English had to cross over them to find Drowning Creek.

Robert Page, a distant relative through Return Page's twin, William Page, traces the Pages back to Suffolk, England. Sellers states of the Pages there were Joseph, Solomon, Thomas, and perhaps David. In addition, I found evidence of David Page from a Bible, copied from a Mrs. Temple, of Lake View, South Carolina, which a Pansy Page Jensen witnessed and made a record. The copy Pansy made of David Page's Bible was given to the Horry County Historical Society web page, and that is where I retrieved it. The Bible lists David Page, son of Abraham and Mary Page.

Return Page Sr. and Sarah Ann Grainger are both listed as the parents on Return Jr.'s death certificate, which connects me to John Grainger. John Grainger fought in the Revolutionary War and was listed on the muster roll as a bombardier in the Corps of Artillery of Captain Stephen Buckland, commanded by Lieutenant Colonel

Ebenezer Stephens. Records indicate he was also at Ticonderoga from November 9, 1776, until March 1, 1777, and White Plains from December 5, 1777, until July 19, 1778. He was promoted on November 24, 1778, to the rank of lieutenant colonel in Lamb's Continental Artillery Regiment—later the Second Continental Artillery Regiment. In 1781, he was one of the artillery commanders at the Siege of Yorktown and was discharged from the army in June 1783.[59] Stephen Buckland was at Ticonderoga in 1776 too. He resigned his commission after four years on April 12, 1780, and, subsequently, became a privateer. He was captured by the British and imprisoned on the frigate *Jersey*, where he died a month later. In a letter to his wife, he'd stated over seven hundred prisoners were aboard the ship, which had been designed for five hundred people.[60]

The David Page Bible indicates that the Page and Grainger families lived near one another and are connected through marriage. Additionally, I found evidence of David Page cited in a land grant made by George II, consisting of three hundred acres in Bladen County, North Carolina. The grant references Tadpole Swamp and Ashpole Swamp, which could entail areas in present-day Columbus County since Columbus was created from Bladen in 1808.[61] The grant references the Province line. Thus, this grant lies on the border between North Carolina and South Carolina. William Tryon signed this grant of land as the governor of North Carolina.

Tryon was governor July 10, 1765, and served until June 30, 1771, when he became governor of New York. In North Carolina, he is most remembered for Tryon Palace, labeled a "monument of opulence and elegance extraordinary in the American colonies" and suppressing the Regulator Movement—local opposition to taxes and abuses of power by government officials—which ended in the Battle of Alamance on May 16, 1771.[62] It seems rather a good fortune Tryon gave David Page the three hundred acres on April 18, 1771, as he certainly was busy suppressing a revolt in North Carolina in May and departing in June of 1771.

Solomon Page secured 170 acres in Bertie County. The land grant was entered on September 19, 1786, and issued on September 13, 1791, on Jumping Run. Jumping Run is located in the northwestern corner of the county near Woodville. An article summarizes how Jumping Run received its name. The origin is said to be because of the impassable swampland in the area. Poles would be laid across to provide a roadbed. However, only a "good" mule could make it across and then only if the driver would "jump and run" beside the mule. What had started as Jump and Run slowly became Jumping Run.

What I discovered written on the back of the land grant of David Page was also very interesting. Another ancestor, Ignatius Flowers, whose entire family moved to Bladen and then to Alabama, was listed as one of the chains or surveyors. Finally, Arthur Dobbs issued Abraham Page, on behalf of his majesty, the king of England, 150 acres on the north side of the Neuse River in Dobbs County.

The Neuse River has one of the three oldest surviving English-applied place-names in the US.[63] Colonists named the Neuse River after its name by the American Indian tribe known as Neusiok, with whom the early Raleigh expeditions made contact. They also identified the region as the Music. In 1584, Sir Walter Raleigh commissioned two English captains, Arthur Barlowe and Phillip Armadas, to explore the New World. They landed on North Carolina's coast on July 2, 1584, to begin their research. In their 1585 report to Raleigh, they wrote favorably of the Indian population and how "the country Neusiok, situated upon a goodly river called Neuse," as the local population called it. Insofar as Dobbs County, it no longer exists.[64]

Dobbs was formed by Johnston in 1758 but did not come into effect until 1759. However, in 1791, residents petitioned to change the name of the county after the Revolutionary War, and later, it ceased to exist when divided into Greene and Lenoir Counties. It was named for the royal governor of the province of North Carolina, Arthur Dobbs. Dobbs was a Scot and a member of the Irish Parliament and served as the seventh governor of the province from 1754 until he died in 1765. He also purchased four hundred thousand acres of North Carolinian land, and at age seventy-three in 1762, he married fifteen-year-old Justina Davis at St. Phillip's Church in Brunswick Town. However, he had a stroke shortly after that and died. Incredibly, there on the land grant to my ancestor is his signature.

In researching these land grants, I understood how the Flowers, Van Pelt, and Strong families, who originated in Maryland, New York, and Connecticut, respectively, came to North Carolina. Almost all the other relatives I have traced came from Virginia. The counties adjacent to the Virginia and North Carolina state lines slowly migrated down to the South Carolina and North Carolina boundary before the Revolutionary War. It is predominately at this point where most of their descendants remained for two hundred years. In tracking the land grants, my speculation is they were taking advantage of the free land grants. For example, the elusive Return Strong, father of Patience and Elizabeth, was granted fifty acres on February 9, 1780, in Bladen County on the south side of Gapway Swamp. This is an area I know as the Jam between Fair Bluff and Tabor City on Swamp Fox Road, which is not far from the state line. Then, Return had another grant of 640 acres granted on August 23, 1779, and issued July 16, 1795, again on the south side of Galway Swamp. Therefore, it may be possible he was traveling back and forth from New England. Lewis Williamson, who also moved from the coast to Duplin, Sampson, and

Bladen—Columbus—Counties, had a land grant of 150 acres entered on January 1, 1793, and issued December 17, 1796. Signed on the back, where the survey was drawn, is Return Strong's signature. He later died in 1794 at age sixty-four or sixty-five.

Both Worley and Page families would, for a few generations, continue to share and cling to the name Return as they had children, signifying its importance. However, as far as I am aware, the last time it was used was when Return Page passed sometime around 1919 and Return Strong Worley in 1880. As the generations passed, the Return name faded into memory.

Return Page was my great-great-grandfather and the twin brother of William Page, born in 1845. The Pages and many others found themselves somewhere above the slaves, the poor White trash, and the planters. Like many young men of the South in 1860, they were of the hardscrabble variety who had no stake in slavery and were minor farmers. For many, President Lincoln's call-up of seventy-five thousand volunteers to put down the rebellious state of South Carolina transformed the war from slavery to defense of their homes and, by extension, their state. Evidenced by the reluctance of the northern tier states in the South to hesitate, today those who fought the war from all occupations, no matter how poor or disconnected from slavery, are labeled racists. To do this without considering the entire history of slavery is unmerited and lumps every individual in the South into a pillar of the planter aristocracy, which is inaccurate on its face and an insult to many poor Whites.

Nevertheless, to think the entire region would rise and welcome a Union army seen as invading does not stand historical merit. The case of Robert E. Lee illustrates this position best.

Offered the command of Union armies by the secretary of war, Lee hedges on the outcome of Virginia's decision to stay or leave the Union.

At that time in history, there was no relationship between people and the national government, as there is today. For generations, each state had developed its own traditions and governing institutions. People thought of themselves as a South Carolinian and a New Yorker before they considered themselves an American.

To summarize, how can one be asked to bear arms against one's family and community, especially when 97 percent of the Whites in the South owned no slaves? Perhaps, for some, this war was a defensive war to protect home and hearth. Opposition to tyranny is a universal trait; it opposes the government in London or the one on the Potomac River. Unfortunately, there was also deference to the leadership of those at the top echelons of state power, considering the actual odds of chances of success. It is as if Boudicca's army challenging the might of the Romans with conviction and perseverance could triumph over superior weapons and superior labor. For many Southerners, the decision to fight was made, from their perspective, by Lincoln and the ruling planter elite. As the record illustrates, this was by no means a unanimous choice. Union sentiment, not abolition, drove West Virginia to break from Virginia. Mountain people in both North Carolina and Tennessee harbored Union sentiment. In my ancestors' case, Return and his brother Abram ended the war "absent without leave. I cannot begin to know why one stayed to the end and the other did not. Perhaps Return saw no reason to risk his life in a war. In his opinion, it was apparent the South was losing. Return's twin William joined the war late, perhaps compelled by a sense of duty. Whatever the reason, it is clear one was there and the other was not. I have found no record of Return Jr. at Appomattox.

Both Abraham and Return served in the Twenty-Third South Carolina Infantry, also known as Hatch's Coastal Rangers, and saw duty outside of Charleston, South Carolina, in the Isle of Palms, which was then a mostly inhabited coastal island known as Long Island. The only importance of Long Island then was its vicinity to the city of Charleston, South Carolina. At some point during the war, the unit was transferred to the defense of Vicksburg, Mississippi. General Grant successfully subjugated Vicksburg's city, and the twin Page brothers were sent back to South Carolina. Now the young Return must have grown weary of the futility of the war or may have simply decided he would not die for others to lead a privileged life of the planter class. He collected twenty-five dollars from the army in Charleston, then disappeared into the swamps of Marion and Horry Counties. Abraham is also listed as AWOL. The Twenty-Third was transferred to the Petersburg, Virginia, area and was with General Robert E. Lee's army at the surrender of his army at Appomattox. Grandma Hazel's grandfather, Absolam Benjamin "A.B." Turberville, also was at Appomattox with Lee at his surrender and was paroled on April 9, 1865. Additionally, A.B.'s brother, George Washington Turberville, served in the Twenty-Third and survived the war. Three other brothers fought in the war: Lemuel, Willis H., and Calvin Turbeville.

Twenty-Third South Carolina Infantry Regiment
The Twenty-Third South Carolina Infantry Regiment was assembled in Charleston, South Carolina, in November of 1961. Most of the men in this unit were from the Horry, Georgetown, Charleston, and Colleton Counties. The regiment was stationed in South Carolina and then moved to Virginia.

During the war, it served under General Evans's, Elliot's, and Wallace's Brigades. It participated in the battles of Second Manassas, South Mountain, and Sharpsburg, then was ordered to North Carolina and later to Mississippi. The unit engaged the enemy at Jackson, Mississippi, returned to Charleston, and in the spring of 1864, was sent to Virginia. The Twenty-Third fought in the trenches at Petersburg, Virginia, and around Appomattox Courthouse. The regiment lost 68 percent of the 225 men.

Return, meanwhile, having perhaps seen too much death in his young years, was sowing his oats, or maybe he was mending his wounds or healing from the trauma of Vicksburg. I envy those who know what happened. From what I have been told, or not told, the spindles of the spider's web of life have long been weaved, and the answers I seek are no longer known. Anyway, at this point, Return had met Elizabeth Cartrette. He may have known of her before the war and met with her in some fashion while seeking solace and relief from the war. In the end, they did not marry but had a child named Daniel Return Page. The name Return stands in our family record like a sentinel on a rocky coast, fraught with the shadows of time and events, sunk to the depths of the graves in Columbus or Horry County. It is like a voice calling from the past, asking me to do what I humbly can to share the story of these people.

Enoch Cartrette, brother of my grandmother Elizabeth Cartrette, served in the Twenty-Sixth South Carolina, which was formed at Blanton's Crossroads Community, known as Green Sea since 1870.[65] Enoch enlisted on February 9, 1864, "at the time, underage, and consent of parents was required."[66] He was present from enlistment until January 20, 1865, when he was given a sixty-day furlough from a Richmond hospital. These inclusive dates place him at the Battle of the Crater, where the Twenty-Sixth suffered seventy-two casualties. Richmond and Petersburg, Virginia, surrendered to Union forces on April 3, 1865, and the last major battle of the war was fought at Saylers Creek on April 6, 1865.[67] Therefore, Enoch was, perhaps, home at this time or not engaged in battle or engaged in battle; I cannot verify where he was at this time. I cannot find Enoch after the Civil War. Like many in the family, he seemed to vanish in the records. Interesting bit here is there is also, according to the *North Carolina Troops in the War Between the States*, published in 1882, an Enoch Fowler in Company D of the Seventy-Third Regiment. Could Enoch have somehow changed units during the war?

The following are records of the Twenty-Sixth South Carolina Infantry, Company K:

- **CARTWRIGHT (Cartrette), ALVA**—Private—Cartwright enlisted in Horry District on February 27, 1864, and was present or accounted for until killed at Clay's Farm, Virginia, near Petersburg on May 20, 1864. See Family No. 1000 in 1860 US Census of Columbus County, North Carolina, showing Alva "Cartrette" as thirteen years old.[68]
- **CARTWRIGHT (Cartrette), ENOCH**—Private—Cartwright enlisted in Horry District on February 9, 1864, underage, as the consent of parents was required. He was present or accounted for through January 20, 1865, when he was given a sixty-day furlough from a hospital in Richmond, Virginia. See Family No. 808 of 1860 US Census of Horry District, South Carolina, showing Enoch "Cartrette" as fourteen years old, born in North Carolina.[69]
- **CARTWRIGHT (Cartrette), RICHARD**—Private—Cartwright enlisted at Blanton's Crossroads, Horry District, on January 1, 1862. He was present or accounted for until muster report of February 29–June 30, 1864, which shows him on wounded furlough in Columbus County, North Carolina, since June 3, 1864. Further records show him wounded across the back on May 20, 1864, at Clay's Farm, Virginia, near Petersburg. He returned to duty on November 15, 1864, and was present or accounted for until captured in a Richmond

hospital on April 3, 1865. He was sent to Point Lookout, Maryland, on May 2, 1865, and released on June 26, 1865, after taking the Oath of Allegiance. See Family No. 1000 in 1860 US Census of Columbus County, which shows Richard "Cartrette" as fifteen years old.[70]

- **CARTWRIGHT (Cartrette), WILLIAM H.**—Private—Cartwright enlisted at Blanton's Crossroads, Horry District, on January 1, 1862. He was present or accounted for until wounded in the first joint of the left forefinger on May 20, 1864, at Clay's Farm, Virginia, near Petersburg, and hospitalized in Richmond on May 21, 1864. He was given a furlough to Columbus County, North Carolina, on May 28, 1864, and returned to duty before December 1, 1864, when he was admitted to a Richmond hospital. Muster roll of February 1865 shows him in the hospital since December date. He was on the list of paroled prisoners dated April 13, 1865, at Lynchburg, Virginia. See Family No. 1000 in 1860 US Census of Columbus County, where William "Cartrette" was seventeen years old. Also, see Family No. 378 in 1850 US Census of Horry District.[71]
- **FOWLER, AMOS**—Private—Fowler enlisted at Blanton's Crossroads, Horry District, on January 1, 1862. He was present or accounted for until discharged for being over forty years old on January 1, 1863, when the term of enlistment was completed. He was the brother of Reuben Fowler of Columbus County, North Carolina, in Company D, Twentieth Regiment, North Carolina Troops.[72]
- **FOWLER, F.H.**—Private—Fowler enlisted on November 17, 1863, in Horry District with the consent of his parents, as he was under eighteen years of age. He was present or accounted

for until August 12, 1864, when he was given a thirty-day furlough from a Richmond, Virginia, hospital, with Fair Bluff in Columbus County, North Carolina, as his destination. He returned to duty before February 1865, when he was noted as sick at Blanton's Crossroads, Horry District. See Family No. 290 in 1860 US Census of Horry District.[73]

- **FOWLER, G.W.**—Private—Fowler enlisted November 17, 1863, in Horry District and was present or accounted for until captured on April 6, 1865, at Farmville, Virginia. He was imprisoned at Newport News, Virginia, and released on June 15, 1865, after taking the Oath of Allegiance.[74]
- **FOWLER, JACOB P.**—Private—Fowler enlisted December 8, 1863, in Horry District with the consent of his parents, as he was under eighteen years of age. He was present or accounted for until captured on April 1, 1865, at Southside Railroad, Virginia, near Petersburg, and confined at Point Lookout, Maryland. He was released on June 27, 1865, after taking the Oath of Allegiance.[75]
- **FOWLER, PETER**—Private—Fowler enlisted January 1, 1862, at Blanton's Crossroads, Horry District. He "ran away from company" at a Savannah, Georgia, depot on August 27, 1863, and returned to duty September 23, 1863. Peter was present or accounted for until admitted to a Petersburg, Virginia, hospital on August 12, 1864. He returned to duty September 5, 1864. No further records.[76]
- **FOWLER, WILLIAM**—Corporal—Fowler enlisted on January 1, 1862, at Blanton's Crossroads, Horry District, and mustered in as corporal. He was present or accounted for until wounded in the right arm on June 27, 1864, at an unspecified location in Virginia, probably near Petersburg. He was admitted

to a Richmond, Virginia, hospital on July 1, 1864, and given a thirty-day furlough on August 5, 1864. No further records.[77]

I have included the Fowler names in this because Enoch was the great-grandson of Peter Fowler—brother of John Fowler Sr. It is accepted that Peter, at one time, lived in Horry County; thus, perhaps there was still family-owned land there. Without a doubt, all of the above are related.

I am not sure what caused the demise of Enoch Cartrette's parents, but evidently, they died, or some tragedy befell his father, and his mother was unable to manage the family, at some time during the period between the 1850–1860 Census. Lancy Folwer Cartrette would be one of my third great-grandmothers and Enoch's mom. Both Lancy and Kinion, his father, seem to sort of disappear in the historical record. Lancy, however, is listed on a later census as living with a relative, but her children are not in the same home.

The year 1860, in South Carolina and American history, would prove to be a watershed year when the nation turned against itself. Relatives killed one another over the rights of states, the issue of slavery, or the issue of whether "all men are created equal" and "endowed by their Creator with certain unalienable Rights," as the Declaration of Independence proclaims. The observation I make concerning these events is personified by the actions of William Page and Return Page. In their case, they were like the twins Jacob and Esau, fighting in their mother's womb. William drudged on to the end at Appomattox, and Return was evidently AWOL at the end. Obviously, in the wake of defeat at Gettysburg and Vicksburg, the industrial prowess of the North was inevitable, and despite the myth of a commitment to the cause, I think many knew the war was over. Why else would the number of missing or absent-without-leave soldiers be such a reality?

Return appears on a list of prisoners captured by Captain Rodgers on the North Eastern Railroad on May 17, 1863. This document places Return, Abram, and A.B. Turberville at the Battle of Big Black River Bridge. This battle involved Major General John A. McClernand's Twelfth Corps and Brigadier General Michael K. Lawler's Second Brigade. Eugene A. Carr's Fourteenth Division led a charge against General John C. Vaugh's inexperienced and pro-Union Confederate East Tennessee Brigade, causing confusion and panic in the defenders. The Confederates hastily took flight across two routes: the bridge they burned as soon as they had crossed and three tied steamboats, *Dot*, *Charm*, and *Paul Jones*. In the aftermath of the retreat, seventeen hundred to eighteen hundred Confederates were captured.[78] Ohioans participated in the battle, and I discovered the following description:

On 17 May 1863, three divisions of Grant's army, commanded by Major General John A. McClernand, caught up with the Rebels. Even though the Confederate position was fronted by a bayou of waistdeep water protected by eighteen canons, the Rebels threw down their weapons.

> [They] fled for the two makeshift bridges spanning the river when the Yankees began their advance. The majority of Pemberton's soldiers made it across, but 1,700 men were stranded and captured when the Confederates burned the bridges to prevent any Union pursuit. The Federals suffered 276 casualties at the Battle of Big Black River Bridge compared to 1,751 soldiers for the Confederates, most of whom were prisoners. The Union victory made the fate of the Rebel soldiers who eluded capture and escaped back to Vicksburg inevitable. Grant invested in the city for the next

six weeks before Pemberton surrendered Vicksburg and his army on July 4, 1863.[79]

The United States had to struggle in its youth and expansion with slavery, and in its early maturity, the issue was decided not in the halls of Congress or state legislatures but through death. As President Lincoln rightly observed, a house divided against itself could not stand. America was to be all-slave or all-free. Lincoln justifiably saw a nation that looked in the mirror and confessed its sins. Matthew 18:9 (NIV) states, "And if your eye causes you to stumble, gouge it out and throw it away." Assuredly, the institution of slavery had to meet a similar demise.

CHAPTER 17
The Cartrettes

Elizabeth Cartrette (Cartwright)

I can only imagine Elizabeth, my second great-grandmother, mother of Granddaddy Gordon's father, Daniel Return, was subject to anguish by the outbreak of the war. Her parents were no longer present, and her siblings and she had ceased to be a family unit. She was entering a period of unprecedented uncertainty. Moreover, she was still more a girl than a woman, personally, and I suspect she was in a fragile place in her life. Unfortunately, as is often the case, history and a tumultuous civil war were to intercede in the ordinary course of events and lay yet another tragedy at her feet. However, she never fled. She accepted her condition and stood with her son, and when God called them both home, she ensured their earthly bodies rested adjacent to one another.

Some months after I began this, recent discoveries indicated that Elizabeth Cartrette's mother, Laney or Lancy, was the daughter of Reuben Fowler, Sr.. Elizabeth's brother Enoch being listed on the 1860 Census in the house of Matthew Fowler now makes sense, as Matthew was the son of Reuben Fowler Sr. and, thus, would have been the uncle of Enoch Cartrette. Matthew is listed as the son of Reuben Sr. aged eighteen on the 1850 Census in Columbus County, North Carolina. On the 1860 Census, in Columbus County, he is thirty and married to Nancy Cartrett, another Cartrett, with three of their children and Enoch who is fourteen. On the 1860 Census in Horry County, South Carolina, Rebecca Cartrette age eighteen, Elizabeth's sister, is listed as living in the house of Traverse Prince. Laney, their mother was forty-five years old and living with her father, Reuben Fowler Sr, age seventy-five, on the 1860 Census in Columbus County. Why is she not with her children? And where is her husband Kinion?

Thus far, I cannot determine what happened to Laney's husband, Kinion. Insofar as Traverse Prince, I am unsure of any relationship to Solomon Prince, but surely, in a community as small as this one, there must have been one. Traverse served in Company B of Manigault's Artillery and is also listed in Company A of Alston's Artillery. He is listed as having died in a Confederate hospital near Columbia, South Carolina, on July 25, 1862. Further, a claim was filed with the Confederate Government on September 18, 1863, for a pension by his surviving spouse. The turn of fate was bitter and cruel to Elizabeth and her siblings.

Accessing this information shows that my Granddaddy Gordon was a descendant of Daniel Fowler Sr. through both his mother and father. There are no records or memories recorded of the events of Elizabeth during the war. Granddaddy may have known her—her tombstone records her to have died at the age of 101—but he never said anything about her. The evidence of those times is solely the birth of an infant Elizabeth was carrying in her womb. There is no knowledge of the circumstances by which she may have become pregnant either. There can only be speculations. I can only imagine that Return was wanted for desertion and possibly aided by family, or even Elizabeth, in keeping his whereabouts unknown. Perhaps he returned to the military in some fashion. I do not know. Sincerely, if there are any facts I am not aware of that demonstrate otherwise, I hope this story prompts those who may know to come forward and bridge the gap that exists between the two individuals. I can only report what I know and any conclusions I may draw. However, given the circumstances of war, the age of both Elizabeth and Return, and the human need for companionship in trying times that test people's souls, I prefer a story that sees them drawn together like a heroine and disillusioned soldier tired of seeing only death and not youthful exploits. Elizabeth's pregnancy is the only physical evidence of an intimate relationship between them. She duly delivered a healthy baby boy, whom she named Daniel Return Page, as I've mentioned before. Return, for his part, evidently realized Elizabeth was not the woman he was meant to build a life with in a war-torn state, for he ended up marrying a woman from the Green Sea community named Ara Floyd.

In many respects, the story of Return and me divides like a fork in the road at this juncture. However, the web of generations in Horry County and Columbus County has forever intertwined the branches of our family trees, the roots beginning with the two sisters who had married into the Page and Worley families. The Return name continued to sprout like a persistent sweet gum until its novelty and separation from the original Return Strong made it an anecdote. Return and Ara sired many children who sprinkled South Carolina and North Carolina with many future generations. They found their resting place in Horry County in a local church cemetery in the Gallivants Ferry community. As the church witnessed the congregation move from the church pews to the sandy burial plots, its membership irrevocably declined. The church was eventually dismantled as the cemetery became full and the benches became empty. Such was the demise of the church, being surrounded by newer tombstones. In contrast, the older ones stand on the opposite side of the road, making a permanent division between them. The descendants of William and Return Page may have departed Horry County, but in death many were returned back to reside with relatives in everlasting peace below Spanish moss draping downward from the oaks and pines.

I can only imagine what Elizabeth was going through. What should have been a blessing was wrapped in the challenges and trials of a postwar world. To be an unwed mother of a child, or multiple children, in a state that had been defeated and subjugated by the Union army indeed makes the difficulties of everyday life seem trivial. My aunt, Pattie Sue Page Powell, relates a story about how Elizabeth was once unable to secure a ride from Loris to Whiteville, so she made the journey on foot. Another story is when she rode in a car with Daniel, and she insisted he drive slowly, lest she be flung out of the car and killed. I have a copy of her obituary, which states she was confined to her bed for a year before she died. Surely, for a woman of such independence and grit, this must have been a difficult outcome in her life. Again, this is conjecture because there are no oral or written stories to be told of how she perceived this blessing or trial. I can also speculate that the baby was welcomed and loved, and she became forever attached to him. The fact that their remains, along with my great-grandmother's, are resting side by side is the only testimony I need of this.

Further research has not cleared the mystery of Elizabeth's parents, but the veil around her mother's family has been lifted. Her mother was Lancy Fowler, and her mother's parents were Reuben Fowler and Martha Hathaway. Reuben was the son of Daniel Fowler and the brother of John Fowler. Their father was Daniel Fowler Sr. Thus, both Daniel and Anna Elizabeth Hattaway Prince merged into Daniel Fowler's family tree. Reuben's mother was Martha Spivey, wife of Daniel Jr.

The fact that Martha was a Spivey in the family and Elizabeth Fowler was the sister of John clarifies why Patience Caroline Fowler Hattaway is buried with her daughter Margarette at Spivey Cemetery in Tabor City.

There is a gap of many years concerning my great-grandparents Daniel Return and Anna Elizabeth that I cannot fill. I do not know what Daniel and his mother, Elizabeth, were doing from the time of Daniel Return's birth until I can place him in Evergreen, North Carolina, when he is married to Anna Elizabeth and has a family. I do not know how Daniel Return and Anna Elizabeth met, but from the interconnectedness of the family, I assume it was in Tabor City. I know absolutely not anything of how their single mothers lived, where they lived, nor how they supported their children. I know Daniel Return lived in Evergreen, North Carolina, in a tenant house and is listed as being forty-four years old in 1910 or 1911 when he worked at the Butters Lumber Company in Boardman, North Carolina. The Butters Lumber Company was the preeminent employer in the area at the turn of the century. Yet, with each log they pulled out of the swamps surrounding the Lumber River, their eventual demise drew nearer. Eventually, the available trees that could be pulled out of the swamps by mules to higher ground and loaded on wagons were exhausted, and the company closed. With its closure, the stores in turn boarded up, and the people sought opportunity elsewhere.

When I was in my teens, I ventured into one of the swamps and saw the silent sentinels of oak crossties neatly laid out as dominoes in a straight line through the swamp. In summer, this area was dry. Nevertheless, during the winter, these square logs were submerged in about ankle-deep water or slightly higher. It was pretty amazing, as this area was remote, and there was no sign of any other activity of humans but the remains of those oak crossties.

I speculate that with the closure of the lumber mill, Daniel Return migrated back to Horry County and had saved enough money to purchase a small farm between Loris, South Carolina, and Tabor City, North Carolina. It is here he spent the remainder of his life, passing during World War II. He lies not two miles from where he lived and is listed in the 1900 Census in Columbus County in Tatum's Township as a thirty-three-year-old sawmill laborer. There is also proof Daniel voted in the 1908 election filed in the Columbus County Courthouse. On the same list is the name E.L. Williamson, who was my mother's great-grandfather. Laney B., known as "Rena," was one of Daniel's children and is buried at the Methodist church in Evergreen, North Carolina. The discovery of Rena in Evergreen has only recently surfaced. I have been there numerous times with my mother, and no one ever made me aware of her grave.

Daniel Return's wife was Anna Elizabeth Hattaway or Hathaway—I have seen both spellings but believe the correct one is Hathaway. Anna Elizabeth, my great-grandmother, was a reverent Christian woman and the daughter of James Erwin Hattaway and Patience Carolina (or so I thought until I saw her death certificate listed Solomon Prince as her father). The only photo I have of Anna Elizabeth is one of her family standing outside the house in Evergreen, North Carolina, dated 1913. Missing from it are the three sons she lost as young boys or infants, who are buried at the George Fowler Cemetery in Tabor City. She was a small woman of stature and stood confidently in the photo. However, the image does not reflect the heartache she endured during her life. Her three male children later died young, and her daughter also fell victim to an epidemic and passed before 1920. That left her with her other three sons, including Gordon, my grandfather, and daughter, Emma, whose two young children had also died in 1915.

Granddaddy Gordon thought very highly of Emma. In 1973, he once drove to Fair Bluff and brought her to the house for Thanksgiving. I remember seeing her there and then hearing about her passing away not long afterward. When I went with Grandpa to clean out her house, I walked into the house and remember thinking it was very modest. I have a bottle from there that says Cape Fear Soda on it, which I still treasure dearly.

After I discovered Aunt Rena is buried in Evergreen, I went to visit her grave. As I stood there, looking at her tombstone, I noticed two small markers in the form of a square with the base cut off and mounted to another floor. It read, "Son and Daughter of E.V. Byrd and Emmer Byrd," who would have been my Granddaddy Gordon's sister Emma Victoria and her husband. It was referring to Herman and Lela. It struck me very profoundly that the Pages had lost six children between Emma's two children and Anna's three boys (William, Hester, and Malloy) and daughter Rena.

Discovering the Fowlers

Daniel Fowler fought in the Revolutionary War as a private in the First North Carolina Line, which was organized in the fall of 1775 at Salisbury and Wilmington. It consisted of ten companies, furloughed at James Island, South Carolina, on April 23, 1783, and disbanded on November 15, 1783. Sadly, the British at the Siege of Charleston captured Daniel.

As I dug my way through the families in my tree, I found one relative by the name of Edward Rackley, who had arrived in Virginia in 1639. He was one of five servants transported by Richard Preston. Preston received fifty acres of land for each of the settlers for whom he paid transportation to Virginia. Edward was indentured to Preston for seven years. Records in this regard are not available, but indentureship was customary. Edward prospered after he was free of his debt to Preston. In 1657, he obtained four hundred acres of land in present-day Essex County, Virginia, which was his reward for paying twelve settlers' transportation to Virginia. In 1658, Edward and Peter Ford obtained 640 acres in Kent County, Virginia, for having paid transportation for twelve immigrants. In 1673, they patented another 640 acres. This is the last documentation of Edward Rackley in Virginia.[80] His date of death is unknown, as is the name of his wife, whom he presumably married after arriving in Virginia. However, it is certain he had a son, John I, who registered a cattle mark in 1670 in Essex County. He married Martha North, the daughter of Anthony and Joane North. Anthony had immigrated to Virginia in 1654 and was a vestryman of Sittingbourne Parish in 1665. John I and Martha had two sons, John II and Anthony. If there were any daughters, there is no record of them.

John Fowler was born in 1747 in a portion of Duplin County, now Sampson County, and was the son of Daniel Fowler and Mary Rollins. According to Richard Gildart Fowler in *A History of the Fowler Family of Southeastern North Carolina*, Mary was a sister of Edward Rollins of Bladen County, North Carolina. Daniel's sons were John, William, Daniel Jr., Richard, Peter, and Francis. Daniel was perhaps the brother of the Sampson County Loyalist D'Arcy.[81]

About 1776, John married Elizabeth Rackley, eldest child of Joshua and Cityvias Rackley. Elizabeth is six generations removed from Edward Rackley, who came to Virginia from England in 1639. John served in the Revolutionary War in the North Carolina Militia and the First North Carolina Continental Line. The affidavit made for the pension in the superior court testimony is affirmed by a witness, Ezekiel Hawes, and resulted in John receiving a pension of thirty dollars per annum, which commenced on March 4, 1831. After the revolution, he moved to Lancaster, South Carolina, where his brothers-in-law, Elijah and Shadrack Rackley, lived. The first land record in his name is from 1779. It records that he deeded the land in the Crane Creek area, patented by his father, to Richard, John's brother. He resided in Lancaster for about twenty years but was living next to his brother Peter Fowler in Prince Georges Parish, South Carolina, in 1790. In 1797, he was back in Lancaster, South Carolina, purchasing one hundred acres on Camp Creek in November and selling in 1802. He was on the 1800 Census in Lancaster County. In 1802, he was back in Columbus County. By 1837, John had amassed one thousand acres of land along Beaverdam Swamp in Columbus County. Still, in 1837, John appointed an attorney-in-fact to handle his affairs in Columbus County and moved to Alabama. He was robbed of his pension papers in transit through Georgia and spent three years attempting to have his pension restored.[82] A letter from Luke R. Simons of Tuscaloosa, Alabama, to J.L. Edwards of the Court of Pensions in the City of Washington, dated December 16, 1840, asks for his assistance in replacing the pension certificate. The letter further establishes John Fowler has relocated to Pike County, Alabama. The documented movement of Richard Fowler to first Alabama and then Louisiana supports the relocation of John Fowler to Alabama—see the monument to Richard Fowler in Louisiana. John's application to restore his pension and his letter back home to Stephen Wright does too.

The following is from a letter written by John Fowler from Pike County, Alabama, on August 25, 1843:

> *Dear son, after my love to you and family, these lines will inform you that I am as well as could be expected of my age. I can tell you that on the 23rd of this instant, I received a letter from you stating that you and your family were all well. And, also saying that the letter I sent you that you went to Messer with, the letter and the order both, and*

he would not pay the money without the order being witnessed by two witnesses, and now I send you an order with two witnesses assigned to it and my mark as you asked. This is all I can do, and if he pays you the money, keep twenty dollars out of it and write to me when convenient, and if he pays the money over (extra) to you, send it to me in a letter. When you write, direct your letter to Thomas Cribb. You stated to Cribb that you want to know where Joseph Blackburne lives, you direct to him Alabama Coffee County Post Office. Thomas Cribb wishes you to state about him as said Henry Cartrett and Jonathan Gore was dead, and he wishes to hear from them all. I can say to you that all of the connections are well at this time, hoping lines may find you and your family the same. So, nothing more at present but remain your father and well-wisher till death. The land that I sold to John Robins was sold before I put Messer in possession of my business. John Fowler[83]

John Fowler died on September 11, 1845, and is buried at the Good Hope Churchyard in Pike County with the Spiveys, who moved from Columbus County to Alabama. Amazingly, his great-granddaughter, Patience Carolina Fowler, is buried with her daughter in the Spivey Cemetery in Tabor City. My impression of John Fowler is one of a restless soul. He was married at least twice, and he moved from North Carolina to South Carolina and then to Alabama, and many of his descendants seemed to share that adventurous characteristic since they are scattered throughout the United States.

John Fowler and Family Connections
In the interest of knowing the details of the pension John Fowler was awarded, I have included the following research:

On June 7, 1832, Congress enacted pension legislation extending benefits more universally than under any previous legislation. This act provided full pay for life for all officers and enlisted men who served at least two years in the Continental Line, the state troops or militia, the navy, or marines. Men who served less than two years but at least six months were granted pensions of less than full pay. Benefits were payable effective March 4, 1831, without regard to financial need or disability, and widows or children were entitled to collect any unpaid benefits due to the veteran at the time of his death. Everyone who claimed benefits under this act was required to relinquish their claims under any prior federal or state pension laws. Still, by amendment on February 19, 1833, invalid pensioners were exempted from the operation of this release of their prior pension benefits.

In his annual report to Congress in 1834, the commissioner of pensions reported that there were then 27,978 pensioners on the rolls claiming pensions under the 1832 Act, claiming benefits of $2,325,000 per year. The entire federal pension rolls in 1834 contained about forty-three thousand claimants. By June 30, 1867, all the Revolutionary pensioners had died, but Congress voted two other soldiers pensions of $500 per year during that year.

The last of those men, Daniel F. Bakeman, died on April 5, 1869. As of June 1869, there were still 887 widows on the pension rolls. Altogether, the number of pensioned soldiers was 57,623, of whom 20,485 were pensioned under the Act of 1818, 1,200 under the 1828 Act, 33,425 under the Act of 1832, and the others under the more limited acts summarized above. The total cost to the federal government as of 1869, when the last surviving pensioned soldier died, was $46,178,000.[84]

Richard Fowler—son of John Fowler, veteran of the War of 1812, and brother of Amelia Ann "Millie Ann" Fowler Wright—and his wife, Sarah Parman, are buried at Taylor-Liberty Hill Cemetery, which was originally the family graveyard on the plantation of Judge John Taylor, an early settler and the first parish judge who arrived in Union Parish in 1837. In 1845, Taylor allowed the Pleasant Hill Baptist Church to build a meetinghouse near his family cemetery. In 1848, this missionary Baptist church dissolved and reformed as Liberty Hill Primitive Baptist Church. Due to its association with Judge Taylor, both Liberty Hill Church and the cemetery became referred to as Taylor Church and the Taylor Cemetery by the latter 1800s. Over the next thirty years after its formation in the early 1840s, the cemetery developed into a community cemetery. In the mid-1900s, it became known as the Taylor-Liberty Hill Cemetery, the name by which it goes today.

After his service during the War of 1812, Richard moved with his wife, Sarah, first to Conecuh County, Alabama, and then to Snow Hill, Alabama, in 1818 or 1819. They were neighbors to Noah Lewis Scarborough, who later married their daughter Samantha Fowler. They resided in Snow Hill until a drought took place in 1847. The Scarboroughs then moved to Louisiana in 1848, and the Fowlers followed in 1850. The marker in Louisiana states both helped found the Bethsaida Primitive Baptist Church in Alabama and Liberty Hill Primitive Baptist in Louisiana.

Elvira Fowler was born on June 24, 1814, in Columbus County, North Carolina, the daughter of Richard Fowler and his wife, Sarah. When she was about five, her parents moved from North Carolina to Monroe County, Alabama, which later fell into Clarke County. Richard Fowler and his family remained there until about 1827, when he moved north to Snow Hill. He bought a plantation outside Snow Hill on the county line between Wilcox County and Dallas County.

Elvira married Amos Robinson on August 20, 1835. They had three children before his death in the early 1840s. Between 1844 and 1846, Elvira remarried Wiley Jefferson Polk. They remained in Clarke County until the winter of 1850–1851, when they followed her parents and sisters to Union Parish, Louisiana. Within a few years, Elvira and Wiley moved west again, this time settling in De Soto Parish, Louisiana. They had no children of their own. It appears that Elvira and Amos's son John R. Robinson died while serving in the Confederate military. In the 1870s and 1880s, Elvira lived near her daughter, Roana Robinson Howell, before she passed away.

The *South Carolina Historical Magazine* published an article by Tommy W. Rogers in January of 1967 entitled "The Great Population Exodus from South Carolina 1850–1860," which indicates a meaningful movement of South Carolinians to the lower South during the antebellum era. Nearly half of all White persons born in the state during the 1800s migrated to another state. The movement of South Carolinians was proportionally more significant than any other state. Of the 448,639 free persons on the 1850 Census born in South Carolina, 186,479 were living in other states. The primary destination for these migrants was Georgia with 52,154, Alabama with 48,663, and Mississippi with 27,908 South Carolinians. The 1860 Census continued the movement of South Carolinians farther west. The state of Texas in 1850 had 4,482 native South Carolinians, but that increased to 10,876 by the 1860 Census.

In a paradoxical twist of demographics, South Carolina experienced no such movement of other peoples to the Palmetto State. In 1850 and 1860, 90 percent of the people living in South Carolina were natives.[85] This large migration out of the state was to spread the ideas of South Carolina throughout the lower South, which still resonates with implications two-hundred-plus years later. From my perspective, it is incredible my ancestors essentially chose to remain straddling the border between North Carolina and South Carolina and did not head for other opportunities out west. North Carolina similarly experienced the same outward movement of people during the early 1800s. It was the third most populous state in the Union in 1790, but by 1860, it had dropped to twelfth. Hundreds of thousands of White North Carolinians fled the state during those years, seeking cheap, fertile land in Tennessee, western Georgia, Indiana, Alabama, Missouri, Mississippi, and other trans-Allegheny states and territories. Thirty percent of North Carolina's native-born population, amounting to more than four hundred thousand persons, was living outside of the state in 1860.[86]

Returning to John Fowler, the testimony he gave, claiming a Revolutionary War pension, stated he served for six months, serving in Wilmington and marching out against the Tories, taking station at Moore's Creek. The testimony also said he served a year under Colonel Alfred Moore while being stationed at Wilmington and marching to Charleston. Additionally, he did the third period of service in a militia company under Captain William Vann for three months. This period of service witnessed British Colonel James Craig advancing on the North Carolinians with a much superior force. John Fowler and company were ordered to retreat and were obliged to toss their ammunition in a river.

The testimony affirms landmarks such as the North River, which originates in the Great Swamp east of Elizabeth City, North Carolina. It ends in a four-mile mouth into the Albemarle Sound. John mentions he was stationed at a place called Holy Shelter, which today is a 48,795-acre game reserve in Pender County. Colonel James Craig is Sir James Henry Craig, who participated in the Battle of Bunker Hill, where he was badly wounded but refused to leave his regiment. He subsequently served with distinction at Quebec, Fort Ticonderoga,

Nova Scotia, and North Carolina. He specialized in leading light infantry troops, and his rapid promotions suggest an unusual degree of initiative and resourcefulness.[87] After the British defeat at the Battles of Saratoga, General Burgoyne wrote in a postscript to his letter to Lord Germain, "Capt. Craig is an officer of Great Merit and is particularly worthy of notice for having Served with unabated Zeal and Activity thro' this laborious Campaign notwithstanding a wound thro' his Arm which he received at Hubbardton."[88] According to the British military historian John William Fortescue, Major Craig "showed very great ability in his difficult post at Wilmington."[89] His superiors commended "the accuracy of his intelligence, the fertility of his resources, and the clearness of his military judgment."[90] However, American historian James Sprunt claimed that Craig displayed "tyrannical conduct that was needlessly cruel to the people of Wilmington."[91]

Today, there is a North Carolina highway marker remembering the Battle of Rockfish Creek in Duplin County, which may be Fowler's reference to the close pursuit. Craig's warning to the people of Cape Fear valley of North Carolina was issued as an ultimatum: "Pledge an oath of loyalty to the Crown and enlist in the Loyalist Militia or suffer the consequences." On August 1, 1781, when the declared grace period ended, the British forces under Craig began to pillage the countryside around Wilmington. Early in their exploits, the British forces, under the command of Colonel Thomas Kenan, encountered the Patriot Militia of Duplin County at Rockfish Creek. General Richard Caswell's forces supported Colonel Kenan's Militia, numbering around 330 men, when they met Craig's troops at Rockfish Creek on August 2, 1781. The North Carolinian Patriots were easily overwhelmed.[92]

The Tories, which Colonel Craig intended to use as the basis for British victory in the Cape Fear region, were routed at the Battle of Elizabethtown on August 27, 1781. Loyalists and British forces numbering between three hundred and four hundred men were headquartered in Elizabethtown. The Patriots, about sixty or seventy men, were driven from their homes and seen their estates ravaged and their houses plundered or burned. Led by Colonels. Thomas Brown and Thomas Robeson, the Patriots knew they would need to rely on cunning and strategy against the militarily superior numbers. They accomplished this by issuing orders to phantom soldiers. When the battle began, "the Tory commanders, John Slingsby and David Godden, were both fatally wounded, and their troops scattered into the darkness." Many of them plunged headlong into a deep ravine near the river, which has been known ever since as Tory Hole. When the smoke of battle cleared, seventeen Tories were either dead or mortally wounded. Not one Patriot was killed, and only four were wounded. Fortunately for the cause of the American Revolution, positions in the British military were given based on birth and not merit, and General Cornwallis, rather than Craig, commanded. Thus, the defeat of his Tory allies and the surrender of Cornwallis at Yorktown, Virginia, negated Craig's accomplishments in the Cape Fear valley.[93]

Stephens-Wright Cemetery and the Wright Family in Tabor City

Outside Tabor City, close to the junction of Peacock Road and Swamp Fox Highway, are the Hardee Woods. Adjacent to Peacock Road is a weathered sign that reads Stephens-Wright Cemetery. Turning down the road, one has to drive for some distance until the road forks, and then they have to guess if they go either left or right. Fortunately, I took the left fork and found the cemetery after traveling for about two thousand feet. There is a dividing mound of dirt that separates the Stephenses from the Wrights, but they lived and died knowing one another. Attorney Richard Wright was able to arrange for many of the old markers to be replaced with modern ones, primarily those of the sons who had served in the Confederacy.

What surprised me when I first visited the cemetery was that Tabor City is on the way to North Myrtle Beach, which means, as a child, I passed through Tabor City many times. All that time, hidden in the Hardee Woods, were the ancestors of my great-grandmother's family, who had given much to the state of North Carolina.

Battle of Malvern Hill, Virginia
Fleetwood and Hanson are the sons of my third great-grandmother Amelia Ann Fowler and Stephen Wright. Both fought at Malvern Hill and died in their service at the battle. The Confederate casualties were fifty-six hundred. I have included a brief summary of the battle since both lost their lives here. On June 30, 1862, the retreating Federal Army of the Potomac finally stopped at the James River at the end of seven days of fighting outside Richmond.

Confident in their support from naval warships behind them on the river, Union commander Major General George McClellan's men selected 130-foot-high Malvern Hill as a defensible position and invited a Confederate attack. Colonel Henry J. Hunt, McClellan's chief of artillery, posted 171 guns on the hill facing west, north, and east. Gently sloping, open fields fronted the Union position. McClellan arranged his infantry with the Fifth Corps on the west slope of the hill and the Third and Fourth Corps on the eastern side. Most of the rest of the army was held in reserve in the rear.

Robert E. Lee believed a sustained artillery barrage could weaken the Union position before his infantry attacked. Around one o'clock in the afternoon, both sides opened an artillery duel, which was largely ineffective. Lee ordered in the infantry, some twenty separate brigades under seven division commanders. The attacks were not coordinated properly and advanced across the open ground at different times;

most attacks stalled well short of the hill's crest. For each Confederate advance, the effectiveness of the Federal artillery was the deciding factor, repulsing attack after attack, resulting in a tactical Union victory. On July 2, 1862, McClellan withdrew the army to Harrison's Landing on the James River and commenced a six-week recovery and rehabilitation period before Washington's authorities transferred McClellan back to the Potomac River in August.[94] Twenty years after the battle, the slaughter at Malvern Hill was resonating in the mind of Confederate General Daniel Harvey "D.H." Hill, who stated, "It was not war, it was murder."

Amelia Ann traveled to Virginia to collect her sons and bring them home to Columbus County.[95] I cannot imagine her anguish and the added sadness of her granddaughter Patience's husband's death.

In doing this research, I came across another relative's sacrifice to Alabama, as shown in her letters. I have kept the original spelling in the letter.

> *John Pittman Lowe is my 2nd cousin 4 x removed. They are part of the exodus from the Carolinas to Alabama. Lucy A. McCarthy Lowe was born 14 April 1849 in Edgefield County, South Carolina and died in Crenshaw County, Alabama, in 1897, age 77 or 78. Lucy gave four sons and her husband to the State of Alabama in its war with the Union. She bore the burden of managing their farm and caring for their small children as her family gave one life after another.*

Below is a letter from John Pittman Low's wife, Lucy. The original letter is located in the Alabama State Archives in Montgomery, Alabama, in the William Hall Collection, Military Records Division.

Lounds County 1 June 1862

Dier husband

I know take my pen in hand drop you a few lines to let you no that we are all well as common and I am in about the same helth that I was when you left I hopes these lines may find you the same I receved a leter from you the 29 of May and you sed that you had not got many leters from me yet I have sent you fore leters besides this one George has got home he got hear the end of May he is very lo yet the boys has come home to sea me on a furlow and stade 10 days they started back yestrday to the camp they don't know whare they wil git to from their they are station at arbon (Auburn) above Mongary (Montgomery) John my corn is out know and I have not drawed anything yet but I hop I wil my crop is nice but pane hes quit and left my crop in bad fix but the neighbors ses they will help us you sed you wanted me to pray for you as for prayers I pray for you all the time I pray for you nearly every breth I draw and I want you to pray for yourself I have give the boys 13 dollars and I bought some 9 bushels of corn and that is all that I give him for his work and I have got 20 dolars yet George is very bad yet and he don't know whether he will ever get able to go back the sergeant give him furlo to stay at home til he was able to rejoin his company and he ses for you to try to get him a discharge from the head one for he never will be able to go back agane and I want you to get one if you can George sesy that you can get one any time you want to Sister ses she wants to sea you and kis you Your baby is the pertyest thing you ever saw in your life She can walk by herself and your little gran son is perty as a pink and growes the fastest in the world you must come home and sea all of your babyes and kis them I have got the ry cut hook sent and cut it for nothing Your old mare is gone blind in one eye and something is the matter with one of her fet so she cant hardly walk your hogs and cows is coming on very wel I want you

> to come home for I want to sea you so bad I don't know what to do I must come to a close by saying I remane your loveing wif until deth
> You must write to me soon as you get this leter goodby to you
> Lucy Lowe to John P. Lowe

[Note: Spelling and punctuational errors have been preserved from original letter.]

Patience Caroline Fowler Hattaway and James Erwin Hattaway had three children: James Calvin Hattaway (Hatoway), Margarette Hattaway, and Annie Elizabeth Hattaway (Prince) Page. It is necessary to note here that I have seen many different spellings for the last name Hattaway, which is why there are many variations included in this book. Granddaddy Gordon spelled it "Hathaway." He also stated Annie's middle name was "Laura," but her tombstone reads "Elizabeth." I have learned, too, that in 1910, Patience said she had four children, but only three of them were still living. I never knew anything of James until I began this research; thus, perhaps the fourth child will still be discovered. Granddaddy Gordon thought he was named after Annie's father, Gordon Hataway, but it was actually James Erwin's brother.

Now the twist in the family here gets more complex. Solomon Prince is listed as the father of Annie on her death certificate, completed by her husband, Daniel Return Page. Fortunately, other researchers have provided further insight into Patience's circumstances. There is documentation in the Columbus County Courthouse that proves Patience filed for a widow's pension on July 1, 1901. It states James Erwin Hataway enlisted in Company D of the Twentieth North Carolina Infantry in April of 1861. He died in Richmond, Virginia, at Howards Grove Hospital of smallpox in January of 1863. Patience is listed as fifty-six years old on the 1901 pension application, which places her birth in 1845 and corresponds to the 1850 and 1860 Census information. According to ancestry.com, the National Archives has a record of a claim against the Confederate Government for any "pay, allowances, or bounties" due to James Erwin Hattaway. Justice of the Peace R.F. Marlow takes her sworn statement she was the said widow of James Erwin Hattaway. The affidavit also bears the testimony of Isaac Wright, presumably her uncle, that Patience and James Erwin were married. Patience received $199.95 due to her husband dying in the line of duty. The rate of pay was $11.00 per month. Of course, the fate of Patience and what happened to her is purely speculative, as I have no evidence. Patience would have been nineteen or twenty in 1863. She evidently had two children to care for and few prospects of gaining the assistance of a man since many of them did not return from the war, and those who did would have their own families. Moreover, she may have been pregnant with Margarette when she was claiming her husband's body. She and Margarette are eternally resting side by side and share a common grave marker.

After the war had ended, Solomon Prince and Patience Caroline Fowler had a daughter named Anna Elizabeth Hattaway. Annie was given the name Hattaway for reasons unknown. One fact is undeniable: both my great-grandparents Daniel and Anna were illegitimate, which explains Granddaddy's insistence on not speaking of the past. What strikes me is that both Patience Caroline Fowler Hataway and Elizabeth Cartrette suffered immensely because of the Civil War, and both seemed to make the best of their lives. I wish there was something written or some oral history that revealed more information about their lives than what I have here.

During the copy editing of this manuscript, I continued to do research on one of the primary missing links of my past: identifying the father of Granddaddy Gordon Page's mother, Anna Elizabeth

Hattaway Page. Granddaddy Gordon told me her father was a Hathaway (Hattaway). However, Anna's husband, Daniel Return Page, lists Anna Elizabeth Hathaway's (Hattaway's) father as Solomon Prince. James Ervin Hattaway, the husband of Anna's mother, Patience Caroline Fowler, died during the Civil War in 1863 while in Virginia. Anna Elizabeth was born in March of 1866; thus, she was conceived perhaps in June of 1865. Since dead men do not father babies, when I discovered James Ervin's death date and Anna's birth date, I realized Granddaddy Gordon was either mistaken concerning the identity of Anna's father or had repeated the story he had been told. When I discovered Anna's father was listed as Solomon Prince, I tried to learn more about him and his family. I have discovered much on Solomon Prince's line. He was a descendant of Joseph Prince, who moved from Hull, Plymouth, Massachusetts, around 1731 to South Carolina. I did find a connection to the Horry (Ouri) Family of South Carolina. Joseph Prince married Elizabeth Mary Horry from Horry County, South Carolina—Elizabeth being the daughter of Daniel Horry (1662–1646), who fled France after the repeal of the Edict of Nantes, which allowed French Protestants (Huguenots) to practice their faith. Daniel came to South Carolina with his brother Elias (1664–1736). Their father, Jean Horry (1646–1686), who was an "Elder of a church in Paris, who died a martyr, for the Protestant faith, when the Edict of Nantes was Revoked by Louis XIV in 1685," according to a mural tablet of Elias Horry, son of Jean Horry, in the French Protestant (Huguenot) Church in the city of Charleston, South Carolina, at the Corner of Church and Queen Streets (geneologytrails.com).

Mary Horry was a widow of Captain Charles Lewis when she married Joseph Prince about 1735. Mary and Joseph had at least one child, Nicholas Prince Sr. The son of Nicholas Sr. was Nicholas Jr., who filed for a pension for Revolutionary War service. He served five months as a private in Captain Dennis Hankins and William Snow's South Carolina Companies. Nicholas Jr. was at Fort Moultrie when the British were driven back. He subsequently reenlisted in August of 1777 and served two years and nine months in Captain John Weekly's Company, Colonel Roberts and Beekman's South Carolina Regiment of Artillery, and was at the Siege of Savannah. He saw Count Casimir Pulaski fall from his horse during the Siege of Savannah in 1779, after being struck by grapeshot. Nicholas Jr. served during the Siege of Charleston and was captured but escaped after thirteen days. He then enlisted with General Francis "Swamp Fox" Marion. Nicholas Prince Jr. was granted a pension in 1833 while a resident of Horry County.

In the *Beatys of Kingston* by Edward Stanley Barnhill, published in 1958 by Furlong and Sons in Charleston, South Carolina, the history of the Horry (Ouri) family is found. It states the Horrys are of a noble family from the ancient province of Angoumois, France, now in the department of Charente. Mary Horry's father was Daniel Horry, who was the great-uncle of General Peter Horry, for whom Horry County, South Carolina, was named. Daniel and his brother Elias were Huguenots who fled France and came to South Carolina in April of 1692 aboard a privateer ship named *Loyal Jamaica* and is vouched for by Isaac Mazyck. Daniel Horry married Elizabeth Garnier, who was also a Huguenot, in August of 1692.[96] Daniel's arrival in South Carolina in April of 1692 is also documented in the *Journal of the Grand Council of South Carolina*.[97]

Elizabeth Garnier's father was Daniel Garnier, who with his wife, Elisabeth Canton, boarded a ship called *Margaret* and came to South Carolina.[98] Most of these French Protestants settled along the Santee River forty miles north of Charleston.

In the article "The Inscriptions on the Tombstones at the Old Parish Church of St. James's Santee, near Echaw Creek" by the South Carolina

Historical and Genealogical Society published in 1911, Daniel Horry's brother Elias is noted as having a memorial there.⁹⁹ There is also a marker in a church in Charleston stating the following about Elias:

> *The venerable ancestor of the Horry's of South Carolina. Elias was born in France in the year 1644, and was the son of an Elder of a Church in Paris, who died a martyr for the Protestant faith when the Edict of Nantes was revoked by Louis XIV. Escaping persecution, he fled to Holland and thence to England and finally South Carolina about 1690 and settled near the Santee, in the Parish of Prince George, Winyah where he resided for 46 years. Elias Horry died in Charleston on the 25th of September 1736 aged seventy-years and was buried in the French Church.*

The marriage of Daniel Horry and Elizabeth Garnier is recorded in the *Court of Ordinary of the Province of South Carolina 1672–92* on page 490 (LLMC Digital). A transcription of the bond appeared in the thirty-second issue of the *Transactions of the Huguenot Society of South Carolina* in 1927 (FamilySearch.com). The bond posted was of a large sum, indicating Elizabeth Garnier was a person of property.¹⁰⁰ The same publication had a transcription of the will of Elias Horry. The will was proved September 29, 1736. Both Elizabeth and Daniel Horry were granted citizenship by an act of Parliament read in the House of Commons on January 5, 1697, passed the House of Lords January 9, 1697, and received royal consent January 11, 1697.¹⁰¹ It is uncertain where Daniel is buried, as no marker has ever been found. Elias and Daniel Horry's father was Jean Horry and their mother was Madelaine DuFrene. Jean Horry, as stated, was thrown in the dungeon because of his Protestantism and was never seen again, falling victim to the precarious nature of King Louis XIV and the revocation of the Edict of

Nantes. Such was the terror directed against the Protestants of France that the wife of one Huguenot, Daniel Strering, found herself alone in Paris at the time of the revocation of the Edict of Nantes while her husband was in England. Baffled in her attempts to escape Paris, destitute and penniless as a result of their property being seized, she resorted to desperate measures. Pleading with a guard at one of the city gates, she needed to search for food. She gave her two-year-old child as ransom and a promise to return. This she did not do but instead found her way to England and was reunited with her husband. The fate of the child was unknown.[102]

The story of the Horrys' immigration to South Carolina seems to be an omen of the effects of wars upon women. Many decades later, Patience Caroline Fowler Hattaway would also find herself a widow during the Civil War as a young woman, and in some unknown circumstances, she and Solomon Prince had a child, my third grandmother Anna Elizabeth. I have no history of what subsequently happened, and that will probably forever be hidden by time. Fortunately, I have been able to determine the father was Solomon Prince and the family connection to the Horrys.

The story of Edward Teach, a.k.a. "Blackbeard," takes place in eastern North Carolina; he is considered to be a prominent figure in its early history. In researching my memoir, I learned my ancestors might have lived contemporarily with Blackbeard. These would be the Blounts. I am extremely grateful to Beverly A. Ramsey for her book entitled *The Blounts of Mulberry Hill: Descendants of Captain James Blount of Chowan County, NC, 1650–1900*. The impressive amount of research provided me with an illustrious history of my ancestors who originated in Virginia and were some of the first to settle in North Carolina.[103] Another book where I discovered information was Deason Hunt's *Out of Mississippi: The John Robert Wingate Family of Nacogdoches County, Texas*. The information in the following paragraphs is taken from Ramsey's and Hunt's books. The parents of Deason's mother, Ozie Mae Moody Hunt, were Fred and Mae Wingate Moody. Thus, the connection to the Wingates is through the brother of John Wingate, Edward Wingate.[104]

Hunt corroborates Edward Wingate was born in 1686 to John Wingate of Chowan County. The record of Edward to his father-in-law, Joun Blount, is attested in the land records. In 1718, John, father of Ann Blount, conveyed a plantation to the couple, located on Queen Anne's Creek in Chowan. In 1723, the plantation was sold to Edmund Gale. Edward later patented land in New Hanover County, North Carolina, on Lockwood Folly River. Edward Sr. and Ann were living in Prince George Parish, Craven County, South Carolina, when they both died. Edward Sr. had participated in the doomed British expedition against the Spanish in present-day Cartagena de Indias, Colombia, in 1740.[105] George Washington's half-brother Lawrence participated in this expedition, served on Admiral Edward Vernon's flagship, and set off with the most significant amphibious force to date against Spain in America.

The British defeat is attributed to the Spanish commander, Blas de Lezo. "A living legend among Spanish sailors, Lezo—nicknamed *Mediohombre,* or 'Half Man'—had literally given life and limb for his country. When Lezo and Vernon first faced each other in battle in 1704, a cannonball maimed Lezo's left leg, which had to be amputated. Two years later, shrapnel claimed his left eye, and not long thereafter, a musket shot took his right hand and forearm." The fighting had lasted sixty-eight days and ended with the British Royal Navy withdrawing in defeat after losing ninety-five thousand men, having seventy-five thousand wounded, and having fifty ships either sink or be severely damaged by enemy fire or be abandoned for lack of crew members. There were nineteen ships of the line damaged, four frigates, and twenty-seven transports lost. Of the thirty-six thousand American minutemen who had volunteered due to being lured by promises of land and pillage of mountains of gold, only three hundred returned; most died of yellow fever, dysentery, and outright starvation. Lawrence Washington, George's brother, was a privileged one who returned back home to rename his Virginia plantation "Mount Vernon" after Admiral Vernon.[106]

Edward Wingate was fortunate to return to Virginia or North Carolina, yet his exploits against the Spanish did not end. When the Spanish attacked North Carolina in the so-called Spanish Alarm of 1748, Edward Sr. and his sons, Edward Jr. and John, served in William Dry's Company to repulse the Spanish raiders.[107] The Spanish incursion into North Carolina resulted in the occupation of Brunswick and was the last of a series of raids into North Carolina.[108]

Returning to Edward Wingate and Ann Blount, Ramsey says family lore states Ann Blount's grandfather, Captain James, was in Virginia by 1645. He was alleged to be a Cavalier and supporter of King Charles I, who was beheaded during the English Civil War. Like many other supporters of the Stuarts, he sought refuge in America. What's certain is he was in Virginia by 1655, as records in England document the passage of three bonded passengers to planter James Blount in America. There is also a deed record dating to May 3, 1673, in Virginia.

On March 24, 1663, King Charles II of England granted to his supporters the Province of Carolina. This grant conveyed with it the right for the lords proprietors to govern the colony, but only William Berkley, who was already in Virginia, chose to take advantage of this. The lords proprietors directed Berkley to reserve twenty thousand acres for themselves and grant ten-acre tracts to colonists. Berkley, anxious to start collecting rent from the colonists, made grants of fifty acres on the Albemarle Sound in North Carolina. The area of the land grants was adjacent to Queen Anne's Creek and became known as

Edenton. Sometime before 1668, Captain James Blount settled on a three-hundred-acre tract on the Albemarle Sound east of Edenton. The lord proprietors were two years delinquent in formulating a constitution for the colony but finally issued the Concessions and Agreements in January of 1665.[109] The twelve precincts into which the colony had already been divided were to remain. The area which is now Chowan, Perquimans, Currituck, Bertie, Pasquotank, and Edgecombe Counties was then one county called Albemarle, which was divided into precincts. Present-day Chowan County originated as the Shaftesbury Precinct, which was in existence from 1671–1681. It then became the Chowan Precinct and finally Chowan County.[110]

Captain Blount appears to have been married in Virginia and had three sons: James, Thomas, and John. James and Thomas remained in Virginia for about three years but eventually joined their father in North Carolina. Captain Blount was politically active in Chowan; he was elected to the council in 1669 but became immersed in more notorious politics known as Culpeper's Rebellion. The rebellion "was an early popular uprising against a proprietary rule in the Albemarle section of northern Carolina, caused by the proprietary government's efforts to enforce the British Navigation Acts. These trade laws denied the colonists a free market outside England and placed heavy duties on commodities. The colonists' resentment found an object in the deputy governor, Thomas Miller, who was also a customs collector. Led by John Culpeper and George Durant, the rebels imprisoned Miller and other officials, convened a legislature of their own, chose Culpeper governor, and for two years, capably exercised all powers and duties of Government. Culpeper was finally removed by the proprietors and tried for treason and embezzlement but was never punished."[111] Beverly Ramsey includes that economic conditions caused by a hurricane, which destroyed the crops in 1670, had amplified the burden of taxes paid by the colonists. Coupled with the indifference of the proprietors to the Carolinians' plight, the resulting rebellion should have been expected.[112]

Further, the Carolinians had become a self-sufficient group who were not wanting to look to England for leadership. Isolated from ocean trade routes and distant from the seat of government, they saw little reason to defer to a king who knew nothing about their life. Like other American colonists, they were slowly being financially strangled by the king in his navigation acts. Beginning with the passage of the first act in the mid-1600s, these laws protected the shipping trade of England while producing a century-long choke hold on the American economy.[113] The rebellion events are compelling and demonstrate the foreboding of an individualistic personality developing in the future Tar Heels. I have included below Ramsey's account of James Blount in the uprising:

> *Capt. James Blount, although one of the Great Council or Assistant to the Deputies is one of the chief persons amongst the insurrection, and although I wrote to him, the speaker and the rest of the Burgesses of Chowan Precinct, yet when the Sheriff or Chief Martiall came with my letter and endeavored to raise Posse Comitatus for keeping the peace and of that your Lordships County, he the said Blount with one Captain John Varnham took the Martiall and his men Prisoners and raised forces against the Government.[114]*

James Blount after the Insurrection

James Blount's participation in Culpeper's Rebellion did not damage his reputation among his peers. He served on the rebel council and was also elected to serve on the restored council from at least 1680 to 1683. In 1682 and 1683, Captain James Blount was a justice on the county court. He may have served in these offices in other years for which records have not survived. Court and land records over the next few years make further mention of James Blount.[115]

Further records show James Blount was holding the position of assistant deputy to the lords proprietors. There are many court records indicating the involvement of Blount in local affairs. Perhaps the most interesting thing about James Blount during this time involves Seth Sothel. When Sothel was finally ransomed and made his way to Carolina to be the governor, both he and Blount became interested in a New England woman who had moved to the area from New Hampshire: Anna or Ann Willix.

When Anna was about ten years old, her mother was robbed and murdered while traveling between Dover and Exeter, New Hampshire. Her body was summarily tossed in a river. Anna had an older sister, Hazelelponi, and a younger sister, Susannah. The three daughters' lives changed after this tragedy. Their father remarried, but all three girls were forced to work as servants for neighboring families. Speculation is that her new stepmother may have become mentally ill and was unable to care for the children. Ann worked for Reverend Timothy Dalton of Hampton, New Hampshire, and endeared herself to the family's wife. Ann later married Robert Riscoe and immigrated to Albemarle District, North Carolina, by 1670. Riscoe was a seafarer and did business between New York and Albemarle. He died, and in 1683, James Blount married Anna and petitioned the courts to be made executor of Riscoe's estate. English law forbade married women from managing their affairs; thus, this is an indication James and Ann married sometime before the petition to the court.[116]

James made his will on March 16, 1685, and named his sons, James, Thomas, and John, and daughters, Ann and Elizabeth. Additionally, he called John Blount, Elizabeth's child. John Blount must not have met maturity because James Blount stated, "John should be maintained during his minority." James died between March 1685 and July 1686. Only one person, Edward Wade, made a claim against his estates and was awarded four pounds, seven shillings, and a ninepence.[117]

Ann married Seth Sothel sometime between July 1686 and January 1689. Ann's new husband may have been a lord proprietor, but he was one of the most unscrupulous men to have governed in Carolina. In 1677, he purchased the Earl of Clarendon's proprietorship of the Carolina Province from his son Edward Hyde, second Earl of Clarendon.

One historian describes him as the "most beastly and detestable man" and says the following:

> He broke up all trade between the colonists and the Indians, so that he might monopolize the profits. He seized and confiscated, without the shadow of cause, merchant ships and their cargoes. He imprisoned Thomas Pollock of Bal-Gray, Bertie County, for attempting to appeal against his rapacity, and George Durant, having expressed disapprobation of his course, received like treatment and further injury. He stole slaves, cattle, and plantations. Even pewter dishes were not exempted from his filthy and rapacious hands. All his sympathies were with villains like himself, and no man could be prosecuted who had money to bribe the governor.[118]

Seth Sothel and tyranny were one until the people of Albemarle revolted, tried him, and banished him from the county. So he fled to Charleston, South Carolina, and, for a time, was governor there from 1690 until November of 1691. He then returned to Albemarle and to a four-thousand-acre plantation he had acquired, legally or otherwise, on Salmon Creek in present-day Bertie County, now called Avoca. He died in either 1692 or 1694, and Ann married again, for the fourth time, to Colonel John Lear of Virginia, sometime between September 5 and October 8, 1694.

For John Lear, that was his second marriage. He was from Nansemond County, Virginia, where he owned at least nine hundred acres at Orepeak, which was patented in 1682. Ramsey points out some claims about how Ann may have been the mother of some of James Blount Sr.'s children but demonstrates that because of the timeline, this is impossible. Anna inherited perhaps twelve thousand acres of land from her marriage and left her sisters as the beneficiaries. This would have been the twelve thousand acres Sothel was entitled to under the Fundamental Constitution written by John Locke, which specified that each proprietor had a right to a *seignor* of twelve thousand acres in each county.[119]

Hazelelponi's son-in-law traveled to North Carolina from New England and successfully secured the land for Anna's sisters. They later sold the land to Thomas Pickering. While Anna is not an ancestor of mine, I have included her story because it illustrates the trade between the colonies and also the plight of a woman owning vast amounts of land yet having to rely upon a husband to manage her estates and affairs. Further, it illustrates how she was able to survive in the eighteenth century.

Thus, with the end of James Sr., I now briefly turn to his son James Blount Jr. His daughter was Anne Blount, who married Edward Wingate. Their son, John Wingate, was born in 1719. About 1739, he married Hannah Sessions. They are shown on the 1800 Census, Bladen Co., North Carolina, Captain Barfield's District. John Wingate also operated a mill near White Marsh in Whiteville when the area was in Bladen County until Columbus became a county in 1808.[120]

A Visit with Judy Carol Worley Williams

"It is in the woods, the jungle," stated Judy Carol Worley Williams, my mom's first cousin and my Grandma Ara Mae's niece. Judy was speaking about the location of the assisted living facility at Tabor City she had been living in since she'd had her stroke. After several attempts to locate the facility, I was eventually directed to the nursing home by an employee at Dale's Seafood. Located down a single-lane road with trees overshadowing it, the facility did indeed seem to be the entrance to some jungle, as described by Judy.

I walked into what, in my opinion, was essentially a barrack for older adults. There was no attendant at the desk, and a central hallway led to the left and right with doors off to each side. A woman dressed in scrubs who clearly worked there came up to me and asked, "Who are you looking for, hon?"

I replied, "Judy Carol Worley."

"We do not have a Judy Carol Worley, but we do have a Judy Carol Williams." She escorted me to a door with the name Judy Carol Williams on the front.

I looked inside and saw her lying on a bed, and she looked as if she were sleeping. Since it had been years since I last saw her, I did not recognize her at first and told the woman, "I do not think that is her."

"Maybe she is in Loris at that assisted care facility, hon," replied the woman.

Judy Carol must have been awakened by us talking because she sat up and looked at us both, giving us a perplexed gaze. The woman asked, "Ms. Judy, were you a Worley?"

"Yes, I am."

At that point, she still did not know who I was until I stated, "I am Dollie's son, Ara Mae's grandson."

Judy smiled and replied, "I declare, Lord, I have not seen you since forever."

I asked, "I have brought some photos and would like to know if you can recognize any of the Worleys in the pictures?"

"Well, dear, my eyesight is not so good since I had a stroke, but I will try." While looking through the photos, she would see my mother's and her siblings' faces and call them by their full names. Occasionally, she would point at someone and say, "That is Uncle Joe," or "That is Aunt Ara Mae," or "That is Dollie Monteen, and that is Priscilla Joe." It was somewhat surprising to hear her call them by their middle names since I had not heard them since I was fifteen. I was extremely pleased to hear those names called out by her. Like my bestowed nickname, "Bo Dean," they had been left in Columbus County, but upon finding someone who still remembered, they were as fresh as the morning dew.

When she saw her father, Barnum Worley, she said, "That is Daddy." Here was a woman who weighed about one hundred pounds, nearing ninety, and still remembered and called her father "Daddy." That was a very touching moment for me, and I'm glad I was able to share it with her.

Judy Carol related a story of how Grandma Ara Mae had wanted "Cilla Joe," who was my mother's sister, Priscilla, to take piano lessons, so she bought their piano. "I was taking lessons, and Mommy told me that if I did not take a better interest in it, she would sell the piano," stated Judy Carol. "Well, she did." Cilla Joe had no interest in taking piano lessons. She did not even have the musical talents of a frog, but Grandma Ara Mae was set on forcing the issue until she finally gave up on her daughter.

When they, my grandparents and Aunt Priscilla, came to pick up the piano, they loaded it onto the trailer and did not bother tying it down. They agreed that the weight of the piano would hold it down, and they would not drive too fast. When they rounded the curve between Cherry Grove and Cedar Grove, "the wind grabbed the piano and slung it out of the truck"—their words. It came crashing down and broke into pieces. The Lord heard the prayers of Cilla Joe, not Grandma Ara Mae.

When Cilla Joe heard the piano's fate, she shouted, "Amen, amen, amen!"

Judy Carol stated, "It was probably a good thing the piano fell and broke since none of them had musical talent. It most likely would have brought more of the boogeyman than the Lord in the house."

Judy Carol then revealed it was Ara Mae who liked the piano. "Your grandma would be at our house and bang out the tune to 'Frog Went a-Courting' and then shout, 'Whooo wheeeee!' Your Grandma Ara Mae sure was a fun person full of herself and laughter. Teresa Rose, my mom's sister, is the most like her of all the children, but your mom favors her the most."

Judy Carol then turned the conversation to my mom. "She is a good person, but she does not take any crap off of anyone. She will sail on you like a hawk in an instant if you wrong her. I know she put your father in his place." That was something Judy Carol did not have to tell me; I knew that very well.

When I had told my mom that the Coleman boys had teased me on the bus one day, she chased the bus down and admonished the bus driver for letting it happen. The next day, Mom was called to the principal's office while I waited outside his office. A bit of a role reversal, for sure. The bottom line was neither of the Coleman boys bothered me again.

Judy Carol had a keen mind and could recall many people's past and their children. She named all thirteen of Grandma Hazel's sister Clara's children in order from eldest to youngest. Aunt Clara lived in the same Cherry Grove community as the Worleys. "Clara never saw the light of day," Judy Carol said. "She was always pregnant and having babies every nine months. She had fourteen. One died." That Aunt Clara had an infant who passed was news to me. "She was a good mother, and

I knew them all and knew them well. We all knew each other from school or the Baptist church. Yes, Clara never saw the light of day with thirteen children."

Later, I spoke to my Aunt Pattie, who confirmed Clara had all her children at home, and one was born a "blue baby." I assume the baby boy, perhaps, was tangled in the umbilical cord and lacked oxygen. Pattie also stated, "Aunt Clara said all Uncle Guilford had to do was lay his pants on the bedpost, and I was pregnant."

That day I visited Judy Carol, she repeatedly told me, "You made my day. You have made my day, seeing you and these photos, and you made my day." She also said I had the Worley mark on me.

I stammered, "Th-the Worley mark?"

"That round face and that grin where the left side of your smile rises and the right side pulls down." I had never heard it called the Worley mark, but she was correct. I have it, and so does my mom. Grandma Ara Mae and several of Mom's siblings do too. "You don't have the boogeyman in you like those Williamsons, do you?" Well, this was a new one too. "Those Williamsons get the boogeyman in them, and feathers go to flying. They are good, hardworking people and can work longer and harder than anyone can, but if you get them riled up, the feathers will go flying. No, you do not want to make them angry or get on their bad side, those Williamsons. Your Grandpa Joe was a lucky man. Aunt Ara Mae was a pretty girl, and she was full of laughter." With that, she again said, "You made my day," and thus ended my short time with Judy Carol Worley.

Judy Worley Williams passed away on May 5, 2021, at the Lower Cape Fear Life Care in Tabor City. I am forever grateful I had the opportunity to speak to her.

PART III

CHAPTER 18
Distant Relations

Annie Mae Page Bellamy

"I am eighty-eight years old," Annie Mae Page Bellamy said as she reached down and picked up another pine cone that had blown from its perch because of Hurricane Dorian. I was on my way to North Myrtle Beach, a journey everyone who lived in Columbus County made for as long as I can recall. When I had passed her house, I saw her in the yard, tossing the remnants of pine branches and debris into the back of a small pickup. Although, in my opinion, Annie's truck was more of a wheelbarrow and akin to a wagon.

I was surprised an eighty-eight-year-old woman was laboring in the humid September weather, but my wife was also not known for being able to stay still. "I need to be doing something," my wife would remark. Evidently, that is a family trait, as I have never met a Page who was more comfortable just sitting. They are always busy at something.

Annie Mae, so named after our Grandma Annie or Anna Elizabeth Hattaway or Prince—only Anna's mother Patience Fowler Hattaway could ever confirm the research based upon Anna's death certificate that her father was Solomon Prince—was the only daughter of Jessie

Caldwell Page and Lillie Frink Page. Annie Mae also had three brothers, Norman, Charles, and David. She told me Jessie and Lillie had planned on naming her after Grandma Ann. As Grandma Annie's health declined, Jessie asked her to hold on for a bit longer because they hoped she would see Annie Mae when she was born. Of course, Jessie did not know if it was a girl or boy, but then Annie told him, "Jessie, the Lord gave me a vision, and it is a girl, and she will be healthy and live long." Grandma Annie died nine days before Annie Mae was born, but the vision proved accurate, and she was named Annie.

Annie stated, "When I was young, we lived at the Webster Place. Daddy bought some land there, and we lived more than a mile off 701, where I had to walk every morning to catch the bus. Sometimes, Daddy would hitch up the mule and take me to the end of the road. If his car was working—it frequently was not—he would drive me to the end of the road." She related how she was happy when they moved closer to 701, as she would not have to walk that two-plus-mile trip every day during all sorts of weather if the mule or car was not available.

When I asked about Daniel Return's mother, she said, "I remember her. She lived to be over a hundred years old and was a very independent woman. She was able to get around really well for her age until she fell going down the steps. After that, she was bedridden until she passed away. She lived with us, and Mommy did not know what to think of her because she would put a sheet over her head and tell us she was soon going to be a ghost. Yes, she walked around with that sheet over her head, saying she was a ghost." She added, "It was sad to see her bedridden like she was, but back then, there was not anything to do for people."

I asked her about Aunt Rena, whom I only recently discovered was buried at Evergreen. She replied, "How terrible ... she died young.

Daddy said she was engaged to be married, had a hope chest, and planned to start a family. She had a vitamin D deficiency, and it contributed to a disease she caught. Oh Lord, she has been dead a hundred years ... unfortunate."

When she saw the photo of her adopted brother, she said, "That is the boy Granddaddy took in and raised. He was just like a brother. He lived over in Marion and worked his way up a company and ended up owning a sawmill. His wife was not a good woman. When he died, she did not even tell us he had passed. I had to read it in the paper. Yes, they all looked upon him as a brother. He was a relative to Elizabeth, Daniel's mother." I wanted her to confirm her adopted brother's identity, but she could not recall his name. I had heard of him in the past through stories from my father and his sisters. When I started talking with her about him, it all came back to Annie Mae, and she confirmed his identity and the fact that his second wife was not very nice. This man was the brother who had promised to help Grandpa Gordon buy a farm. The same wife who did not tell the family of his death also persuaded him that there were better ways to invest one's money than helping a brother. It seems strange, as the Pages had taken him in when his mother had passed and reared him as one of their own.

Another aspect of this is that Jessie had some disfiguring disease that affected his back. Perhaps it was scoliosis. Annie Mae said they'd had to carry him up and down the stairs when he was younger. I recall Grandpa Gordon telling me about this and how he would work with Jessie and try to help him move around. Annie said, "It got better, but when he got old, he started to pull together again."

She also spoke of the only surviving daughter of Daniel Return and Anna, Aunt Emma Victoria Page Byrd. "I used to go to Fair Bluff and spend a week at a time with her in the summers. She was a delightful woman. She taught me to sew. She had two babies to die very young and had only one son. His name was Aldridge. I do not know what happened to him or where he is. Yes, she was such a sweet lady." This remark by Annie Mae confirmed the newspaper clipping a resident, Bob Morgan, had run in the paper about Emma. Mr. Morgan's family lived next to Aunt Emma, and he said she was the salt of the earth, and his daughters loved to visit with her.

Thus, my trip to the beach proved beneficial. My loving and very patient wife dutifully sat there at the table and listened to me discuss people she did not know. I found out a few more bits of information, which allowed me to piece together more about people I wish I knew more about. I am quickly exhausting any living relatives whose memories predate the World War II era and even the stories they may have heard back to the early 1900s.

Extended Families in Columbus, Robeson, Brunswick, Marion, and Horry Counties

In researching this material, I have developed a relationship with the people and families I have found. Their triumphs and tragedies have become my own. The times they lived in have been turbulent, joyful, and marked with progress unparalleled in recorded history. They lived as I have lived—with hopes, dreams, and optimism. When I consider how, from one day to the next, none of us know what the day will bring to our doorsteps, I remember the Thomas Hardy poem "Hap"—living in the face of the dice being played by those three blind doomsters playing with their lives:

> *If but some vengeful god would call to me*
> *From up the sky, and laugh: "Thou suffering thing,*
> *Know that thy sorrow is my ecstasy,*
> *That thy love's loss is my hate's profiting!"*

Then would I bear it, clench myself, and die,
Steeled by the sense of ire unmerited;
Half-eased in that a Power fuller than I
Had willed and meted me the tears I shed.

But not so. How arrives it joy lies slain,
And why unblooms the best hope ever sown?
—Crass Casualty obstructs the sun and rain,
And dicing Time for gladness casts a moan....
These purblind Doomsters had as readily strown
Blisses about my pilgrimage as pain.

The Pages of Lake View, South Carolina, and Marietta, North Carolina

Apparently, and confirmed by DNA testing, Abraham Page, who had died in the Revolutionary War, was either a son or brother of Thomas Page. Abraham Page's wife was Mary Lamb. Thomas Page originated in the Isle of Wight, Virginia, and his estate was probated in Bertie County, North Carolina. The probate records were signed by Solomon Page, which established a connection of Solomon Page, who is buried down from Bear Swamp Baptist Church in Lake View, South Carolina.

According to Quaker meeting records, Thomas Page and his wife, Isabell Lawrence, were Quakers and married in 1701 in the house of Francis Denson. My working hypothesis is that the Quakers in Virginia did not last that long, and once the Pages moved to North Carolina, they became Baptist. They moved from Bertie County to the North and South Carolina border of Marion and Robeson Counties, which is where many of their descendants live today. I based this assumption on the biblical names most of these Pages share, which indicates a common religious background. What I know for sure is David Page Sr. received a land grant on the Providence Line, and today, many Pages live in and around the same area of the original land grant. The paternal DNA of the Page males is M-253, Scandinavian in origins, with the highest percentage being represented in Sweden and Finland. Thus, their English origins perhaps mask a Viking ancestry, which results from the Norsemen incursions into the British Isles.

Rebecca Gore

I am related to the Gores of Brunswick and Columbus Counties through Rebecca Gore, who had married into the Isham Williamson family. It seems the Gores are English but were sent to Ireland by Queen Elizabeth to establish Englishmen in Ireland. Sir Bart Gore made his way from Ireland to Virginia. Three generations later, Joshua Gore made his way to Brunswick County. His son Jonathan received a land grant of one hundred acres in the fork of Horse Pen Branch in Brunswick County in 1800.

The Gores came to Virginia with John Gore, Sir Bart's son, and emigrated in 1654. They, like others, later moved into North Carolina and the lower Cape Fear River area. Supposedly, the Gores originated in Northern Ireland with an Englishman, Sir Bart Gore, a baronet, and Isabella Wycliffe. A baronet is a British hereditary order of honor and made up of commoners designated by "Sir" before their name. Sir Bart was a baronet of Magherabegg in County Donegal. His wife, Isabella, was the daughter of Francis Wycliffe and the niece of the first Earl of Strafford. I cannot find any hard evidence of my family's connection to Sir Bart in the only report I have discovered. However, the wife of Jonathan was a Simmons, and there are Simmonses in Brunswick County, and his son Joseph's wife was a Best. Thus, I am confident of the ancestry until it departs Brunswick County back to Virginia and then Northern Ireland.

I should mention the word "gore" is Old English for "a triangular piece of land."

Pierce Godwin

John H. Williamson of Davidson, North Carolina, sent me an email stating he had some information for me if I could travel to Davidson on Sunday and get it. Visiting John is indeed always a pleasure, and the traffic on I-77 to Davidson from Rock Hill is relatively light on a Sunday morning. Thus, I readily agreed and traveled to Davidson to have lunch with him. Afterward, we walked back to John's room, and he presented me with over four thousand pages of research on the Williamson family and associated families.

Since William the Conqueror had defeated Harold Godwinson in the Battle of Hastings in 1066, making him the master of England, the name Godwin was one I took much interest in learning more about. The information John gave me had been compiled by a relative on the Wright side of my family, Jason Bordeaux, commissioned by John H. Williamson. Nancy and Alley Godwin were two of the daughters who married into the Williamson family. My connection is to Nancy, who married Joshua Williamson.

Pierce Godwin's will is dated April 25, 1845, in Columbus County, North Carolina—Will book A, page 55. He names daughters Alcy, Nancy, Susan, and Emily. Pierce also names Maranza Ann Williamson and the heirs of Elias Godwin, Ireny Moncrieff and Ithamar Tatum. He also names grandson N.L.—Nathan Lewis, presumably—Williamson. All these names are associated with Columbus County in which I was reared. Laban and Dennis Williamson, Joshua Williamson's sons, signed the will.

Pierce Godwin was the son of Solomon Godwin, who died before 1763 and was from Johnston County, North Carolina, and Martha

Pearce. The research did not establish who the mother of the Godwin daughters was. Still, speculation is he married later in life to Clary Green Tatum—her father was Simon Green—the widow of Richard Tatum Jr., who died in 1829. The children named in Pierce's will in 1845, Ireny and Ithamar, were her children.

Another note of interest is that on January 2, 1798, Pierce Godwin, Ephraim Nichols, and William Faulk witnessed and deeded from John Coleman to Elias Nichols three hundred acres of land on the south side of Porter's Swamp. Once again, the last names here are all family names connected not only to the Williamsons and Worleys but also the Lewises and Pages of Marion and Horry Counties.

Richard Tatum Sr. was listed on the 1789 Bladen County tax list in John Yate's District. On March 14, 1789, he purchased two hundred acres on the east side of Drowning Creek and the south side of Cow Branch from Francis Lawson for seventy British pounds. On the 1790 Census, he is listed between John Shaw and Williams Sibbet. Lewis Williamson, Hamilton Hilborn, and Goldsbury Flowers are all listed nearby. On July 16, 1795, he was granted another five hundred acres on Cow Branch. In 1797, he witnessed a deed from Simon Bright Sr. to Wynn Nance. Lewis Williamson and Simon Bright witnessed the deed. Richard Tatum is mentioned in a deed relinquishing the rights to 180 acres of land by Joshua Tatum, Richard Jr., and Jesse Tatum to Laban Tatum.

Moving forward to Richard Tatum Jr., on April 5, 1828, he and James Griffin witnessed a deed from Fanny Wells to Goldsbury Flowers for one hundred acres. There are many other deeds and many land sales by Joshua Williamson as the first sheriff of Columbus County. I have included this information on the Godwins because the recorded land transactions will substantiate the interconnection of the original families of the Williamson's Cross Roads area and Cerro Gordo. It appears the Tatums, like the Flowers, eventually sold their lands and moved to Georgia, Alabama, and Mississippi. However, their legacy remains in the blood of their descendants and the records of Columbus County Courthouse.

One final note is that Cow Branch is adjacent to Macedonia Baptist Church.

The Stricklands (Borderlands)

From my research on Grandma Dalmas's, "Goggi Ma's," line of Strickland ancestors, there's some Scottish and northern English blood in our veins. In his seminal book *Albion's Seed: Four British Folkways in America*, David Hackett Fisher states the following:

> *The border area of England and Scotland derived its cultural character from one of decisive historical fact. For seven centuries, the Kings of Scotland and England could not agree on who owned it and constantly meddled in each other's affairs. At Penrith, a market town halfway between Carlisle and Kendal, there is a great red sandstone beacon high on a barren hill, where the warning firs were lighted when the Scots came over the border.*[121]

Many of the clans of this area were described as "Scottish when they will, and English at their pleasure."[122] Fisher documents the later Scot-Irish immigration primarily in the later seventeenth century to the backcountry of the British colonies—for example, two-thirds of which took place from 1765–1775, just short of the year of independence.[123] The evidence suggests the Stricklands were the trickle, which began in the early 1700s, to Virginia. Encouraging people to migrate to Virginia was not an easy task, as the obstacles to success were many at the time. Thus, the English Crown used creative means to increase emigration. One way was by using a system of headrights. The English used headrights to increase emigration to Virginia when the tobacco economy grew beyond the means to be effectively harvested by the population. The Library of Virginia states:

> *To encourage immigration into the colony, the Virginia Company, meeting in a Quarter Court held on November 18, 1618, passed a body of laws called Orders and Constitutions, which came to be considered "the Great Charter of privileges, orders and laws" of the colony. Among these laws was a provision that any person who settled in Virginia or paid for the transportation expenses of another person who settled in Virginia should be entitled to receive fifty acres of land for each immigrant. The right to receive fifty acres per person, or per head, was called a "headright." The headright practice was continued under the royal government of Virginia after the dissolution of the Virginia Company, and the Privy Council ordered on July 22, 1634, that patents for headrights be issued."* [124] *Describing these immigrants from the Borderlands of Scotland and England, one Philadelphian observed, "Their speech is English, but they spoke with a cadence that rang strangely to the ear. Many were desperately poor. But even in their poverty, they carried themselves with fierce and stubborn people that warned others to treat them with respect."* [125]

I cannot state whether my Stricklands were "desperately poor," but no truer sentiment rings true in their unyielding demand of respect. They originated from the area of Westmoreland, which faces the Irish Sea. Many different peoples have ruled this part of England or Scotland. The Romans advanced and retreated across this area, building walls to keep people out and then again moving northward into Scotland only to retreat again. Vikings from Dublin, Ireland, raided the coast and sacked Dumbarton Castle in 1870. Dumbarton, built on a volcanic rock, "was a mighty stronghold in the Dark Ages and the capital of a kingdom of Strathclyde. The Viking assault, led by King Olaf and Ivar of Dublin in 1870, besieged the fortress with two hundred longships and carried off much treasure and slaves."[126] Without any reservations, the hardships and trials of invasions, and even the environment, nurtured each generation of Stricklands until an indomitable spirit set root in America. This spirit continued to manifest itself in times of war.

One of the primary occupations by every social class was the practice of reiving—raiding or plundering—along the border area. From the fourteenth century until the seventeenth century, the borderlands of Scotland and England were an area where there was not any allegiance to the sovereign but only to the family or clan. Scottish Border Reivers would as readily raid fellow Scots as they would the English. The English Border Reivers operated by the same rule. Many times, they would unite and raid both sides of the border. From a reiver's perspective, the constant warfare between the kings of England and Scotland reduced their lands to wasteland. The people were left with no other viable option but to find alternative subsistence by raiding and pillaging. There was no need to plant a crop if an English or Scottish army would burn it before being harvested. One story was related that a wife of one famous border reiver demonstrated that her larder was empty by serving her husband his spurs on a plate instead of his dinner. The message was clear: either mount up and go reiving or go hungry.[127] Except for the Scottish Highlands, the Borders were the last part Britain brought under the rule of law.

One of the most notorious and famous of the reivers was Walter Scott, Fifth of Buccleuch, First Lord Scott of Buccleuch. Scott brazenly rescued another reiver, Kinmont Willie Armstrong, who had been captured by the English in violation of a truce and subsequently imprisoned in Carlisle Castle on March 17, 1596. Scott attempted to secure Armstrong's release by diplomacy, but he raided the castle and freed Armstrong when those attempts failed. The raid on one of Queen Elizabeth's forts nearly caused a war between Scotland and England until Scott surrendered himself to English authority. He was sentenced for the crime, sent to London, and presented to the Queen herself. When Elizabeth I asked how he dared to undertake such a desperate and presumptuous enterprise, Scott replied, "What is it that a man dare not do?" Not accustomed to such brazen and frank remarks, Elizabeth replied, "With ten thousand such men, our brother in Scotland might shake the firmest throne of Europe."[128]

Scott's kinsman, the author Sir Walter Scott, transcribed a well-known ballad about the raid entitled "Kinmont Willie" in his collection *Minstrelsy of the Scottish Border*.[129] Upon the ascendancy of James VI of Scotland to the throne of England as James I in 1603, King James I, famous for commissioning the King James Bible, declared no border between the two nations and ruthlessly sought to end the era of the reivers. "The chiefs and lairds were apprehended and hanged or drowned most often without trial." The King took lesser clan and family members and transported them to Northern Ireland, where they eked out a precarious living from the bogs of Roscommon. Still, the Crown sent "others, the young and able-bodied men were sent to the cautionary towns of the Low Countries to aid the Protestant Dutch in their war with catholic Spain."[130]

Both the demise and the origins of the reivers began with Scottish kings, King William I in particular. William was captured by the English during the Battle of Alnwick in 1174. He had foolishly charged into a group of English knights and was thrown from his horse and captured. Imprisoned at Falaise in Normandy—the birthplace of William the Conqueror—he was only released when he agreed to pledge an oath of fidelity and subordination to King Henry II of England. William was powerfully built, redheaded, and headstrong. He was an influential monarch whose reign was marred by his ill-fated attempts to regain control of his paternal inheritance of Northumbria from the Anglo-Normans. The Scots briefly regained Northumbria when Richard the Lionhearted sold it back to Scotland to finance his crusade to the Holy Land. However, in 1237, under the Treaty of York, Alexander II of Scotland met his brother-in-law, King Henry II of England, at York and abandoned his ancestor's claim to Northumbria and Cumbria. Afterward, the boundary of England and Scotland was set between Solway and Firth in the west and the mouth of the River Tweed in the east.

The tendency to make one's mind up certainly was characteristic of Sampson Strickland during the American Revolution. As the youngest son of Mathew Strickland and Anne Braswell, he steadfastly refused to swear allegiance to the state of North Carolina in 1777. Like many of my ancestors in Columbus and Horry Counties, the Stricklands had originated in England and entered colonial British America in Virginia at the Isle of Wight. The families were not recent arrivals to America. Based on his background, Sampson Strickland's loyalty to King George III seems at odds with his origins and his family. Perhaps he was illustrating the English tendencies to do what was in their self-interest. The ancestors of the Stricklands made decisions based upon an allegiance to survival of the Stricklands and not a monarch, as did many on the border of England and Scotland. With the majority of Sampson's family being Patriots, his choice of supporting the king of England three thousand miles across the Atlantic Ocean could be either heroic or shortsighted. Unfortunately for him, his allegiance to the Hanoverian monarch seemed to end his connection to the state of North Carolina, and he was banished. His widow reported the value of his estate after his death in 1781. Sampson's principled stand and banishment did not leave a deficiency of Stricklands in the Carolinas, as the name grew in abundance. Most North Carolina Loyalists were Highland Scots and not Lowland Scots. However, there were many Highland Scots who settled around Wilmington and Cross Creek (Fayetteville) and in the Piedmont, Anson, Guilford, Rowan, and Surry Counties.[131]

The difficulty in the Revolutionary War was many citizens remained loyal to the crown and, though they may not have taken up arms against the colonists' effort to win independence, they nonetheless were remembered as Tories—supporters of the king of England—after victory and were subject to having their property and land forfeited. A later North Carolina court case, *Bayard v. Singleton*, which concerned the North Carolina legislatures seizing and selling confiscated Tory property, was a precursor to United States Supreme Court's *Marbury v. Madison* decision and the establishment of judicial review of legislative acts by a court and their ability to rule them unconstitutional.

The final observation I have noticed is that after four generations, my Stricklands, Nathaniel and Sally Ann, married and were both descendants of Mathew Strickland II and Ann Braswell through their sons William Abner Strickland and John B.—I assume Braswell—Strickland. In researching the Stricklands, I came across work done by Forrest King entitled "Descendants of Mathew Strickland (1648–1696) Through Four Generations." His research summarizes the will of Mathew Strickland I, which states the land he gave his children may only be sold to other Stricklands.[132] My interpretation of this is a confirmation of the clannish nature of his origins in the border areas. I may mention, now, Elizabeth Campbell's—wife of John Strickland—pedigree is very admirable and rooted in Scottish lore as much as the thistle is.

Concerning the Stricklands, there may be a connection to Sir Thomas de Strickland, who was the standard-bearer for Henry V at the Battle of Agincourt on October 25, 1415. Thomas and a group of archers known as the Kendal Bowmen served valiantly, and as an esquire, Thomas fought dismounted with a sword and without a shield, as the man who carried the banner of St. George would be protected by his men during the battle. Thomas also fought at the Battle of Shrewsbury on July 21, 1403, when the Lancastrian King Henry IV and a rebel army led by Henry "Harry Hotspur" Percy from Northumberland clashed. This battle was the first battle in which English archers fought each other on English soil, with devastating results on both sides. When the battle ended, King Henry had lost more men, but Percy had been killed when he lifted his visor during a charge and was struck by an arrow. To squelch rumors that Percy was not dead, Henry had his body disinterred. It was subsequently salted, impaled on a spear, and set up in Shrewsbury between two millstones in the marketplace pillory with an armed guard. It was later quartered and put on display in Chester, London, Bristol, and Newcastle upon Tyne. His head—still on a spear—was sent to York and placed on the north gate, looking toward his lands. In November, his grisly remains were returned to his widow Elizabeth. If Sir Thomas de Strickland is indeed in the family, I am glad he chose the side of the Lancastrians.

Coleman

The Colemans originated in Essex, England, and the first one to come to Virginia was Robert Coleman I, who arrived in Virginia around 1639. His wife was Elizabeth Mott Grizzell. Robert Spilsby Coleman III and his wife, Susannah, moved from Virginia to Edgecombe County, North Carolina—the same place the Worleys had moved to when they left Virginia.

Since the Colemans, Worleys, and Stricklands continued to marry into each other's families, it has been a real challenge tracing their lineage. However, what is certain is they had spread across the South, and James Plemon Coleman became the fifty-second governor of Mississippi.

Worley/Gaskill/Southwick

From the research I have found, the first Worley came to Virginia in 1654 from England. Nicholas Worley Sr.'s father—Edward Worley—was married to Mary Elizabeth Gaskill, the daughter of Samuel Gaskill. Samuel was married to Provided Southwick. Provided was the daughter of Lawrence Southwick. Their story is a testament to religious freedom in early colonial British America.

Samuel Gaskill was arrested on June 29, 1658, in Salem for attending a Quaker meeting at the home of Nicholas Phelps.

The following is from author Joseph Barlow Felt's *The Annals of Salem* and is provided for reference:

> *June 29th. The Court, being informed of a Friends' meeting, held at the house of Nicholas Phelps last Sabbath, called those there to an account. Among them were William Brend and William Leddra, who had come from England. They escaped to Newbury but were brought back and sentenced to the house of correction in Boston. Nicholas Phelps, Lawrence Southwick and his wife, with their sons, John, Josiah, Daniel, and Provided, Samuel Shattock, Joseph Pope, Anthony Needham, Edward Wharton, Samuel Gaskin, Henry Trask and wife, the wife of Joseph Buffum and his son Joseph, and Thomas Bracket, were tried for attending the meeting. Others, under a similar indictment, but who did not appear, were Robert Adams, the wives of Needham, Phelps, Pope, and of George Gardner. [...] Such*

> *excommunications were evidently for adherence to the doctrines of the Friends. Lawrence Southwick and his wife and son Josiah, Samuel Shattock, Joshua Buffum, and Samuel Gaskin were sent to Boston, confined, and whipped. They forwarded a petition of July 16th to the Court here for a release. Shattock and Buffum were set at liberty. The rest were kept imprisoned for about twenty weeks.*[133]

The Southwicks were persecuted for their Quaker beliefs by the Puritan authorities and eventually fled to Shelter Island in New York. There, Lawrence and his wife, Cassandra Burnell, died within three days of each other due to deprivation, starvation, and exposure. Their daughter, Provided, and son, Daniel, were sentenced to be sold into slavery in Barbados for unpaid fees relating to their unauthorized Quaker beliefs and activities. Thankfully, the sentence against the two siblings was not carried out.

The marriage of Samuel Gaskill and Provided Southwick is recorded in the minutes of the Salem Friends Monthly Meeting as occurring on December 3, 1662. Samuel and Provided suffered cruelly, and they lived to see the persecution turned away so the Friends could meet in peace. With Daniel and Josiah Southwick, Samuel was a trustee for the Salem Monthly Meeting in the conveyance to them of the first meetinghouse and landed in America on October 13, 1690. On October 3, 1716, this meetinghouse was sold, and the deed was executed by Daniel Southwick, Samuel Gascoyne, Caleb Buffum, and Samuel Collins as surviving trustees on November 18, 1718.

Samuel Gaskill served as constable in Salem and was warned for militia duty in April of 1677, but there is no record that he was called and refused compliance, as he was sure to have done. There is also no record of the death of Samuel. In the will of his son, reference is made to the care of "his Aged Mother, Provided Gaskill." The will is dated

September 1, 1725, and considering there is no mention of Samuel, it is evident that his death occurred previously. Provided died in 1727, outliving her husband and her eldest son.

Chappell

One of the most interesting things I have discovered in doing this research is the number of Quakers who have been in my ancestry. I would have never in my life imagined this.

John Thomas Chappell was captain of the ship *Speedwell*, which was the sister ship to the *Mayflower*. The two ships were to sail to America together, but the *Speedwell* developed a leak and had to turn back to England. She eventually sailed for America on May 28, 1635. John Thomas was the son of Sir Robert Chappell of Nottinghamshire. His son Thomas sailed from Gravesend, England, June 23, 1635, and settled thirty miles upriver from Jamestown on what became Chappell's Creek.

Tatum Family

Richard Tatum Sr. was born about 1728 in Halifax County, North Carolina, and died about 1790 in Sampson County, North Carolina. His first marriage was to Susannah Trotter, who was born about 1733. His second marriage was to a woman named Mary. Many sources list Joshua Tatum as the father of Richard, but there is no conclusive proof. Evidence suggests his son Richard Jr. lived in Bladen County on Cow Pen Branch, and his other son Jesse lived on the north side of Cape Fear.

Numerous land records place Lewis Williamson in Duplin County in what eventually became Sampson County. The first one, in 1784, lists him with three hundred acres. In February of 1788, he was in court to settle a boundary dispute. Apparently, he and Mary moved to the north side of Dunn's Swamp near Cerro Gordo. His last will and testament named sons Richard, Lewis, Joshua, Laban, and Seth, and daughters Rebecca, Nancy, Peggy, and Susannah. Lewis's landholdings in Sampson County were close to those of many Tatums. Interesting speculation since Richard Tatum had children named Joshua, Richard, Laban, and Susannah. Thus, Mary Tatum Williamson may have named her children after her siblings. Finally, while I know of no Tatums in the western part of Columbus County, their name remains in the legacy of this part of the county being Tatum Township, and there is also a Tatum Road.

Faulk Family

The Faulk family originated somewhere in France, although there is very little French heritage in my ancestry. Nonetheless, the story of these Protestant Huguenots fleeing religious persecution in France resulted in a significant impact upon the history of the Carolinians and the United States. After Louis XIV revoked the Edict of Nantes in 1685, he forbade the French Protestants from leaving France. If they were caught, the men were executed or sent to be galley slaves on the French fleet in the Mediterranean, women were imprisoned, and their children sent to convents. Despite these penalties, approximately two hundred thousand fled France, of which fifty thousand settled in England. For example, Horry County, South Carolina, is named after Peter Horry, whose family is of Huguenot origin. All eight of his great-grandparents were Huguenot refugees who were part of a two-wave migration, first moving from France to England and then moving from England to South Carolina. Gabriel, the father of Francis "Swamp Fox" Marion of Revolutionary War fame, was also a Huguenot.

Charles Benjamin Schweizer was born in Maplewood, a suburb of St. Louis, in 1913. His mother was Alice Kendrick Faulk, daughter of

Lorenzo Kendrick Faulk. He did extensive research on the Faulk family and had even been to Columbus County. He published a book, but it is out of print, and I have been unable to find a copy. Thus, what I have found is from web searches.

Richard Foulke—the original French spelling of Faulk—an immigrant, came to Virginia with forty-six other persons on a "Certificate of Import" provided by Captain Francis Page, son of the scion of the Page family of Virginia. He arrived in York, Virginia, in 1688 and paid quitrents on one hundred acres of land in Nansemond County, Virginia, in 1704.[134] He died in Chowan County, North Carolina, in the year 1712. Like many of these Protestants from Virginia, their stay in the Albemarle Sound region of North Carolina was brief. Eventually, the Faulks migrated down the coast and settled in Fair Bluff, North Carolina. Richard's great-great-great-granddaughter Absillia M. Nance married Emory Lorenzo Williamson, and they were the grandparents of my grandfather Joseph Nathan Williamson. In turn, my mother's sister Priscilla Jo is named after Absillia, who was called "Apsy" on her son James Carlie Williamson's death certificate.

The Faulks also married into the Colemans, and their descendant married into the Worleys. Louisiana Faulk married Moses Coleman Jr., Richard Faulk's daughter Keziah Faulk married Theophilus Coleman Sr., and Theophilus Jr. married Ada Jernigan. Their daughter Sarah Jane Coleman married Daniel J. Coleman, and their daughter Mary Gray Coleman married Ashley Gray Worley and brought the Gray name into the family—my mom's other sister is named Glenda Gray. It seems these families started in Edgecombe, Chowan, or Bertie County and settled in Columbus and intermarried more than once. Thus, the people I thought were strangers when I lived in Columbus County were actually related to me in an intertwined web involving the same families who settled in Columbus County before its formation.

Records in the North Carolina Archives and the respective North Carolina counties show that the brothers William and John Faulk purchased land south of the Tar River, downstream from the present Rocky Mount, North Carolina, in 1740. John Faulk—known as John Faulk Sr. in most of the period's records—moved about the area as documented in various Edgecombe and Johnston County records. In 1764, he purchased land on both sides of Little River about a mile above the point where Interstate 95 crosses the Little River. He built a bridge across Little River known as Faulk's bridge, probably a toll bridge. It was still shown on the USGA map of 1904. A concrete bridge crosses the river today, but it appears that a bridge once existed just south of the concrete bridge. In 1769, John gave the land he owned north of Little River to his beloved son Thomas, and in 1780, according to the Johnston County deed book index—the deed book is missing—he gave the land he owned south of the Little River to his son William S. Faulk. William Faulk was the same man who moved to the present Fair Bluff, North Carolina, area about 1784.

Gathering the information from the majority of my family ancestry, almost all of the families originated in Britain and then Virginia. There are a few exceptions: those Huguenots from France, the Van Pelts from Belgium, and a few others from German lands in Europe. From Virginia they migrated into North Carolina Albemarle Sound and then spread throughout the South. This tendency to have family spread across the South is certainly the case concerning the Faulks. When I was at Cerro Gordo Elementary, the librarian was Mr. Faulk. He seemed a rather dapper fellow and managed our small library, consisting of two walls of books and a shelf of magazines, in a diligent fashion. Never would I have fathomed I may have been related to him.

The information I have gathered on the Faulks is that they were part of the French Huguenot exodus, who came to England and America.

The term "Huguenot" refers to French Protestants. Some attributed the word to the fact that Protestants at Tours, France, used to assemble by night near the gate of King Hugo, whom the people regarded as a spirit. A monk declared that the Lutherans ought to be called Huguenots, as kinsmen of King Hugo, since they would only go out at night as he had. Others believe the term comes from the word *aignos*, derived from the German Eldgenosen—confederates bound together by oath—which used to describe the patriots of Geneva hostile to the Duke of Savoy between 1520 and 1524. The spelling of Huguenot may have been influenced by the personal name Hugues. Regardless of the origin, the word has a common thread with the Faulks. While France remained Catholic, the reform influenced many French to convert to the Protestant belief. Naturally, this conflicted with the French monarch, who was an avowed Catholic. In 1685, Louis XIV revoked the Edict of Nantes, which had allowed Protestants a degree of freedom in France. This resulted in many Walloons and Huguenots fleeing France. Louis XIV's new Edict of Fontainebleau declared Protestantism to be illegal in France. The result was both a disaster for France and the Huguenots. Out of the 180,000 of France's most talented artisans and intellectuals, "the hardworking Huguenots were among the most prosperous citizens of France. Their work ethic had made them masters of the crafts in which France excelled. When they fled, they left behind most of their possessions but carried with them their skills."[135] France's enemies gained talented French men and women who enriched their new nations. The National Huguenot Society claims eight presidents have Huguenot ancestry: George Washington, Ulysses S. Grant, Theodore Roosevelt, William Howard Taft, Franklin D. Roosevelt, Harry S. Truman, Gerald Ford, and Lyndon B. Johnson.[136]

Cahoon or Colquhoun

John Faulk Sr.'s wife was Mary Calhoon. They are both buried in Johnston County, North Carolina, at Old Beulah Cemetery. Their children married into several families in Columbus County, and I have numerous Faulks on my mother's side.

The Cahoon name originated in Scotland. William Colquhoun—pronounced *Ca-hoon*—was the first Cahoon to come to the colonies from Dunbartonshire, Scotland. His descendants are now in almost every state in the Union. His descendants spelled their name several different ways: Calhoon, Cahoone, Cohoon, Colhoon, Cahloun. He was the second child of Alexander Colquhoun and Marion Sterling. The Colquhoun Clan originated at Old Kilpatrick on the River Clyde, and through the marriage of Robert Colquhoun to the daughter of the Laird of Luss in 1358, the Luss lands came into their hands. The lands in the Loch Lomond area of Scotland have been held within the Colquhoun family since AD 1150, when the lands were granted to the Laird of Luss. The Colquhoun lands of the Barony of Colquhoun, which runs eastward from Dumbarton for six miles toward Glasgow, were granted around 1240. Since those times, there has been a constant Colquhoun presence in the area.[137]

William made an error and joined the army of Charles II and was captured along with five thousand other Royalist soldiers by Oliver Cromwell's forces at the Battle of Dunbar during Kirk's War. The seventeen-year-old William was then marched to Durham Cathedral. During the march, fifteen hundred of the prisoners died from starvation and sickness. William survived only to be sold and sent to North America as a laborer. He arrived in Massachusetts around 1651, where he was purchased by Beck and Company and sent to the Bog Iron Works in New England. The purchase price was assumed to be twenty or thirty pounds per man.[138] At some point, William married

Deliverance Peck, daughter of Joseph Peck, and had seven children. He contracted with the town of Swansea as a brickmaker and made brick for the residents.

War brought William to America, and war would end William's life in America. Hostilities broke out between the Native Americans and the colonists, and a group of colonists was attacked by the natives, who took refuge in a home surrounded by stone walls. William, who was in the house with his wife, Deliverance, and their seven children, volunteered to make the very dangerous journey from Swansea to Rehobeth in order to bring back a doctor. The natives ambushed William, and his body was discovered three days later, terribly mutilated.

One of his sons, Samuel, disappeared from Massachusetts, but he later appeared in the Isle of Wight in Virginia when he appointed John Giles as his attorney. Evidence suggests his character was incompatible with that prevalent one of Puritan New England. He was listed with 240 acres in Nansemond County, Virginia, in 1704. Records indicate he had six children, and one of his sons, Captain John Cahoon Sr., moved to Bladen County by 1771, patenting two hundred acres east of White Marsh in 1771 and one hundred acres in 1779. His will is dated 1781.

Another son, William, who may be the father of Mary Cahoon, was also in the area. Mary's mother was Sarah Powell. William's will, dated 1789, lists Mary. The connection to John Faulk is made with John Cahoon Sr.'s son Micajah, who was born in Edgecombe County in 1761.

John Faulk witnessed a deed. He first settled in Brunswick County but then joined his relatives in Bladen with a patent of one hundred acres in 1774 and two hundred acres in 1779.[139] One day, I hope to travel to the cemetery where Mary Cahoon and John Faulk are buried and pay my respects to Mary for contributing such an illustrious story to my family history. The Cahoon motto of *Si je puis*, "If I Can," resonates with me because it implies the will to do so.

Cartwright or Cartrette

The Cartwrights made their presence in Columbus County when Hezekiah's daughter Catherine married David Strickland. There are also Cartwrights who settled around Tabor City. The first Cartwright in America was John, who had come from Aynhoo, Northhamptonshire, England.

He arrived in Jamestown in 1624 to witness John Rolfe's marriage to Pocahontas. The Cartwrights found their way to Pasquotank County, North Carolina, and there are several mentions of Thomas and Robert in Quaker meeting notes. Hezekiah is mentioned in the will of his father, Robert, who died in 1746. He fought in the Revolutionary War, and his records are on file with the state archives. Elizabeth Cartrette would be a descendant of these Cartwrights. My assumption is that part of the Cartwrights—and other families from northeastern North Carolina—came into Columbus County shortly before the Revolutionary War.

Barfield of Marion County

The Barfield Family is also discussed in Sellers's book on Marion County. Emily Barfield married Levi C. Hays, and their son Norfolk Hayes married Edith Spivey. Their daughter Bertha Hays married "Shep" Turbeville, and their daughter is Hazel Turbeville Page, my grandmother. Concerning the Barfields, Sellers states they were in the Hillsboro area of Marion County, which placed them near the Hays family. They are descendants of Barrett Barfield, who, in his thirties, resided in Hillsboro, just below Gaddy's Mill and on the plantation owned by his grandson Captain R.H. Rogers. Barrett reared a family of twenty-two children by the same wife. He and most of the family departed for the West. One of his sons, Barrett "Writ" Barfield, remained in Marion. He is buried in the Barfield Cook Cemetery in Dillon. Barrett Sr. was a son, nephew, or brother of the celebrated Tory, Captain Barfield. Sellers states, "A distinctive characteristic of the Barfield family was the beauty of the females. The men were as agile as a deer. They were hard to handle in a brawl of a fight, even by larger men and greater strength. Ms. Appey Barfield was as beautiful in 1835 as the fabled Venus."[140] In Georgia, I found Barrett Barfield Sr. buried at the Jesse Barfield Cemetery. His birth date was 1750, and he died before 1860.

Grainger Family

The Grainger family may be traced back to Joshua Grainger Greasley from Nottinghamshire, England. He migrated to New Hanover County, North Carolina. John's wife was Charity Buffkin, a family still found in the area. The Grainger tie is through his descendants who married into the Pages and the Stricklands. Research indicates that in 1729, Joshua moved to Province, North Carolina, where he resided until his death.

About 1730, a settlement began on the Cape Fear River, opposite the junction of its two main branches. The settlement was named New Liverpool until 1732, when it was changed to Newtown. Eventually, it was changed again to Newton. King George II granted John Watson 640 acres of land in New Hanover Precinct. Watson laid this off into lots and sold large sections to Michael Higgins and Joshua Grainger. The court executed Grainger's deed in 1737, and he became active in settling the new village, selling numerous lots through the years. He was made justice of the peace in 1735. In 1739, the town was incorporated and its name changed to Wilmington in honor of Spencer

Compton, Earl of Wilmington. Among the industries in which early settlers engaged, shipbuilding was one of them, and Joshua Grainger founded one shipyard at the foot of Church Street. He was probably a Quaker, as early recorded New Hanover deeds were proved by his "affirmation," which was accepted by courts as sufficient since Friends refused to make oaths.

Goodyear Family

On April 11, 1872, an article in the *Charleston Daily Courier* referenced John Goodyear as one of the oldest persons alive in Marion County who lived on the Little Pee Dee.[141] Sellers states John had only one son, who died in the war, but he reared ten daughters. One of those daughters, Sarah, married into the Grainger family. John's wife was Zenith Miller. I am not sure of her parents, but Sellers states the Millers lived in northern Marion County. Sellers further relates the Millers "were raised in the day when the muster-field bully was honored and feared more, much more than those who did not aspire to bullyship." The story relates that about 1830 on the Carmichael Bridge on the Little Pee Dee, the Millers and the Barfields, both of whom I am a descendant of, "got into a row and a general fight. In the melee, Thompson Barfield, a small man, not weighing over 120 pounds but active as a cat and fierce as a tiger, cut Edmund Miller across the abdomen. His intestines came out, and he gathered them in his hands and walked twenty-five yards to a place he could sit down. Dr. Robert Harllee of Marion County, the only physician east of the Great Pee Dee, was able to secure the intestines and sew up Edmund." The Millers lived by fighting, as Sellers notes, and a similar circumstance occurred across the state line in North Carolina between the Millers and Gaddys.[142] Today, a road inside Robeson County is named Gaddy's Mill Road, attesting to their presence in the area.

The Abbott and Arnett Families

Benjamin Arnette's wife was Sarah Abbott, and I found the Abbotts first in Pasquotank County, North Carolina. Holloway Abbott, Sarah's father, has a record of the administration of his estate, which states he was of the Little Pee Dee.

Sellers mentions the Arnetts and Lupos in his book but does not have much information on them. He states they resided in the Hillsboro area of Marion County. "They were an honest and hardworking people, primitive in their modes of living and habits."[143] I found records of an Arnette Cemetery in Dillon County and one at Piney Grove Baptist Church in Gaddy's Mill. Benjamin and his wife, Sarah, are buried in an old cemetery located one mile west of the Arnette Cemetery. The cemetery was in the middle of a field and has been plowed over. One larger marker has been placed on the spot of the location of the cemetery. It reads, "To the memory of those buried in this abandoned graveyard the identity of whom is known but to God." The cemetery at Piney Grove has many Millers, Lupos, Turbevilles, and Arnettes.

Hollowell Family

John Hollowell was one of three men to donate five hundred pounds of tobacco to build a Quaker meeting house in Nansemond County, Virginia, on the south branch of the Nansemond River in 1702. There were three Johns, and one was not a good businessman since, in 1766, his farm of 250 acres was auctioned for debts. William Hollowell's daughter Courtney was born in Virginia but married the father of John Abbott and later resided in Pasquotank County, North Carolina.

Hinnant Family

The wife of Richard Faulk was Sarah Hinnant, who died in Fair Bluff, North Carolina. Her father was William Hinnant. Research indicates this family was Huguenot and originated in the Hainaut region of Belgium and France. The spelling was originally *Aunaut*. The original immigrant was Jean Aunaut, son of Jean Aunaut and Sibelle Dumas. The immigrant's wife was Marie Soyer, a native of Dieppe, Normandy.[144] Both Jean and Marie are listed as passengers from London to Charles Town, James River, Virginia, being French refugees in the ships named *Peter* and *Anthony*, Galley of London, Daniel Perreau, Commander. To become anglicized, they changed the name to reflect their new roots in the Anglican American colonies. In doing so, they hid their origins from me, until I did this research. Again, I was unaware of the number of Huguenots composing my heritage. I am delighted to have uncovered it! More interesting is my neighbor is a Hinnant, and I never knew the significance of his name. William Hinnant's will was probated in Johnston County, North Carolina.

Hardee Family
The Hardee, or Hardy, family I am connected to originated from Col. John Hardee of Pitt County, North Carolina, and Susannah Tyson. John Hardee received a land grant of 640 acres in 1775 on Swift's Creek. He was a member of the Committee of Public Safety during the Revolutionary War. His son William Andrew Hardee relocated from Pitt County to first Brunswick County, North Carolina, and then to Horry County, South Carolina. The pension application for William Hardee, who was the brother of my ancestor Andrew, has Andrew Hardee witnessing and confirming his Revolutionary War service.

The first Hardee in North Carolina was John Noble Worthington Hardee, who was born in 1638 in Pembrokeshire, Wales. I have discovered that the Welsh seemed to adapt to their new home in North Carolina and eventually became indistinguishable from their English counterparts. As the Hardees went down the line, a descendant of the

Hardee line, Arabella Grainger, eventually married Moody Strickland and had a child, who was my grandmother Ara Mae Worley's mother, my great-grandmother.

Meares Family

Thomas Meares was born in England in 1602. He immigrated to America in 1637 and was granted three hundred acres of land for transporting six people. The land was on the Elizabeth River in upper Norwalk. One of his sons was Bartholomew Meares, who had a patent of three hundred acres of land in Accomac County, Virginia, dated April 6, 1666. His will was probated in 1682. There is a record of him being sponsored to Virginia in 1655 by William Taylor in North Hampton, Virginia.[145] Bartholomew had sons Richard, Bartholomew, Robert, William, and John.

Spivey of Marion (Dillon) County, South Carolina, and Columbus and Robeson Counties, North Carolina

Bertha Hayes's mother, Edith Catherine Spivey, was the daughter of Jesse Spivey and Sarah Sallie Baker. Sallie's parents are Joseph Baker and Lucy Ada Green of Marion County, South Carolina. Edith Spivey married Nophrlet Hayes in Robeson County on December 15, 1879. Jesse Spivey and his wife, Sarah "Sally," were married by Reverend F.A. Prevatt, Baptist minister in White House Township. Witnesses were L.C. Hayes, Henry Spivey, and Jessie Spivey.[146] Henry is an older brother and a veteran of the Fifty-First North Carolina Infantry Company F. Edith is not on any census past 1900. These Spiveys are the descendants of Elizabeth Fowler Spivey and Edmund Spivey, who fought in the Revolutionary War with Elizabeth Fowler's brothers Daniel Fowler Jr. and John Fowler. I have corresponded with a

Spivey in California, who confirms the Spivey male DNA is the same DNA of the Pages, which is M-253.

Blackwell and Jung (Young)

Return Strong Worley's wife was Helen Amanda Coleman. According to records, her second great-grandfather was James Glenn Blackwell IV. James Blackwell married Catherine Young, whose parents emigrated from Westphalia, Germany. John Young—a.k.a. Johanis Jung—and his wife, Mary Young—a.k.a. Anna Maria Baeumer Jung—arrived in Philadelphia, Pennsylvania, on the ship *Hope*. He originated from Trupbach, Siegen-Wittgenstein, Nordrhein-Westfalen, Germany—known as Westphalia today. John, along with his wife and their three children, Gerderuth, Harman, and Elizabeth, soon joined members of the original 1714 and later settlers at the German colony in Orange County, Virginia. He became the leader of the Lutheran church in the Little Fork. The Blackwells lived in this area of Little Fork in Culpeper.

The German colony in Virginia was encouraged by Lieutenant Governor Alexander Spotswood. German immigration consisted of two phases of settlement, one in 1714 and one in 1717. Perhaps Catherine Young's family was part of this recruitment, which led her to meet the Blackwood family and marry into it. The family later moved into Burke County, North Carolina, and then into Abbeville, South Carolina. Like my other ancestors, they traveled throughout the South in subsequent moves. This connection does not mesh with the connections of the Colemans. James Blackwell was born about 1730 and died about 1783. Catherine was born about 1735 and died between 1802 and 1810. Still, Helen Amanda Coleman's mother must have been from western North Carolina for it to be plausible that a Coleman from Columbus County could have found their way into the mountains and perhaps married into the Blackwell family as they migrated through North Carolina. I included this information for future researchers who wish to verify and because this is the only German connection I have been able to locate in my ancestry.

Flowers

Hannah Flowers and the Flowers family came from Maryland into Bladen County and stayed there perhaps three generations before moving to Alabama. Their name is found on many land grants in Williamson's Cross Roads, but today, there is no one I know of named Flowers in the area. Nonetheless, Hannah Flowers's marriage to Lott Williamson connects me to Elizabeth Greenberry and her father, Colonel Nicholas Greenberry.[147] Elizabeth Greenberry's grandson was Ignatius K. Flowers Sr. who migrated from Maryland, was given several land grants in then Bladen County, and was known as a provider of supplies to the Patriot forces during the Revolutionary War. Colonel Greenberry was the fourth Royal Governor of Maryland and commander of the military forces of Anne Arudel and Baltimore Counties. According to Maryland land patents, he and his wife and children arrived in Maryland in 1674 aboard the *Constant Friendship*. The parents of Nicholas are not known; however, Charles Francis Stein, who studied the seal impression left by Nicholas and his son, proposes a theory: The shield, having a bend with three lozenges (diamond shapes), can be seen without much difficulty, and the crest above the knight's helmet, seemingly a horned animal's head in profile, was most evidently a unicorn. Pursuing the matter further, I discovered that there was one family arms listed as having the combination of a band with three lozenges on the shield with a unicorn's head for the crest. This is the English family of Carrington, a family of ancient noble descent. According to Burke, the chief line of the Barons of Carrington became extinct in the time of Queen Elizabeth. Colonel Nicholas Greenberry was born a generation later, in 1627. It would seem probable that he was closely related to the Carringtons. Could it be that his mother was a Carrington and his father perhaps a member of the royal family?

Of course, this is all speculation, but it makes for a wonderful story.

Godwin

Pierce Godwin's daughters married into the Williamson family, and his father was Solomon Godwin from Johnston County, North Carolina. Solomon married Martha Pearce in 1738 in Johnston and died in Columbus (Bladen) in 1800. Solomon's father was James Godwin, born in Virginia in 1679 and died in Johnston County in 1762, and his wife was Mary Parker. His grandfather was William Godwin, whose wife was Elizabeth Gibbs.

Pierce Godwin named his daughters, Alley Williamson, Nancy Williamson, Susan Floyd, Meranza Ann Williamson, and Emily Powell, in his will, which is dated April 25, 1845. He listed his grandson N.L. Williamson as the executor. Labon and Dennis Williamson were witnesses to the will. Pierce married an unknown Green woman, who may have been the sister of William Green and daughter of Simeon and Ann Green. This information is provided by my relative John Hybert Williamson of Davidson, North Carolina.

Nancy Godwin Williamson married Joshua Williamson, the first sheriff of Columbus County. There is an interesting story concerning his time as sheriff. A deed dated June 2, 1847, transferred ownership of 52,960 acres, known as the Big Survey, originally acquired by a Mr. Rhodes, then acquired by Uriah Flowers, who failed to pay the property taxes. Sheriff Joshua foreclosed the property and auctioned it at the courthouse. The amount of taxes owed was $2.75.[148] The highest bidders were D.F. (Doctor Fredrick) Williamson and Nathan Lewis

Williamson; he is buried on the south side of Dunn Swamp in land now owned by the Hilbourn Family. I visited this cemetery in 2019. A second track went to Lott's wife, Hannah Flowers Williamson, and a third went to Lott's son-in-law, Harrison Coleman.

Hannah was the sister of Uriah Flowers, Nathan Lewis was Joshua's son, Doctor Fredrick was Joshua's nephew, and Lott was his brother. (Information provided by John Hybert Williamson.) My great-grandfather James Carlie Williamson and Jessie Lee Williamson are both descendants of Lewis Williamson and Mary Tatum—James through Joshua and Jessie Lee through Joshua's brother Lott. Two generations separate them from the brothers. Joshua and Lott were the sons of Mary Tatum Williamson and Lewis Williamson, who moved from Duplin sometime between 1787 and 1790.

In December of 1787, Richard Horn sold to Lewis Williamson four hundred acres on the north side of Dunn Swamp. The 1788 Bladen tax list shows Lewis owned 950 acres in Captain Yates's District. Lewis later secured a grant for one hundred acres in 1799, also on the north side of Dunn's Swamp.

Pearce

Martha Pearce's father was Richard Pearce, born in the Isle of Wight County, Virginia, in 1712. Her grandfather was Phillip Pearce, also born in the Isle of Wight in 1670. Phillip's father was George Pearce, born in 1640 in Bristol, England. George's wife was Alice Ann—last name unknown—born 1645. Phillip Pearce's will is recorded in Virginia. His wife is only referred to as "Sarah" in his will. Richard Pearce's will of 20 November 1780 was recorded in Johnston County, North Carolina. In his will, Richard names Martha as Martha Nichols, and he bequeaths to her five shillings. Martha's paternal great-grandparents are George Pearce (1641–1705) and Anne Gaynor (1645–1718 or 1725), daughter of William Gaynor. George, a Quaker, was from Somerset, England, and Anne from Gloucester, England. Both came to America and were married in 1679.[149]

Fulghum

Martha Pearce was wife of Solomon Godwin (1732–1763), married in 1760, and mother of Pierce Godwin and was born in 1730 in Johnston County, North Carolina. Her father was Richard Pearce from the Isle of Wight, Virginia, and Sarah Fulghum is Martha's mother. From what I am able to piece together, Solomon died and Martha then married William Coleman Nichols, who was the son of William Nichols and Edith Coleman. Martha Pearce and Coleman Nichols's son Averitt Pearce Nichols Sr. was the man who was born in 1767 and whose children migrated to Nichols, South Carolina. Averitt married Mary Van Pelt Lewis, which again connects me back to William Lewis and Mourning Van Pelt. Thus, Martha Pearce is the mother of two different sets of descendants of my ancestors Averitt Nichols Sr. and Pearce Godwin.

Sarah Fulghum's father was John Fulghum, who was born in 1700 at the Isle of Wight, Virginia, and died in Johnston County, North Carolina, in 1790. His father was Captain Anthony Fulghum who was born at Walton Hall, Derby, Derbyshire, England, in 1610 and died at the Isle of Wight, Virginia, in 1699. Captain Anthony's father was Hercules Foljambe, son of Godfrey Foljambe and Elizabeth Draycott, who had three children. Godfrey died at age thirty-three, and Elizabeth got remarried to a James Hardwick in 1551. Godfrey Jr. would inherit the lands of his father but had a childless and unhappy marriage and only left an illegitimate son. Thus, at Godfrey Jr.'s death, Hercules inherited the lands of his brother. Unfortunately, he would later risk and lose his fortunes and lands in a risky venture to attack San Juan, Puerto Rico, with George Clifford, the third Earl of Cumberland.

Hercules was a gambler, so he was easily lured by the seduction of adventure as personified in Clifford, whose love of adventure was strong, and he staked his money on the success of his cruises in much the same spirit as when he bet on the speed of his horses or the turn of his dice. And he spared his body no more than his purse. His courage was unimpeachable, and the temper that he showed in times of difficulty won him both credit and popularity.[150] Sadly, he lost all the great wealth he'd gained from his buccaneering in jousting and horse racing, and he was eventually obliged to sell his inherited lands.[151]

The Fulghums are of Norman origins and came to England with William the Conqueror and may be traced back to Ragnar Lodbrok. The University of Virginia has a collection of Fulghum material.[152]

Wingate

Rebecca Wingate, the daughter of John Wingate and Hannah Sessions, married Goldsbury Flowers. Their daughter Hannah Flowers married Lott Williamson before 1812. Rebecca Wingate is listed on the 1840 Census in Columbus County, but her sons moved to Alabama after Goldsborough's death. Rebecca died and is buried in Pike County, Alabama. Goldsbury was the son of Ignatius Flowers and Susannah Gray. He was born in Bladen County in 1765 and died in Columbus in 1838. Susannah was of "excellent blood, and she was of good Irish blood." This description was taken from a note written by Uriah Goldsboro Flowers to his great-niece Lillian Gray in 1907.

There is an indenture dated 22 January 1840 between Ignatius Flowers, James Griffin and wife, Mary, Samuel Bright and wife, Susannah, Lott Williamson and wife, Hannah, John Flowers, Richard Flowers, Luke Flowers, and Goldsbury Flowers of the state of Alabama and the county of Pike, all of the one part, and Isham Williamson for $500 for one hundred acres on the east side of Cow Branch, fifty acres on the east side of Cow Branch, fifty acres on the southeast side of Cow Branch, and fifty acres on the south side of Cow Branch. The witnesses are John Wingate, Sr., N.L. Williamson, J.C. Powell, and T.T. Toon.

John Wingate was born in 1710 in Chowan County, North Carolina. He was the son of Edward Wingate and Ann Blount. John married Hannah Sessions. Lott Williamson and Hannah Flowers's son was James Isham Williamson. Isham was born in 1815 in Columbus County and died in 1872. He married Rebecca Ann Gore. Rebecca was the daughter of Daniel Gore and Mary Ann Grissett.

I have included the division of the lands of Isham, which took place in 1881:

- **Lot 1**—belongs to Francis Carolina Williamson and Andrew Morgan Williamson; 100 acres on Porter Swamp; 70 acres more or less near Williamson's Cross Roads
- **Lot 2**—belongs to Candas Ann Williamson; 344 acres on and in Cow Branch; includes an old plantation
- **Lot 3**—belongs to Hannah Missouri Williamson; 73 acres on the south side of Cow Branch and both sides of Panther Branch; 125 acres on the west side of Big Button Branch
- **Lot 4**—belongs to Princess Ann Williamson; 148 acres on Big Button and Cow Branch. Princess Ann Williamson was married to Ashley Benton, who came from Duplin County to Columbus. The name of this plantation, Evergreen, replaced the name of Griffin Crossroads for the town that grew up there.
- **Lot 5**—belongs to Margaret Joanna Williamson; 100 acres on the south side of Cow Branch; 125 acres on the west side of

Big Button Branch; 70 acres known as the Nelson Tract on Gum Branch
- **Lot 6**—belongs to William Williamson; 196 acres
- **Lot 7**—belongs to Daniel Williamson; 400 acres in Cattail Bay; 100 acres on the side of Cattail Bay, and both sides of Barnes Canal; 65 acres near Jonathan J.C. Gore and Thomas Ward

Also, to make equitable, Lot 2 pays $125 to Lot 3; Lot 2 pays $15 to Lot 4; Lot 5 pays $33 to Lot 4; Lot 6 pays $28 to Lot 4; Lot 7 pays $37 to Lot 4. All of which was signed by Jonathan C. Lennon, J.A. McCloskey, and Solomon Shaw.

Wade

Enoch Wade was born in Virginia, and he came to Columbus County and married Elizabeth Meares. Their daughter, Dollie L. Wade, married Andrew Morgan Williamson on March 28, 1898. I do not recall many Wades in Columbus County when I was young, but a newspaper article from the period states his farm was outside of Fair Bluff.

Dollie Wade, Andrew Williamson, their daughter Lizzie, and her small child Wavey are buried in a family cemetery in the middle of a field on Haynes Lennon Road, north of Dunn Swamp and south of Williamson's Cross Roads.

Session

The Sessions family tie is to George Session, who came to Virginia in 1634 from Chipping, Lancashire, England. Hannah Sessions would have been the great-granddaughter of George. Hannah's father was John Sessions Sr., who moved from Henrico County, Virginia, into Chowan County, North Carolina. Hannah is listed on the 1800 Census in Captain Barfield's District in Bladen County. Hannah married John Wingate.

Best

John Best was born in 1736 in Virginia and died about 1798. John moved to Duplin County, North Carolina. In the Revolutionary War, he served in the North Carolina Militia and wrote his will on May 10, 1798, which was filed in 1799 in the WB-A/13 Duplin County archives. His will gives everything to his wife, Hannah. Together, they had ten children: Patty, Benjamin, John, Rebecca, Elizabeth, Absolam, Howell, Henry, Ethelred, and Redden. Their son John Jr. married Martha Williams in Duplin County in 1783. John Jr. and Martha's daughter, Mary Ann Best, married Daniel Gore. John Jr. served in the Revolutionary War and moved to Georgia.

Jernigan

When I was attending Cerro Gordo Elementary School, there were a brother and sister named Jean and Ricky Jernigan. Ricky was a couple of years younger than I was. Jean was older by maybe a year, and she was quite attractive. It is strange, but the thing I recall most about her was she said she sunbathed nude on top of the packhouse. What I did not know then was both were perhaps related to me.

Aidy Jernigan married Theophilus Coleman Jr. Their daughter Sarah Jane Coleman married Daniel J. Coleman. Their daughter Mary Gray Coleman was the second wife for Ashley Gray Worley, the father of Bruce Eddie Worley, who was the father of Ara Mae Worley Williamson, my grandmother. These Jernigans originated in England and immigrated to Virginia and then into North Carolina. I have not been able to conclusively put together this puzzle. I am not confident Thomas Jernigan, born around 1614 in Somerleyton-in-Suffolk,

England, died around 1700 in Somerton, Nansemond County, Virginia, and married to Elizabeth Thompson, is the progenitor of the Jernigans in Columbus and Horry Counties.

Records show different birth years for Thomas Jernigan, the immigrant, but all point to a birth no later than 1643. He was still living in 1704. He was termed "Master" in a grant to him of 250 acres in the "county of Nanzemund" at Somerton on May 16, 1668. At the session of the general assembly in Virginia, which met in November 1682, he was awarded payments in tobacco assessed against Nansemond County "for carrying publique letters into Carolina." In 1685, as Thomas Jernigan Sr., he patented an additional 330 acres "at Somerton in the upper parish of Nansemond." On the Nansemond Quitrent Roll of 1704, he was listed as holding 165 acres; probably by this time, he had given all his lands except for his manor plantation to his son and heir.

I came across sources that may provide information on these but have not been able to locate a book in print. The first is *The Worley Clan: A Gathering of the Descendants of Nicholas Worley of Duplin County, North Carolina, particularly his son Nicholas Worley of Columbus County, North Carolina* by Velma Prevatt Worley, John Franklin Worley, and Lillian Jernigan Worley. The other book is *Jernigan Reunion: A Gathering of Some of the Descendants of Thomas Jernigan, Immigrant 1635 of Nansemond County, Virginia, Particularly the Family of His Great-grandson Henry Jernigan (Ca. 1710–1783), Planter of Johnston County, North Carolina* by Lillian Jernigan Worley.

Other references are the following:

The Virginia Genealogist vol. 50 no. 1 (January–March 2006):73–74. "A Royal Descent for Thomas Jernigan," by John Anderson Brayton.

The Virginia Genealogist vol. 48 no. 3 (July–September 2004):163–169. "The parentage of Thomas Jernigan of Nansemond County, Virginia," by Neil D. Thompson.

The trail, albeit not conclusive, begins with David Jernigan I and Temperance Moore, then moves on to their son David L. Jernigan II and his wife, Alice Faye Page. She arrived in Virginia in 1724, with their son Jessie Jernigan Sr. and his wife, Jerusha, and their son Jessie Jernigan Jr. and wife, Susannah, and then Aidy Jernigan. I have proof of a land grant in Bladen County issued May 18, 1789, to Jesse Jernigan Jr. for one hundred acres of land on the west of Drowning Creek on the Katt Swamp. I have no clue where Katt Swamp is. I have the will of Jessie Sr. made October 25, 1785, in Bertie County. It mentions Jerusha, James, Jesse, Farribe, Sarah, Alice, and Elizabeth Jernigan. It further names Thomas Bond, Benjamin Jernigan, and Nathaniel Vezey as the executors. There is a land grant to Jesse Sr., issued April 29, 1768, and entered April 16, 1779, for one hundred acres of land on the south side of the Neuse River. David, not sure which one, had a two-hundred-acre grant in Dobbs County on the north side of the Neuse River at a pond called Wildcat, dated September 26, 1766. I have a copy of David Jernigan II's will, which confirms his wife's name is Alice. David III's will references his son Page Grainger, which should confirm the last name of his mother, Alice, being a Page. There are three David Jernigans who left wills in Wayne County, North Carolina. Records show David II serving as a captain in the Wayne County Regiment during the Revolutionary War and Jesse Jr. serving as an ensign. According to the state of North Carolina, known battles and skirmishes they fought in are the Siege of Charleston, Little Lynches Creek, and Camden.

One of the greatest assets in my search for information has been those people who have done research before me and then those reference librarians who have been outstanding in assisting me in obtaining pertinent information from books in their respective collections. One such person is Simone at the McClung Collection at the Knox

County Library. From the information she assisted with, I learned that Jesse Jernigan, son of David Jr., married Susannah Stoughenborough and moved to Robeson County, North Carolina, about 1787. The 1790 Census of Robeson listed Jesse as Captain Jesse Jernigan. He was commissioned to help lay out the town of Lumberton and erect a courthouse. According to Robeson County deed book F, page 188, Jesse Sr. sold land to Ezliel Adams in 1795. Susannah Jernigan and Jesse Jr. witnessed the deed. In 1805, Jesse and Susannah moved into Horry County.

The author of *Jernigan Reunion: A Gathering of Some of the Descendants of Thomas Jernigan, Immigrant 1635 of Nansemond County, Virginia, Particularly the Family of His Great-grandson Henry Jernigan (ca. 1710–1783), Planter of Johnston County, North Carolina* documents two children, Jesse Jernigan Jr., who married Lucy Holmes, daughter of Charles Holmes of Wayne County, and Susannah, who married Cornelius Wingate before 1780, as some of her children are mentioned in Jesse Sr.'s deed. Susannah was living in Robeson County at the same time as her father, but there are no other records. There were other children in the home because the 1790 Census documents this. A Willis Jernigan received a land grant in Horry County in 1791. Charles Jernigan of Columbus County was either a son or a grandson of Jesse Sr. Charles was on the 1850 Census in Columbus County as sixty years old and born in South Carolina. His wife was Sarah Coleman, and their children were Andres, David, Wilson, Martha, Margaret, and Willis. A final note on the Jernigans—*Historical Sketches of Southern Families, Volume IV*, written by John Bennett Boddie, Lundie W. Barlow has an article entitled "Jernigans of Somerton, Nansemond County, Virginia." It was almost certainly the Jernigans who'd descended from the seventeenth-century immigrants to Nansemond County, Virginia, and lived in the Carolinas and Georgia, and who were a junior line of the

Jernigans of Suffolk, England, another branch of whom became Barons of Stafford. The first Jernigan gave the name of origin as Somerton. Further, he was accorded the title of Master in Virginia records in 1668.

In 1910, the then Lord of Stafford wrote to Mr. Thomas R. Jernigan of New Bern, North Carolina, "As your ancestor settled in America in the seventeenth century, I should think he was as the son of Sir Edward or Sir Richard Jernigan." His sons were Thomas, John, and Henry, according to the Virginia patent book vi, 146, vii, 452, and John was born about 1670 and died in 1734. Further, the coat of arms of the Jernigans in Georgia, dating from colonial times, is the exact representation of the Jernigans of Suffolk. Alas, when I discovered Ashley Gray Worley was married to Arrena Strickland and later Mary Coleman, my connection to Aidy Jernigan and Theophilus Coleman Jr. became one of a great-uncle and aunt, not grandparents.

In researching the Worleys, I discovered Nicholas Worley Jr.'s son, Elias, brother of Elijah, married Susannah Jernigan. Susannah was Jesse Jernigan Jr.'s daughter. Susannah and Elias named a son Gray Jernigan Worley, who died in Alabama. Like many of the people in Columbus County, many of Elias Worley's children moved to Alabama, Mississippi, and later Texas.

CHAPTER 19
Stories of the Counties

Walters of Robeson County

William Walters was born in Dobbs County, North Carolina. Before 1784, he married Celia (Selah) Dawson, daughter of Joseph Dawson and his second wife, Patience. The family lived in the Walnut Creek section of Dobbs County, where their first eight children were born. Around 1794, they moved to Robeson County, where the last seven children were born.

Pittman of Robeson County

Thomas Pittman arrived in Virginia in 1667 and, according to Nell Nugent's *Cavaliers and Pioneers*, was in North Carolina around the Albemarle Sounds. His descendants made their way to Robeson County. Thomas Pittman's will from the Isle of Wight County is dated March 3, 1727. Witnesses to his will are Joseph I. Strickling, Thomas S. Pittman, and Edward Hood.[153]

Absilla Spier and her husband, Rev. Isham Pittman, migrated from Edgecombe County to Bladen County—it later became Robeson. Evidence suggests they had no children of their own and that I descend from their adopted daughter, Absilla "Appy" Pittman, who may have been a Spier. She married William Walters Jr., and they lived out their lives in the Barnesville area of Robeson County. All references I have seen concerning Absilla, Isham's wife, were from Craven County, North Carolina, or near the Neuse River. This Absilla was "highly educated" for a woman of that time and kept a daily diary—wish I knew what happened to it! Absilla would go back to visit her family from time to time. She was there when a relative died, and Absilla and Isham adopted the girl, Appy Monroe. At the time of the adoption, Isham and Absilla lived in Robeson County. I believe Absilla "Appy" and William Walters may have married there. Appy and William's daughter Zylphia Walters married Daniel Faulk Nance. Their daughter Absilla M. Nance married Emery Lorenzo Williamson, and their son was James Carlie Williamson.

John Smith IV of Marion County Bear Swamp

John Smith was born between 1710 and 1715 in Chowan County, North Carolina. John IV was the son of John Smith III and Ann Jasper. Ann's parents were Richard Jasper, who left a will, and Sarah Clark. Sarah was a widow of Dr. Henry Clark.[154] John IV married Abigail Commander, daughter of Samuel Commander and Elizabeth, on October 4, 1737, at Prince Fredrick Parish, Georgetown County, South Carolina. He married a second time to Sarah Ford, daughter of Stephen Ford, on September 10, 1742. His final marriage was to Mary Johns in 1748 in South Carolina. John left a will on June 10, 1797, and it was probated on January 20, 1802. John Smith died in Marion County in 1802.

Hays or Hayes Family

Concerning the Hays family, Sellers says they are of Hillsboro Township. Their common ancestor was Benjamin Hayes. He further states one was a citizen near Buck Swamp Bridge. The bridge near the Pages was the only bridge across the swamp. They are and have always been a peaceful, orderly, and law-abiding group of people. They were and still are honest, industrious, and frugal, attend strictly to their affairs, and do not meddle with others. Their name seldom appears on the journal of the court records. Sellers mentions that Levi H. Hayes, the youngest son of Benjamin, married a daughter of Captain William Page and lived near Buck Swamp Bridge. Levi Hayes's will names his wife as Elizabeth and mentions any portion of the estate he has in William Page's estate.[155] My research, however, shows Levi also married Nancy Ann Whittington. Nancy and Levi are buried at Old Bethlehem Methodist Cemetery, Brownsville, Marlboro County, South Carolina, near Highways 34 and 38 just inside Marlboro County.

My Grandmother Hazel Turbeville Page's mother was Bertha Hays, or Hayes. I only have two photos of her and one of her husband, Shep Turbeville. I heard that these families originated in South Carolina and confirmed they came from the Marion County area and originally Orangeburg area of present-day South Carolina. The first Hayes was James N. Hayes, who originated in Bickdor, Gloucestershire, England. There are many Hayes and Harpers buried in the Brownsville community of Marlboro County. To my surprise, I also discovered the Whittington family, who came from England to the Cheraw area of South Carolina. Ironically, upon moving to Mississippi, I dated a girl named Whittington and now wonder if she may have been a descendant of a Whittington who had migrated to Mississippi from the Carolinas like many other South and North Carolina families had in the 1820s and 1830s.

Bryant Family

Concerning the Bryant family, Sellers states they are an old family. Jesse Bryant is said to have been the first of that name in the county. He came from England and married a Ms. Turbeville, sister of Rev. William Turbeville. According to Bishop Gregg, William came over about 1735 and settled at Sandy Bluff on the Great Pee Dee. Several brothers came with him, who now have descendants in Marion. Old Jesse had sons: William, Stephen, and Jesse.

William married Rebecca Miller. He lived and died some twenty-five or thirty years ago on the road just below Ebenezer Church, at age eighty-nine. Sellers concludes that many of the Bryants have immigrated to other parts of the country, and that he is not reasonably sure his account is correct in every particular manner.[156]

Lewis Family

According to Jerry Dale "J.D." Lewis in *My Neck of the Woods: The Lewis Families of Southeastern North Carolina and Northeastern South Carolina*, William Lewis Jr. moved to Nichols, South Carolina, around 1768, coming from upper North Carolina near present-day Pasquotank County. He grew up in Bertie Precinct, which was established in 1722 from Chowan Precinct and later became Bertie County in 1739.[157] In the 1927 publication of the Society of the Daughters of the American Revolution, William Lewis Jr. enlisted in November of 1775 and served in General Francis "Swamp Fox" Marion's unit. He also sold provisions to the United States.

According to Major General Roderick L. Carmichael in *The Scottish Highlander Carmichaels of the Carolinas*, the Lewis family name appears as members of Clan McLeod of Lewis, one of the Western Isles of Scotland. There is an extensive family of this name in Marion and Horry Counties in South Carolina, descendants of William Lewis, an

Ulster Scot who settled first in Virginia before the Revolution and later moved to Horry County. His ancestors were undoubtedly members of the great Ulster Scot group.[158]

William Lewis Sr.'s parents were Isaac Lewis and Margaret Hooker of Chowan Precinct. Isaac's parents were Edward Lewis and Bridgett Browne Lewis. Edward's parents were Thomas Walker Lewis Sr. and Elizabeth "Ann" Wood, last name unknown. Thomas came from Peters Church, Hertfordshire, England, to Albemarle in 1664. Margaret Hooker's father was William Hooker Sr. William Hooker Sr. left a will in Chowan Precinct in 1717 specifically leaving his daughters out of his will. Here is an excerpt: "My daughters Bridgett Man, Margaret Lewis, Jane Brown and Elizabeth Sisemore being already married have received what I desire they should have and my desire that they come in for no more of my estate."

The wife of William Lewis Sr. was Janet "Jane" Blewett Banks. This is confirmed by a deed of gift which Thomas Banks issued on November 10, 1736:

> *For sundry good causes and considerations me hereunto moving but more particular for the good will and Affection which I have and do bear to my son in Law William Lewis of Bertie Precinct Cordwainer [...] give [...] one certain Plantation and Tract of Land lyeing and being in Bertie prect aforesaid Chinckapen Neck Containing by Estimation two hundred acres (more of lefs) Bounded thus Viz Beginning at a marked Oak Thence running along a line of mark trees to John Vanpelt's land it being my Plantation in Plum tree Neck formerly Conveyed to Abraham Bewlet from William Bush as Records will appear.*

This deed of gift also corroborates the fact that John Van Pelt owned land there. Janet "Jane" Banks' mother was Jennet Maule Banks, but she had been married sometime before 1715 to an Abraham Blewett, an immigrant from Switzerland, who died after 1722. Jennet and Thomas Banks legally separated on November 17, 1725, and she died about 1793. Janet "Jane" Banks may have actually been the daughter of Abraham Blewett.[159]

After living in North Carolina, William Lewis married Mourning Van Pelt and moved to the Georgetown District around 1768. William died in 1811 and was buried in Horry County. Both J.D. Lewis and W. W. Sellers say Mourning was from Holland. She was Dutch, but she came from New York. J.D. Lewis further mentions that William and Mourning moved with kin to Horry County. They settled near the junction of Cedar Creek and the Little Pee Dee. They purchased much land in Horry and Marion Counties. William Lewis Jr. and Mourning Van Pelt reared seven sons and two daughters; the sons were William, James, Isaac, Hardy, Joel, Jonathan, and Patrick; the girls were Polly and Zilpha. Their daughter Mary Polly Lewis married Averitt Nichols Sr. around 1787, and it is from her I descend.

Van Pelts

The son of John Van Pelt, Daniel, is the father of Elizabeth Van Pelt Meares. Elizabeth married Mark Meares, and they are the parents of Joab Meares, born in 1780 in Dobbs County, North Carolina. Mark Meares had a land grant of 410 acres of land in Dobbs County, North Carolina, in 1767 on the north side of the great Contentrey Creek and Cattail Swamp. I came across Elizabeth Van Pelt some weeks earlier and thought there must be a connection to Mourning Van Pelt, who married William Lewis. The Van Pelts—being Dutch—were both mariners. They were both operating out of New York and in North

Carolina and South Carolina. William may have become acquainted with Mourning not in Charleston but perhaps in North Carolina at Bertie County. His service during the Revolutionary War was to the state of North Carolina. Like many of those in the northern corner of North Carolina, he migrated down to the new counties in North and South Carolina after the Revolution. Thus, the story that Old Man Van Pelt died on a voyage back to the Netherlands to collect his family and move to South Carolina is probably not true. More likely, the travel was up and down the coast of the United States, and once Mourning married Lewis, he and his family traveled the distance to New York when they moved to South Carolina.

Between 1720 and 1725, the volume of trade between New England and the ports of Roanoke, Currituck, and Beaufort, North Carolina, peaked at fifty-five ships sailing annually. In contrast, Virginia's volume of trade was only half of North Carolina's. Certainly, it is possible that a daughter accompanying her father on one of these voyages may have met her future husband in North Carolina and not in New York or New England. Interestingly, the removal of the pirate activity by Edward Teach "Blackbeard," Stede Bonnet, and Charles Vane around 1718 also contributed to increased shipping activity from the Carolinas, New England, and even the West Indies.[160] The relative safety of travel may have persuaded the Van Pelts to travel with their daughters to the Carolinas.

Once Mourning married in the South, her connections to her Dutch roots in New York were terminated. In his addition to the *William Lewis of Horry County, South Carolina*, William Lewis Johnson states the key to tracing Mourning Van Pelt begins with a deed in Bertie County Deed Book 1, executing the sale of property she inherited from her grandfather Hendrick Van Pelt. Mourning and William received sixteen pounds for this land, which is roughly 2,500–3,000 British pounds today and may have been the reason they moved to South Carolina.[161] Johnson states the original Van Pelt was Teunis Jansen Lanen Van Pelt with his third wife, Grietje Jan, and six children who came from Liege, Belgium, on the ship *Rosetree* in 1663 and settled in New Utrecht, part of present-day Brooklyn, New York. The oldest son was Jan "John," and he married Marytje "Maria" Pieterse in 1668. Their son, Hendrick, was born in 1677, and he married Teitje Andrisse about 1695. Around 1735, many of the Van Pelts moved to Bertie, North Carolina. (Again, the Van Pelts and Lewises were neighbors in Bertie County.) The exact parents of Mourning are not known, but one of the speculations Johnson proposes is she may have been the daughter of Hendrick Jr. History records Hendrick Jr. as being born in 1720 and baptized on January 1, 1721, in Port Richmond, New York. But he left no footprint in North Carolina. Hendrick Sr. died in 1747, when Mourning would have been about two, thus did Hendrick Sr. give the land to Mourning because it was to go to her father and he had died before 1737? Maybe this could be the origin—incorrect—that her father died at sea on the way back to Holland. Perhaps he did perish but on a journey to and from New York and North Carolina? However, her Dutch blood has been revealed now. Mourning's relative Elizabeth Van Pelt, daughter of Daniel Van Pelt, married Mark Meares. The Meares family are alleged descendants of Thomas Meares, who was born in England in 1602. He came to Virginia in 1637 and was awarded three hundred acres on the Elizabeth River in Upper Norwalk, Virginia, for transporting six people to Virginia. He served in the House of Burgesses from 1644 to 1647. His sons are assumed to be Bartholomew, William, and John Sr. Bartholomew's son was John Meares Sr., and his son was Mark Meares. Mark Meares's son Joab Meares migrated from Dobbs County, North Carolina, to Fair Bluff, North Carolina, and his wife was Mary Coleman, daughter of Moses Coleman Jr. and Louranna Faulk, which reconnects all those families who originated in the upper northeast corner of North Carolina in what became Columbus County.

Nichols

The Nichols family sprang up from Averitt Nichols of Columbus County, North Carolina. His youngest son, Averitt Nichols Jr., settled in Marion County in 1830. He lived in what is today called Nichols and died at ninety-three on January 7, 1896. He raised a family of ten children—eight daughters and two sons. One son was at Second Manassas on August 30, 1862. Averitt Nichols was an exemplary man; he had the faculty, in large degree, of attending to his own business and of letting other people's business severely alone. He amassed a large property, raised a sizeable, respectable family, and would not go into debt. He had several thousand dollars in the bank at Wilmington. When it failed, his money was also lost. In his later days, he partially lost his mind and control over his affairs, financial and otherwise. He was never informed of the loss of his money and died knowing no different. My connection to the Nicholses is through Averitt Sr. and his daughter Martha Nichols Nance, who married Daniel Holmes Nance. Martha's daughter Dorothy Nance married Elias Williamson.[162]

The Goodyear family of Marion County, South Carolina, is also discussed in Sellers's book. He states, "The Goodyear family, so far as Marion County is concerned, sprang from William Goodyear, who died in 1800. His wife, I think, was a Ford or a Grainger." William's sons, or grandsons, were Love Goodyear and John Goodyear. The Goodyear family is of English extraction and was one of the early settlers of the county. John Goodyear's daughter Sarah "Sallie" Goodyear married Fredrick Grainger, and their son William Henry Harrison Grainger married Nancy Lee. William and Nancy's daughter was Arabella Grainger Strickland, who married Moody Strickland and, thus, are the parents of Dalmas Cotas Strickland Worley. John Goodyear married Zenith or "Senita" Miller and had an extensive family.[163]

In Sellers's *The History of Marion County*, he states the Nicholses were from Ireland. I suppose they are English and came to America by way of Ireland. Sellers also states Mary Polly Lewis, daughter of William and Mourning Van Pelt Lewis, married Averitt of Columbus County, North Carolina, and was the mother of the venerable Averitt Nichols Jr. of Nichols, South Carolina.[164] Averitt Pearce Nichols Sr. was born in Bladen County, North Carolina, in 1767. His wife was Mary Polly Lewis, and he was the son of Coleman Nichols and Martha Pearce.

In her book, Mary Lewis Stevenson makes light of the fact that W.W. Sellers wrote the obituary of Averitt Sr. and states that when he was a young boy, he attended a Baptist convention at Porter's Swamp Baptist Church in Columbus County in 1828 or 1829. W.W. Sellers states he and his mother, along with 150 other people, spent the night at Averitt Sr.'s home. Everyone was fed, housed, and entertained at the expense of Averitt Sr. No one seemed happier than he.[165] Coleman Nichols, Averitt Sr.'s father, appears to have been the first Nichols to come to Columbus County. He was awarded land grants in Bladen County in 1775 and 1794 on the east side of Drowning Creek and the west side of Porter Swamp, respectively. Moreover, his first name hints at a connection to the Coleman family, who settled in Columbus County.

An interesting connection to the Nichols family is Averitt's great-grandmother was Mary Ligon (1694–1749), who was the daughter of Richard Ligon (1657–1724) and Mary Worsham (1658–1737). Richard was a surveyor of the five-thousand-acre Huguenot settlement at Manakin Town, now in Powhatan County. This was a place for French Huguenot refugees fleeing persecution in France. Colonel Thomas Ligon of Madresfield, Worcestershire, England, came to Virginia in 1641 and, with the help of his kinsman Royal Governor William Berkley, became a surveyor. Thomas Ligon was the grandson of a second son and stood little chance of inheriting any wealth and, thus, at sixteen came to Virginia. He married Mary Harris, daughter of Captain Thomas Harris, and they reared seven children. He was also a surveyor and a militia colonel and served as a member of the House of Burgesses at Jamestown.

William D. Ligon authored a book on the Ligons which was published in 1947 entitled *The Ligon Family and Connections*. The book is over nine hundred pages and contains many references to deeds and wills affecting the Ligon (originally Lygon) family in Virginia. Eventually, like many, they migrated to other places to include North Carolina.

Simmons

Isaac Simmons received land grants in Brunswick and Columbus Counties, North Carolina. Fifty acres on the northwest side of Hawkins Branch in 1809 and one hundred acres in Brunswick County were entered on January 20, 1780, and issued on October 15, 1783. He married Sarah Hall from Nottinghamshire, England.

Whittington

Nancy Whittington's father was Nathaniel C. Whittington, and her mother was Ann Nancy Summerford. Nathaniel Whittington's father was Francis Whittington. Francis moved to the Cheraws from Portsea, Hampshire, England.

Concerning the Cheraws, in 1768, South Carolina eliminated all the original counties and established seven new "overarching districts" with judicial seats in each district. The British Parliament nullified the act creating these new districts, but the reintroduction of the law in

1769 was approved. From 1769 to 1785, these districts remained intact. However, the district seats did change some during that timeframe. After the American Revolution, in 1785, South Carolina reestablished the concept of counties, and thirty-four "new" counties were defined and established. These new counties were "subsets" of, and subordinate to, the "overarching districts" that had been in existence since 1769. Some of the newly defined counties were abolished between 1785 and 1800, whereas other newly defined counties were created.

In 1785, South Carolina created three newly defined "counties" wholly within the existing Cheraw's District—Chesterfield, Darlington, and Marlboro—but the overarching Cheraw's District remained intact. At this time, the district seat was relocated from the town of Long Bluff to Cheraw. In 1800, South Carolina abolished all "overarching districts" and essentially went with the county concept from that year forward. However, in 1800, all counties were called "districts" and would continue being called such until after the US Civil War. In 1868, South Carolina reverted to the term "county," which has been used continuously since then. The boundaries of the original Cheraw's District remained the same from inception in 1769 until 1792, when the newly defined Salem County was established and now included within the Cheraw's District. Those lands had previously been considered part of the Camden District.

The first United States Census was taken in 1790, which enumerated each of the original seven "overarching districts." By the 1800 US Census, all the original seven "overarching districts" had been abolished, and new counties were enumerated separately in that census. Around 1700, the Cheraw Indians came to Cheraw. The tribe had come earlier to the Carolinas after being driven out of Virginia by the Iroquois. Their principal village was on the present site of the town. The Cheraw were of Sioux extraction and were an agricultural people. They were more potent and warlike than the nearby Pee Dee Indians. In North Carolina, they were the Saura Indians.

In the 1730s, the first White settlers came to the Cheraw area. The Welsh Baptist land grant in 1737 had the effect of forcing immigrants already in the region to move farther up the river. The earliest of these included English settlers, the Ellerbes and the Youngs. The first slaves came with some of these early settlers. By the 1730s, almost all the Cheraw Indians had left the region and joined forces with the Catawbas. Subsequently, in 1738, smallpox decimated these tribes. Some of the Cheraw remained with the Catawbas, and others went to live in the Lumber River region of North Carolina.[166]

The following is the transcript of Nathaniel Whittington's Revolutionary War claim:

> *Declaration in order to obtain the benefit of the Act of Congress passed June 7th 1832*
> *State of South Carolina, Marion District: Court of Common Pleas Fall Term 1832.*

> *On this the tenth October AD 1832, personally appeared before the Judge of the Court of Common Pleas for the District & State aforesaid Daniel Whittington a resident of the Same State & District aged Seventy years on the 7th February last – who being first duly sworn according to Law doth on his oath make the following declaration in order to obtain the benefit of the provision made by the act of Congress passed June 7th, 1832. – That he was drafted at or about the beginning of the Revolutionary War & entered the Service of the United States under Captain Tristram Thomas in Marlborough District, South Carolina. Colonel Simmons [sic, Maurice Simons] was an officer of the highest rank he at present recollects. Under him, this*

Deponent marched from Marlborough to Orangeburg – Black Swamp & to Purysburg about fifteen miles from Savannah, Georgia. At one of these last-mentioned places, he was stationed some time as a guard but was compelled to retreat on the approach of the British from Georgia & fled to Charleston, South Carolina, where his time expired & he returned home. He was out at this time three months ten days. He was drafted again for a month at a time at different times & served under Captain Morris Murphy [sic, Maurice Murphy], with whom he went to General Francis Marion's camp in the Swamp of Santee River about Thirty miles from Charleston, South Carolina. At one time, he was stationed at Watboo [sic, Wadboo] Bridge (as he believes) to prevent the British from passing up the Country.

Colonel Tarleton [sic, Banastre Tarleton] was stationed at the same time about three miles from Charleston. Marion sent out a party under Colonel Mayam [sic, Hezekiah Maham] to reconnoiter Tarleton's Camp. This party consisted of about thirty men & they succeeded in getting so near to Tarleton's camp that they killed the Sentinel. Tarleton rushed out upon them & they were compelled to recross Santee River & go on back to Wadboo Bridge. At this place, the British Scouts fired on Marion's picket guard & drove them in. Marion's men were placed behind a fence on each side of the road where there was a lane & as the British rushed through, Marion fired on them & killed four or five men & horses. Upon this, the British retired.

Deponent does not recollect any other engagement or anything else which occurred when he was out at that time worth mentioning. When the time for which he was drafted had expired, deponent returned home & was drafted again under the same Captain

(Maurice Murphy) under Colonel Lem Benton [sic, Lemuel Benton]; he marched down to Scott's Lake Fort about forty miles from Santee River, which was in possession of the British about nine hundred in number. The Americans under General Marion & Colonel Lee [Henry "Light Horse Harry" Lee], in number about sixteen hundred, attacked the Fort & were repulsed with the loss of Thirty or Forty men killed. The Fort was only accessible on one side — This side Marion entrenched & put Colonel Lee's regulars to fire on the Fort, through the Port Holes made in the mound of earth thrown out of the Ditch. He also made a rolling battery & when the British refused to Surrender, he moved up his Battery to the Fort, & as the British showed their heads outside the Fort, Lee's regulars picked them off. In this manner, the Americans succeeded in getting up to the Fort & taking possession of it. After this engagement, deponent returned to Marlborough & soon afterwards was drafted again, marched under the same Captain to Birch's Mill about three miles below Mars Bluff on the Pee Dee River in Marion District where he rejoined General Marion — Marion then moved up the River to Castaway ferry [sic, Cashua Ferry] & crossed over to Boling Green [sic, Bowling Green?] in Marion District where he proclaimed free Pardon to all the Tories who would lay down their arms.

To this proposition many of them acceded & joined the Americans. Deponent was drafted at other times under Captain Hinson, Moses Pearson, _____ Standard. He can't tell whether he ever received a discharge, if he did, he has lost it. He was always under Marion & if he ever received a discharge it was from him. He has no documentary evidence of his Service and knows of Samuel Cox & William Cox of Marlborough District now alive who can testify to his services. [Whittington] was born in Marlborough District, South Carolina

the 7th day of February 1762 — his age is recorded in a Family Bible at the House of Betsy McTyer in Marlborough District. He has lived in Marlborough since the Revolution, except during the last twenty years which he has spent in Marion where he now lives. He is known to David S. Harllee, Samuel Bigham, Thomas Godbold, Thomas Evans & many other gentlemen of respectability who can testify as to deponent's character for veracity and their belief in his services, as stated in his declaration. He hereby relinquishes every claim whatever to any pension except the present & declares that his name is not on the Pension Roll of the Agency of any State.
S/ Nathaniel Whittington, W his mark
Sworn to & subscribed in the year & day aforesaid.
S/ B.J. Earle, Presiding Judge in open Court at the court of Common Pleas & Sessions for the District aforesaid at Marion CH.[167]

Rackley

Amelia "Millie" Ann Fowler's father was John Fowler, who was the son of Daniel Fowler Sr. and Mary Rollins. John Fowler married Elizabeth Rackley, the oldest daughter of Joshua and Cityvias Rackley. Elizabeth was the sixth descendant of Edward Rackley, who came to Virginia about 1639.

Edward Rackley was from the village of Compton Bishop, Somerset, England. He sailed from Somerset, England, and received land grants from Charles I for paying for the passage of thirteen persons to Virginia. Edward and his son acquired vast tracts of land in Virginia and lived among the Powhatans on the south side of the Rappahannock River, twelve miles above Nansemond Town. On May 18, 1663, Edward Rackley and Peter Ford received a patent for 640 acres in New Kent County situated on the north side of the Mattaponi River upon Timber Branch of Dragon Swamp, running over Chiskiak Path. This grant was for the transport of thirteen persons. This tract was located nearby to the other two patents awarded Peter Ford and was in the vicinity of the future location of King and Queen County Courthouse south of Apostique Creek.

John Rackley II was born in Essex County, Virginia, in 1670 and died in Henrico County. His wife was Jane Mills, daughter of Robert Mills of Virginia Colony. This is confirmed by a map showing the locations of early homesites noted as Rappahannock and Tappahannock Rivers. It is believed John Rackley passed away two to four miles away from "Hobs in his hole," Virginia.

John Rackley III moved his family to the swamplands of eastern North Carolina, where his family hired Lumbee Indians to remove the timber out of the swamps, canals, and docks, and levees were made to drain out the water. Precious walnut and cypress trees were harvested out of the swamps and shipped to England and abroad. Also noted is that the Rackleys became fluent in the Lumbee Indian language. John Rackley III died in Bute County, now Franklin County, North Carolina. Joshua Rackley and his wife Cityvias, who was also a Rackley, were first cousins. Their fathers were brothers, Anthony and John III. Their grandfather was John Rackley II.

John Rackley IV owned vast plantations of farmland in the area of eastern North Carolina, Halifax District. Most of the farms were once swamplands drained of the water; the cypress timber was cut and exported overseas, and the land became farming land. The Rackleys had hired Lumbee Indians to do most of this work, and it is noted that John Rackley IV married one of the Lumbee Indian women during that time. John Rackley III may have left his son John Rackley IV out of his will for that reason. John Rackley IV lived among the Lumbee Indians in eastern North Carolina. It is in the belief that he left the Halifax District, North Carolina, and went to live with the Lumbee Tribe.

He then relocated to Franklin District of Georgia, living among the Creek and Cherokee Tribes. He built a small log home on the Hudson Fork River, where he was a trader of goods among the early pioneers.

Joshua Rackley is listed on the 1790 Census of the United States.[168]

Hathaway or Hattaway

As I mentioned in a previous chapter, this name has been spelled many different ways, but nonetheless, they are all the same family.

Isaac Wright, who settled in the Tabor City, North Carolina, area, was married to Ann Hathaway. They are the parents of Stephen Wright.

Ann's father was Thomas Hathaway Jr., who appears on the 1790 Census in Pitt County, North Carolina. His father was David Hathaway. David received a land grant from Francis Corbin, Esquire, acting as an agent for the Earl of Granville, addressed to Captain William Haywood to lay out a plantation of four hundred acres of land in Beaufort County. His father, Francis Hattaway, was granted sixty acres on the south side of the Tar River and the west side of Cocovinly Swamp on February 18, 1750, in Pitt County, from William Robson.

Spiveys of Tabor City

John Fowler's sister Elizabeth Fowler was born about 1760 and is listed on the 1850 Columbus County Census as ninety years old and living with her son Caleb Spivey Jr. Her husband, Edmond Caleb Spivey Sr., died in 1798. He left a will in Robeson County, North Carolina. Elizabeth gave birth just prior to his death, and she moved to Columbus County to be near relatives. Her testimony for a pension is on file, and an extract of it is included later in this section.

The Fowler family of Columbus County and Horry County are descended from Daniel Fowler and Mary Rollins, who were natives of Nansemond County, Virginia. Daniel and Mary arrived in Duplin

County, North Carolina, in a section that became part of Sampson County by 1753 and purchased much property from 1753 until 1773 along Cane Creek, Six Runs, and Buck Horn. Daniel's property was near that of the Wright family, and his granddaughter Amelia Ann Fowler married Stephen Wright in Columbus County in 1819.

John Fowler was born in Duplin County, North Carolina, and was a Revolutionary Patriot at the Battle of Moore's Creek Bridge in 1776. There are extensive records on his war service at the National Archives in Washington, DC.

Daniel's daughter Elizabeth was born in 1760 and later married Edmund Spivey in 1776 when she was about fifteen years old. Edmund Spivey, John Fowler, Daniel Fowler Jr., and William Fowler all served the Patriot cause during the American Revolution. Edmund Spivey joined the army near the beginning of the war in Sampson County, then called Duplin. Soon after his expiration of every term of six months or longer, he would rejoin the army. He continued in the service until the close of the war.

Elizabeth Spivey lived with her husband until his death in 1798. Elizabeth did not remarry. During her testimony to claim a pension as a war widow, the following is recorded:

> She does not know whether her husband was in any battle, but she is inclined to believe he was not. Sometimes during the war, her husband would hire a substitute to take his place in the army, and he would stay at home some months. She does not know the name of the regiment or company in which her husband served. She believes the captain's name was Robert Meritt, and her husband was drafted. She recollects distinctly that at the Battle of Moore's Creek [Bridge] on February 27, 1776, her husband was at home, and a man named John Newton was hired to go in his place.

Her testimony reads:

> "At that time, she was confined to her bed, having just given birth to a daughter. This Declarant claims the pension to which she is entitled under the act aforesaid as the 'Widow of Edmund Spivey for six months' service as a private in the Militia' of the United States under Captain Robert Merritt in the War of the Revolution."[169]

On July 5, 1853, Elizabeth Spivey, about ninety-two years old, appeared before a justice of the peace in Robeson County, North Carolina, seeking a pension. Her claim was based on a law Congress passed on February 2, 1848, granting pensions to widows of persons who had served during the Revolutionary War.

Elizabeth's daughter Martha Beverly Spivey married Daniel Fowler Jr. and had a son. Simply amazing that, apparently, Daniel Jr. married his niece. Reuben Fowler Sr. was the father of Lany Fowler, the mother of Elizabeth Cartrette, and Elizabeth was the mother of Daniel Return Page. Perhaps that is the source of the name Daniel Return. Edmond Spivey was granted three hundred acres of land in Duplin County in 1779, and one of the chain bearers is Daniel Fowler, which I assume to be Daniel Jr. His name is there on the grant as clear as a bright day.

Another note concerning the Spiveys is the Spivey Cemetery on Will Inman Road in Tabor City is the burial location of Patience Carolina Fowler Hattaway Prince. It has puzzled me as to why Patience is buried there and not at the Stephens-Wright Cemetery.

CHAPTER 20
Is this North or South Carolina?

I suppose I'll pause here and say something about the area north of Lake View, formerly known as Page's Mill, and the area of Fair Bluff and Robeson County, which is drained by Bear Swamp and Ashpole Swamp. It seems many of my ancestors were the first to settle this area, as I established with the land grant to David Page. Judge Z. T. Fulmore states, "One of the first acts passed by the first Congress of the United States was a provision for the census of the population."[170] This shows all heads of families substantially in Robeson in that year.

One of the drawbacks was the uncertainty about the exact lines between North Carolina and South Carolina and the county lines between Richmond and Robeson. The federal census is an invaluable aid in ferreting out family history, even if all the names are not included on the 1790 Census. I have depended upon it to identify the families of the Ashpole Community in 1790 and show the early settlements of old English, Welsh, and Scotch Irish descent settlers who made their homes on Ashpole Swamp and its tributaries.

Another aspect of this community I have been brought to is determining the heritage of Samuel Grainger's wife, Elizabeth Tyner.

There are many Tyners in Robeson County, and the original Tyner came out of Nansemond County, Virginia, and into North Carolina, as many of the other people in Columbus, Marion, Horry, and Robeson Counties. What I have found is speculative, but I shall propose this since the movement out of Virginia is the pattern.

Nicholas Tyner was born about 1637 and died about 1708 in the Isle of Wight County, Virginia. I believe he is the ancestor of Benjamin Tyner Sr., who served in the Revolutionary War from Wayne County and settled in Robeson County. He filed for a pension in February of 1833, at the age of ninety. Company F of the Fifty-First North Carolina Regiment was known as the Ashpole True Boys and was raised in Robeson County. It entered service in Wilmington on April 21, 1862. There were Tyners in its ranks. Thus, my conclusion and speculation are that Elizabeth Tyner was one of these Tyners related to Benjamin Tyner.

Samuel Grainger's father is buried in South Carolina between Fair Bluff and Nichols and thus near Bear Swamp and Ashpole, and his daughter Sarah married Return Page. Thus, the families seem connected. Benjamin Tyner II's sons William and Nicholas served in Company F of the Fifty-First. William enlisted at age thirty-nine and was captured at Cold Harbor on June 1, 1864, and confined to Point Lookout, Maryland, until July 12, 1864, when he was transferred to Elmira, where he died of a "contusion" on July 18, 1864. Nicholas enlisted at age forty in March of 1862. He was listed as a deserter between September and October in 1862. He returned to duty on an unspecified date but deserted again on December 15, 1862. He, once again, returned to duty in January 1863. He was present or accounted for until October 1864, when he was reported absent because of a sickness. He returned to duty in December 1864.

PART IV

CHAPTER 21
The Military Section

The United States is a relatively young nation but has fought many wars during its history. My discovery of this research has indicated that many of my relatives have participated in these wars. I have tried to include the information I have found to provide the benefit of having this information in one place so others will know what their relatives did during our collective history. All the persons below are related to me. I am confident I have missed some and apologize for that oversight. Nonetheless, here is what I have.

Revolutionary War
Caleb Abbot. Appeared on the muster roll of Colonel Robert Murden's Regiment, Pasquotank County, North Carolina.[171] Caleb died in Pasquotank County, North Carolina, in 1785.

John Fowler. While a resident of Sampson County, North Carolina, Fowler enlisted under Captain Richard Clinton and James Kenan and was in the Battle of Moore's Creek Bridge. Next, he served under Captain Alfred Moore and Colonel Moore in the First North Carolina

Regiment. He also served at some time under Captain William Vann. Fowler was allowed a pension on his application executed November 12, 1832, while residing in Columbus County, North Carolina. In 1837, he moved to Pike County, Alabama, to be near his children, who I think would be Richard Fowler, his son, who also served in the War of 1812.[172]

Edmund Spivey Sr. Husband to Elizabeth Fowler, sister to John Fowler, Peter Fowler, and Daniel Fowler Jr. According to Elizabeth's testimony on July 5, 1853, for an application for a pension before a C. Leon Harris in Robeson County, North Carolina, Edmund had joined the army at the beginning of the war while in Sampson County. He renewed his service every six months and continued in service until the end of the war. She stated she'd married Edmund when she was fifteen years old and was married to him until his death in 1798. She believed he'd served under Captain Robert Meritt. She recalled distinctly that during the Battle of Moore's Creek Bridge on February 27, 1776, he had been home, and John Newton had been hired to take his place. She further stated that Edmund had been home because she had given birth to a daughter and was confined to bed and needed him to be at home. This record is on file with the National Archives. Edmund was awarded a land grant in Duplin County of three hundred acres on April 1, 1780. Daniel Fowler—either senior or junior; I'm not sure which—was a chain bearer for the survey. Edmund Spivey made his will in 1798.

Daniel Fowler Sr./Jr. Born in Chowan County in 1714 and died in 1783. Daniel Fowler Jr. was born in 1752 and died in 1820. One of them, more than likely Daniel Jr. because of the age, served in Armstrong's Company from Duplin County from June of 1776 until June 28, 1779. Daniel Jr. was the brother of John, Elizabeth, and Peter

Fowler. Daniel Jr. was my great-grandfather five times removed, and Daniel Sr. my great-grandfather six times removed.

John Hardee. A member of the Committee of Public Safety in Pitt County, North Carolina.[173] His son Andrew Hardee moved from Pitt County, North Carolina, to Horry County, South Carolina. John's wife was Susannah Tyson, and her family may have been Dutch or German. Her father was Mathis Tyson but originally was Mathissen den Smet Mathijssen den Smet Thijssen. Records show he emigrated from Wales to Philadelphia, Pennsylvania, in 1709.

John Smith IV. Supported the Patriots during the Revolution and fought at the battle of Bowling Green. The battle took place on June 8, 1782. Brigadier General Francis Marion and his force attacked and captured a group of Loyalists under the command of Major Micajah Gainey. The Loyalists, except for Colonel David Fanning, Major Samuel Andrews, and Major William Cunningham, were paroled after accepting an offer from General Marion to pledge allegiance to South Carolina and serve for six months under him. In his 1833 pension application, North Carolina militiaman Isham Dickeson (R2823) asserts the following:

> *Soon after joining General Marion, they set out in pursuit of a Col. Fanning, a celebrated Tory Colonel, who was committing great depredations about Drowning Creek, Raft Swamp, Shoe Heel, and Little Pee Dee Rivers. When they reached a place called the Bowling Green, General Marion selected from his troops one hundred footmen to go out as spies and scouts—of which number this declarant was one—who were placed under the command of Capt. Robert Ellison. After leaving the Main Army, they traversed the country for several*

days to discover, if possible, the hiding place of the Tories. On the night of the third day, they fell in with a small body of them with whom they had a considerable skirmish, having killed and wounded several—the number not known—without losing a man.[174]

Francis Whittington. Appeared on the muster roll and list of Colonel George Gabriel Powell's Battalion serving in the late expedition against the Cherokee from October 11, 1759, to January 15, 1760, under the command of His Excellency William Henry Lyttleton, Esquire, governor and captain-general of the expedition. He is on the list of Captain Peter Kolb's Company as a clerk. He also is listed as serving in the company of General Marion and present at the fall of Charleston, South Carolina, and served thirty-seven days in the militia in 1782.[175] Additionally, he took part in the Cherokee Expedition of 1756–1760.

Nathaniel C. Whittington. Drafted under Captain Tristram Thomas and Colonel Simmons. Next, he served under Captain Morris Murphy and General Marion. Nathaniel participated in the skirmish at Wadboo Bridge with the British and helped take Scott's Lake Bluff or Fort Watson. He additionally served under Captain Clayborne Hinson, Moses Pearson, and William Standard.[176]

James Allison Hayes. Served as a sergeant in the Second Dragoons under Captain Isaac Ross, Colonel Charles Middleton, and General Sumter during 1781.[177]

William Lewis II. Served with the Second Regiment commanded by Lieutenant Colonel Francis Marion as a private, but that is not in his testimony. He states he was at the battle of Stono, and afterward, he returned to Halifax, North Carolina, and stood guard over prisoners taken at Stono. He then participated in the pursuit of Lord Cornwallis and was doing so at the declaration of peace. After the war, he was granted 887 acres in Horry County.

Daniel Nance Jr. Owned land on Jacob Creek, Mecklenburg County, Virginia. He lived in Prince George County (Bristol Parish) in 1728 and received a land grant while living in Brunswick County in 1733. He eventually moved to North Carolina in 1770 and was believed to be the first Nance in the state. He served as a scout for the North Carolina Militia in Bladen County, North Carolina, from 1776 to 1783.

Daniel Nance III. Served in the military before 1770 as an army scout in the North Carolina Militia from Bladen County, North Carolina. He is listed in the 1790 Census and 1800 Census as living in Bladen County.

Lewis Williamson. Appeared on General Cashwell's list as a Patriot at Moore's Creek Bridge.[178]

Richard Tatum Sr. Father of Mary Tatum Williamson. He was paid two British pounds, nine shillings, and sixpence on a claim dated May 3, 1779, and paid out March 16, 1782, for service during the Revolutionary War. His parents were Joshua Tatum and Amy Chappell. Amy Chappell's great-grandfather was Captain John Thomas Chappell II, captain of the *Speedwell*. The *Speedwell* was a sister ship of the *Mayflower* but developed a leak and could not make the voyage. However, it did sail to America on May 28, 1635, from Southampton to Virginia.[179]

Nicholas Worley. Appeared on a list as serving in the militia in Captain Nathaniel Bradford's Company as a corporal in the Edgecombe County Militia, North Carolina. He served in the Wilmington area, and his pay voucher is listed in the North Carolina Archives as 3663.[180]

Absolam Turbeville. Brother of George Turbeville and was killed during the Revolutionary War. His wife, Lucy Wyndham, was awarded a pension.[181]

George Turbeville. Served as a corporal in the Fourth Regiment under Captain H. Davis during January 1780. George Turbeville was the son of Charles and Susannah Sanders, one of the first settlers in what became Williamsburg County, South Carolina. The following is taken from *History of Williamsburg: Something About the People of Williamsburg County, South Carolina from First Settlement by Europeans about 1705 until 1923* by William Willis Boddie, first published in 1923:

> *Priscilla Campbell, John and Elizabeth Kelly, John and Elizabeth McDonald, Thomas and Dorothy Jenkins, Richard and Elizabeth Jones, John and Philadelphia Turbeville, John and Margaret Lee, Stephen and Elizabeth DuBose, John and Rebecca Hodges, John and Mary Singleton, William and Sarah Purvis, John and Arabella Scott, Lodowick and Anne Hudson, Daniel and Susannah McGinney, William and Jane Green, John and Elizabeth Dozier, John and Hannah Davis, James and Mehitabel Boyd, John and Mary Britton Sinkler, William and Sarah Tompkins Dinkins, Moses and Hester Jolly Britton, Alexander and Elizabeth Ball Davidson, Charles and Susannah Sanders Turbeville, Moses Britton, Daniel and Elizabeth Hyrney Britton, George and Hannah Saunders, and Peter and Isabel Tamplet.*

These people settled along the Black River from the point where it turns abruptly northward, just after entering Georgetown County from Williamsburg County, and along the present Williamsburg-Georgetown County line to the Pee Dee River. This settlement was called Winyaw, and this was the first part of the present County of Williamsburg that was inhabited by White people. Some of these people lived there in 1710. They organized Prince Frederick's Church in 1713. Reverend William Screven and his Congregation of Dissenters from the Church of England were the first permanent settlers in the Winyaw section. They were granted a large part of the territory on both sides of that section of the Black River flowing through ancient Winyaw. While Reverend Screven was a militant Antipedobaptist, many of the Dissenters who came with him were of the Presbyterian faith. The Saunders family were from Banffshire, Scotland.

Hezekiah Cartwright. Served in Robert Murden's Regiment and is listed on the payroll as being paid for service in the Revolutionary War by the Edenton District fifteen pounds and eight shillings, on April 1873.

Theophilus Coleman. Awarded $48.33 for service in the American Revolutionary War and enlisted as a private in the Bladen Militia under Captain Daniel Shipman in the fall of 1777.

According to the testimony, the Bladen Militia was surprised by a British attack because General Ashe had not expected one and had not adequately prepared. Coleman and the militia crossed the Pee Dee River into South Carolina and then proceeded to the Savannah River and Georgia. They encamped at Brier Creek between the creek and the Savannah River. The Patriots "only made one fire before retreating by swimming across the Savannah and recollected at a place called the

Ridge."[182] This battle is undoubtedly the Battle of Brier Creek, which took place on March 3, 1779.

The following is an account of the fight. British Lt. Colonel Mark Prevost's troops approached in three columns. Baird's light infantry was on the left, the First Battalion of the Seventy-First was in the center, and Carolina provincials and "rangers" formed the right. Prevost held in reserve the light dragoons and grenadiers. Both sides opened fire at long range, and then Colonel Samuel Elbert's men of the Continental Army moved forward to close the distance between the British and the Patriots. Two things then occurred to create a gap in the American line. Elbert's men drifted left as they advanced, partially screening the fire from the New Bern men, and British cavalry threatened the right, drawing the Edenton, North Carolina, men away from the center. Seeing this opening, Prevost ordered his British troops to fix bayonets and charge.

Most of the Patriot Militia did not have bayonets. Seeing the British charging at them, many broke and ran without even firing a shot. The Edenton, North Carolina, men fired a few rounds and then abandoned the fight. Elbert's Continentals held formation in the center while the militia around them fled for the swamps and was eventually surrounded, forcing Elbert to surrender.[183] The two hundred men came up to the battlefield late in the fighting but quickly withdrew before getting drawn into the rout. The British counted five killed and eleven wounded. The carnage on the American side was never fully tallied, as many militiamen retreated to North Carolina, and an unknown number drowned in the swamps. Prevost claimed that 150 American bodies were found on the battlefield and 227 captives were taken, mainly from Elbert's Continentals.

Anthony Lytle, the commander of the American light infantry, dispersed his men to avoid capture. General Ashe was seen riding after the militia companies and was widely blamed for the disaster, often amid claims that he had led the retreat. A court-martial acquitted him of charges of cowardice but did convict him of failure to secure his camp. Brier Creek stalemated American attempts to force the enemy out of the new state and guaranteed British domination of the region.[184]

Brier Creek has a length of approximately eighty miles (130 kilometers). In many places along the length of its course, it is thirty to fifty feet (nine to sixteen meters) in width. Near its mouth, it is sometimes as broad as eighty feet (twenty-five meters). Much of the lowest portion of the creek is bordered by the Tuckahoe Wildlife Management Area, which contains a significant amount of the battlefield. In the foreground is the historical marker for the battle site. Brier Creek can be seen in the background. The joining of Brier Creek with the Savannah River forms a significant geographic constraint upon movement in that area between the forks formed by the creek and river. The land surrounding the stream and river is often swampy, and moving across both waterways is significantly constrained. This lay of the land contributed to the location and consequences of the battle.[185] The defeated remnants of the American army marched back across the Pee Dee and into North Carolina, met at Cross Creek, and joined General Rutherford.

At Cross Creek—known today as Fayetteville, North Carolina—Theophilus Coleman's enlistment expired, but he was substituted for three months' service for his father, who was detailed from Captain Ames's Company to the Bladen Militia. He was sent to Captain Shipman and formed with other militia under Colonel Brown and Colonel Lillington. According to Theophilus Coleman's testimony, they marched to Thompsons Mill in South Carolina and then to the Blue Ridge in North Carolina with the Back Country Militia under General Rutherford. They were stationed for four weeks. They were ordered to accompany the baggage trains back to Fayetteville to avoid General

Cornwallis but were met by Colonel Brown and told to return home and meet him at Livingston Creek in Brunswick County, North Carolina. Colonel Brown was not there, but the testimony states they met him after his defeat by Tories. They met at Long Creek and were told by Colonel Edward Wingate to repair Hood's Creek Bridge but were met by a body of British from Wilmington, North Carolina.

Theophilus Coleman states the British were kept in check for a day by Captain Simmons, but Simmons was killed. North Carolina history confirms this to be the battle of Hood's Creek in September 1781, and Simmons was a captain in the Brunswick Militia under Colonel Wingate. Colonel Brown ordered the men to disburse, and he went home. He then volunteered to serve in a company of light-horse militia under Captain John Grantham of Bladen County. Grantham was preparing an expedition against Tories in upper Bladen County and the state of South Carolina. He marched to the Pee Dee and then to Mars Bluff on the Pee Dee. He served for three months and upon marching back to Lumberton, North Carolina, received a verbal discharge. Coleman again volunteered when Cornwallis was marching back to Wilmington, North Carolina, after his defeat at Guilford Courthouse. This service was with a Bladen light-horse militia under Captain Legget.

Coleman formed with the Back Country Militia under General Butler and Colonel Thomas Owen, who had led the Bladen County Regiment at the battles of Little Lynches Creek, Camden, Tory Hole, Brown Marsh, Raft Swamp, and the Evacuation of Wilmington.[186] They then marched on Marsh Castle, encamped along a cornfield at Baldwin's Old Field, which was where the battle of Brown Marsh was held in September of 1781, and were attacked by the British. The Back County Militia fled, but the Duplin and Bladen Militias under Colonel Owen and Captain Dodd held until they were forced to retreat by a superior number of British. Theophilus Coleman was again verbally discharged but called again to act against Tories in Bladen County for two more months. In 1781, he also served under Col. Thomas Brown in the Bladen County Regiment. He fought at Moore's Creek Bridge, Brier Creek, Rockfish Creek, Brown Marsh, and Evacuation of Wilmington.[187]

After their victory at Tory Hole in Bladen County, the Patriots tried to confine or contain the efforts of the British forces occupying Wilmington. Lt. Col. Jacob Leonard of the Brunswick County Regiment took about thirty men. He set up a camp just outside of Wilmington to cut off incoming supplies and prevent slaves from flocking to the British occupiers. Leonard's camp was a severe threat and annoyance to Major James H. Craig, who soon resolved to break it up. Craig sent out a detachment of British Regulars to establish an ambush site at the bridge on Hood's Creek in nearby Brunswick County. Another detachment was to be sent behind Leonard's camp to cut off any retreat. Loyalists were strictly ordered to give no quarter and to kill every Patriot with arms in their hands. When a Loyalist guide heard these orders, he decided not to take the second detachment to the Patriot camp ... at least not directly. Many of those in that camp were his neighbors. The Loyalist guide wandered in the woods from swamp to swamp until he reckoned that the camp had noticed their approach and reasoned their intent. At Hood's Creek Bridge, the British force became impatient and sounded a horn to let the Loyalists know that they were ready.

The Patriots heard the horn, but they were not aware that a second enemy group was wandering nearby, ready to attack. They sent out two brothers named Smith to Hood's Creek Bridge to learn what the horn signified. When they reached the bridge, they quickly wheeled their horses under a volley of musket fire. One brother had his hat shot off, and the other was severely wounded and fell off his horse. The

British rushed forward and bayonetted him to death. The Patriot camp heard the shooting and quickly withdrew to safety with no additional injuries.[188]

In his 1834 pension application, Theophilus Coleman recounted the following:

> They, however, received orders from him [Col. Thomas Brown], through Colonel Edward Wingate, to repair to Hood's Creek Bridge where a small body of Brunswick Militia was stationed under Colonel Wingate & Captain Simmonds. While there an attack was made on the detachment by a body of British from Wilmington under Major Manson. The British who made their appearance about daylight, were kept in check for a short time by a small body of men at the Bridge under Captain Simmonds—but Captain Simmonds having been killed—the detachment was ordered by Colonel Wingate to disperse & returned home. [189]

Note Coleman's testimony established Edward Wingate as in the area of Bladen County.

The Battle of Brown's Marsh, Bladen County, North Carolina

I know from testimony that John Fowler, perhaps his brother Daniel, and Absalom Powell were at the Battle of Moore's Creek Bridge, but I have not found testimony they were at Brown's Marsh. Although, since this battle took place near present-day Clarkton, chances are they may have been there. I have included a description for the reason this battle marked the high point of Tory success in the area of Bladen and Columbus Counties.

American Brigadier General John Butler had missed his chance to rescue Governor Thomas Burke, and he missed his opportunity to capture Major James H. Craig and his forces at Livingston's Creek on September 23. He knew the Loyalists would be coming back to the upper Cape Fear River area to return home, so he planned to retaliate against the men who had committed the raid on Hillsborough and transported their prisoners to Wilmington. Major James H. Craig, the occupying commandant of Wilmington, had received intelligence that Brigadier General Butler and his army had gathered near Brown Marsh in Bladen County. Major Craig sent Major Daniel Manson with 180 provincials from Wilmington to escort Col. Duncan Ray and his Loyalists as far as Brown Marsh.

When the provincials and Loyalists arrived, Major Manson divided his forces and placed guides with each element. Three groups were to strike Brigadier General Butler's camp from different angles: The Royal North Carolina Regiment, Col. Duncan Ray's Anson County Militia, and Col. David Fanning's Regiment under the command of Capt. Stephen Holloway. This plan quickly fell apart when the guides became lost in the Brown Marsh. Major Manson and Capt. Holloway were able to move out of the swamp and get into position, but Ray's men were lost. They could be heard moving through the swamp, breaking brush, and getting tangled in vines and bushes. The Patriots heard all this and set up a defensive position facing the swamp. Unaware of this, Major Manson ordered the attack to begin before sunrise. Brigadier General Butler was facing the swamp where he had heard the noisy Loyalists under Col. Duncan Ray, and he did not expect an attack on his flanks. When Major Manson fired the first volley, Brigadier General Butler assumed the British had fieldpieces, and he ordered a retreat.

As before, Lt. Col. Robert Mebane—a Continental officer—did not retreat and repeated what he had done successfully at Lindley's

Mill. He disobeyed Brigadier General Butler's order and continued to fight. Owen's Bladen County Militia joined him, and they fought until they were overpowered and forced to retreat. In less than an hour, the Loyalists had the Patriot's camp. They had lost three killed and five wounded. The Patriots reported they had lost three killed and two injured. However, Major Daniel Manson wrote the following to Major James H. Craig in Wilmington:

The Rebels were completely dispersed, leaving twenty dead and five and twenty prisoners. They also had many wounded who, in the darkness of the night, got off. We took between thirty and forty horses, but the militia the next day got upward of a hundred more who were running loose in the woods.[190]

Pierce Godwin. Served in the Revolutionary War. He was awarded a Revolutionary War pension under the Revolutionary Claims Act of 1832 in March of 1833, in the amount of fifty dollars.

Court testimony states he volunteered for service in a company of Bladen Militia commanded by Captain Thomas and Lieutenant John Gates in 1776, shortly after the commencement of hostilities. The company was formed with the Bladen Regiment commanded by Colonel Thomas Robeson at Elizabethtown, North Carolina.

This regiment was one of many under the command of General James Moore. Their objective was to march to Rockfish Creek seven miles below Fayetteville, then Cross Creek, to drive the Tories under McDonald and McLeod, who had collected in force there. Pierce Godwin's sworn testimony states General Moore feared his inferior numbers threw up entrenchments on the north side of the creek. However, the Tories crossed the Cape Fear at Campbelltown. In pursuing the Tories, Moore learned of a defeat of other Tories by Patriot General Caswell at Moore's Creek Bridge, whereupon he discharged the militia.

However, the company of Captain Ames, of which Godwin was part, was sent to South Carolina to collect Tories in that area and require an oath of allegiance from them. He was engaged in this service for one month. In the month of May or June 1776, he again volunteered in the Bladen Militia for two months, once again, in Captain Ames's Company with Lieutenant John Yates and Ensign William Oliphant. The company redeployed to Marsh Castle. On their way, they joined another company of Bladen Militia under Captain Josiah Hendra and then joined two companies of Duplin Militia under the command of Colonel Thomas Brown of Bladen. They remained in Wilmington for two weeks and then relocated to Jumping Run. Godwin received a written discharge from Captain Ames.

In the spring of 1778 or 1779, he was drafted. On arriving at Campbelltown, he was assigned to forage for supplies up and down the Cape Fear from Fayetteville to Wilmington in order to supply the Patriot army. His testimony is supported by the testimony of Absolum Powell, Caleb Stephens, and Everitt Nichols. His will is on file at the Columbus County Courthouse dated, April 1845, and confirms four daughters: Alcy Williamson, Nancy Williamson, Susan Floyd, and Emily Powell. It also references Miranza Ann Williamson and the heirs of Elias Godwin, Ireny Moncrief, and Ithamore Tatom. A grandson N.L. Williamson is the executor of the will, and Laban and Dennis Williamson witnessed it.

Abraham Page. Died during the Revolutionary War on September 26, 1778. I have not discovered if this was from action in battle or some other cause. Abraham Page appears on a list of Dobbs County, North Carolina, militia with William Lewis and John Grainger. The Provincial Congress authorized the regiment on September 9, 1775, consisting of thirty-five existing county militias. The Dobbs County

Militia was active until the end of the war. Abraham Page was given 150 acres of land in Dobbs County, North Carolina, on April 2, 1761. Document states the land was given at Wilmington. His son David Sr. was given three hundred acres of land on April 18, 1771, on the southwest side of Tadpole Swamp. His son Solomon was given seventeen acres on Jumping Run on September 13, 1791.

Abraham Page's son David Page Sr. was awarded a land grant in Marion County, South Carolina, at what became Lake View and possibly on the North Carolina side of the state line. David's brother, Solomon Page, also received a land grant and was also a veteran and is buried in Lake View.[191]

John Grainger. Served as a matross—an artillery person, ranked below the gunner, whose duty was to assist the gunner in loading, firing, and sponging the cannon—in Stevens's Corps of Artillery, the organization in which he enlisted on November 8, 1776. He was transferred to Steven Buckland's Company, Third Artillery Continental Troops. His name appears on a roll and receipt for material in September 1779. The date of his discharge is not given. He was paid eight dollars for building a hut at Valley Forge, Pennsylvania, in 1778.

Caleb Grainger Jr. Served as a captain in the First Regiment North Carolina Battalion from its first establishment September 1, 1775, to September 1, 1778. He was promoted to major but resigned his commission at White Marsh (Whiteville) on April 26, 1777.

John Best Sr. Served in North Carolina Militia during the Revolutionary War.

John Best Jr. Served for twelve months in 1781. His testimony made on April 6, 1835, in the Inferior Court of Screven County for pension states he was born in Dobbs County. However, he served from Duplin County under Captain Joseph Rhodes, Major Blount, and Colonel James Armstrong, who received seventy-two thousand acres of land in Tennessee for his military services.[192] John fought under General Nathaniel Greene at the Battle of Eutaw Springs and was wounded. He also served with David Quinn and Thomas Canaday. The Battle of Eutaw Springs on September 8, 1781, in present-day Orangeburg County ended any designs the British had envisioned in keeping South Carolina. John, among others, is listed as serving in the Revolution in North Carolina.[193] His unit also served at Stono Ferry on June 20, 1779, and the Siege of Augusta from May 21, 1781, to June 1, 1781. Thus, perhaps John was at the Siege of Augusta. The British commander there surrendered to Continental soldiers from North Carolina, which further indicates John may have been there.

Seven years of British determination to bring South Carolina to her knees met failure. The spirit that had long resisted royal edict and church canon, the fierce desire and indomitable will to be masters of their own destinies, and the dauntless courage that had carved a new way of life from a wilderness were again threatened by oppression; so little difference was felt among nationalities and creeds, causing a unity to grow among the new-world "peasants and shepherds" that shook the foundations of old regimes.[194]

John Best's war records of ninety pages are on file at the National Archives.

Noah Lee Sr. Served in the Revolutionary War and listed on a payment record of Colonel Moses Hazen's Regiment of Foot as being paid by Captain Moses White for services from June until October of 1778.

During this period, the unit was transferred from the Second Maryland Brigade to the Northern Department for a planned invasion of Quebec. However, the planned attack was plagued with staffing and supply issues, so Congress called it off in March. The unit was reassigned to the Highland Department in April, relieved of this assignment in July, assigned to the New Hampshire Brigade, and sent to White Plains, New York, to guard British-occupied New York. Noah is included in the 1932 North Carolina Daughters of the American Revolution book, *Roster of Soldiers from North Carolina in the American Revolution*.[195]

William Walters Sr. Born in Dobbs County (now Lenoir), married Celia Dawson from Wayne County, and served as a captain during the Revolutionary War. He and family moved to Robeson County in 1794 and lived near the Lumber River. His great-granddaughter, Absillia M. Nance, married Emory Lorenzo Williamson.

Absalom Powell Sr. 1752–1832. State of North Carolina, County of Columbus: Court of Pleas and Quarter Sessions November Term 1832.[196]

On November 12, 1832, Powell, then eighty years old, appeared in open Court before the Worshipful Moore Lennox, Bythel Haynes, and Lot Williamson Justices of the Peace—Lot Williamson is also an ancestor through my mother—"who being first duly sworn according to law, doth on his oath, make the following declaration, in order to obtain the benefit of the Act of Congress passed June 7, 1832. That he entered the service of the United States under the following named officers, and served as herein stated."[197]

He entered the service as a private in a company of Bladen Militia commanded by Captain Thomas Amis (pronounced "Amy")[198]— John Yates was lieutenant and Barnabas Stevens was ensign—in the month of March 1776, shortly after the commencement of hostilities with Great Britain. He then resided in that part of Bladen County, now called Columbus. The company was called into service to prevent the Tories, who had collected in considerable force at Fayetteville (then Cross Creek) from making their way to Old Brunswick below Wilmington, where a British vessel of war, called the *Old Cruiser*, was stationed. On his first tour of service, Powell participated at the Battle of Moore's Creek Bridge.

The pension statement reads:
> Shortly after this expedition, the country was in such a troubled state, that the influence of the laws was scarcely felt, and no regular commissions could be obtained—one-half, or nearly so, of the population of Bladen County, then embracing within its limits the counties of Robeson and Columbus, and part of Cumberland, were disaffected. The Tories would frequently collect in large bodies, as the tide of affairs would take a favorable turn for them, plundering and murdering the peaceful inhabitants, who would not take sides with them. At that juncture, and about three years before the close of the War, he received a brevet Commission as Captain of a Militia Company, in that part of Bladen, now called Columbus County, from a regimental Court Martial, which convened at Elizabethtown Bladen County, and as well as he recollects the Commission was signed by Colonel Thomas Robeson and Colonel Thomas Brown, Field Officers of the Bladen Regiment.[199]

Of significant note is two of my other grandfathers provided testimony to Powell's service:

Pierce Godwin and John Wingate personally appeared in open court on the 12th day of November 1832. Pierce Godwin and after being duly sworn according to law doth on his oath depose as follows: That he recollects that Absalom Powell, the above applicant for a Pension, was a Captain of a Company of Bladen Militia for two or three years before the close of the Revolutionary War. Godwin states he was frequently engaged in active service against the Tories, in different parts of the Country that this Deponent was in two or three expeditions under Powell as a Private against the Tories, but he has no recollection of the particulars.

John Wingate, who after being duly sworn according to law, doth on his oath depose as follows: That he recollects that Absalom Powell, the above applicant for a pension was a Captain of a Company of Bladen Militia at the close of the Revolutionary War.[200]

Powell was frequently engaged in expeditions against the Tories in the adjoining country. Wingate went with him twice as a private in his company against the Tories, over Drowning Creek. On May 14, 1839, Powell's wife Mary Browne Stephens filed for a widow's pension under the 1838 Act, stating she is the widow of Absalom Powell; she married him on March 7, 1774; and he died on October 14, 1834. Powell appears on the North Carolina 1835 pension rolls along with Theophilus Coleman, John Fowler, and Pierce Godwin.

Interesting note on Powell—my research indicates he purchased around fifteen hundred acres near Fair Bluff. The cemetery where my grandparents Gordon and Hazel, brother Patrick, and great-aunt Emma Page Byrd are buried is known as Powell Cemetery and may be land which Absalom originally owned.

Barnabus Stephens. 1730–1978. Was the father of Mary Browne Stephens Powell. His first land grants in Bladen (Columbus County) are dated 1767. He served as an ensign in a body of county militia raised in March of 1776 and later served as a colonel in the county militia. Records indicate he was granted two hundred acres of land on the branch of Western Prong and around Porter Swamp. Mary inherited his lands in Western Prong and later sold to Thomas Wooten.

Felix Kenneth Powell Sr. 1785–1850. Participated in the Florida Wars and served in Harllee's Battalion, South Carolina Militia. He additionally served in the War of 1812 in Gasque's Battalion, Captain Elisha Bethea's Company of South Carolina Militia, rising from a private to a sergeant. He was the son of Absalom and Mary Stephens Brown. Fleix and Mary Fipp's daughter Elizabeth Powell married Caleb Spivey Sr., and their son Jesse James Spivey married Sarah "Sallie" Baker, whose daughter Elizabeth Spivey was Grandma Hazel Turbeville Page's maternal grandmother.[201]

William Baker. 1739–1823. Was the great-grandfather of Sarah Baker Spivey. He is noted in Sellers's *History of Marion County* as moving from New Bern, North Carolina around 1740 and settling in Marion County, South Carolina. Sellers states he was prominent in the Revolution and noted for his dedication to the cause of liberty.[202] His Revolutionary War service is documented by the South Carolina Archives and a Sons of the American Revolution application in File AA 252, Indent # 308 Book R at the State of South Carolina Archives.

Nicholas R. Prince. 1758–1839. On my great-grandmother's death certificate, her father is listed as Solomon Prince. Solomon's grandfather was Nicholas R. Prince. On the eighth day of November 1833, he appeared in court in Horry County, South Carolina, and filed a testimony for a Revolutionary pension. He stated that he was born in Robeson County, that while he was young his family moved to Catfish in Marion County, South Carolina, and that when he was about three years old, they moved to Horry District (County), then called Kingstown Parish. He entered service in June of 1776 in Captain Dennis Hawkins's Company, and then that company and several others were placed under the command of Captain William Snow and were sent to Sullivan's Island, South Carolina. He was at Fort Moultrie when the British were repulsed. The regiment marched to Savannah, and he witnessed the siege of Savannah and saw Count Pulaski fall when he was hit by "grape shot." Prince states, "after a bloody and obstinate engagement with the enemy of two hours' duration the American Army was defeated with great loss." The regiment marched back to Charleston and was there when Charleston fell to the British. He states this took place in March of 1780. He was taken prisoner by the British for thirteen days but "effected his escape." He then joined the army of General Francis Marion (the Swamp Fox) at a place called Watboo (Wadboo), not far from Charleston.

War of 1812
Richard Fowler. My fourth great-uncle and son of John Fowler served as a private under Captain Caleb Stevens, Major Lindsay, North Carolina Militia.

William Walters Jr. Served in the Eleventh Company, Robeson County Regiment.

Elijah Worley. Served as a corporal in Major Lillington detachment, North Carolina Militia.[203]

Corneilus "Cade" Neil Barfield. Served in First Regiment Robeson County, North Carolina.

Joshua Williamson. Sheriff of Columbus County during the War of 1812 and first sheriff of Columbus County, North Carolina.

Joseph Gore. Served as a private in Captain Caleb Stephens's Company, the Fourth Regiment North Carolina Militia. He enlisted on October 10, 1814, and served until March 10, 1815.[204]

Hinnant Faulk. One of my grandfathers four times removed is listed in muster rolls of soldiers of the War of 1812 under Captain C. Stephens. Detached from the Militia of North Carolina in 1812. Hinnant's pension application for the War of 1812 can be found in the National Archives. Hinnant lived in the southern portion of Robeson County and complained to the sheriff in December of 1867 that a Bundy Ford and a Sally Page stole and killed and ate two of his hogs. Evidently, he had interactions with the Pages of that portion of Robeson County where they straddled the state line. The relationships with Hinnant's neighbors may explain why there is an advertisement for the sale of his plantation in 1850 in the newspaper. The ad notifies the public the plantation consists of two thousand acres on the junction of Ashpole and Hog Swamps in the White House community of Robeson County, fifteen miles south of Lumberton on the Georgetown Road.

John Lee Sr. Served in Captain Woodward's South Carolina Militia from November 7 until December 15, 1814.

Civil War

The following are children of Amelia Ann "Millie" Fowler and Stephen Wright of Tabor City, Columbus County, North Carolina. They're all third great-uncles and brother of Ann Wright Fowler (my third great-grandmother).

Isaac Wright, Second Lt. Fifty-Seventh Regiment, Columbus County, Fourteenth Brigade; listed in the Fifth Regiment Home Guard under Captain Frink on November 25, 1864.

Zechariah Wright. Home Guard, Columbus County; served under Major B. Smith in Whiteville.

McLennon Wright. Home Guard, Columbus County; served under Major B. Smith in Whiteville.

Isaac Fowler. Husband of Ann Wright Fowler and son of Peter Fowler; served as a private in Captain David Callihan's Company, Eighth Senior Reserves.

James Calvin Wright. Home Guard, Columbus County; served under Major B. Smith in Whiteville.

Richard Wright. Served in Captain McDugald's Company and in Company E in August of 1863, Second Regiment; discharged for disability in November of 1863.

John Wright. Served in the Seventh Company, Fourteenth North Carolina Infantry.

Kinyon Wright. Company D, Twentieth North Carolina Infantry, wounded at Gettysburg, paroled at Appomattox Courthouse; served the entire duration of the war.

Stephen Wright Jr. Served in Captain McDugald's Company.

Fleet Cooper Wright. Company D, Twentieth North Carolina Infantry, wounded at the battle of Malvern Hill; died on September 4, 1862, in Richmond, Virginia.

Simpson Wright. Company D, Twentieth North Carolina Infantry; served in the Home Guard in Columbus County in 1864, listed with rigidity of the joints and rheumatoid arthritis.

Hanson Wright. Company D, Twentieth North Carolina Infantry; killed at the battle of Malvern Hill.

The following are all first cousins, four times removed, and nephews of Anne Wright Fowler, my three-times-removed great-grandmother:

Manuel Wright. Company D, Twentieth North Carolina Infantry, son of Isaac Wright and Elizabeth Norris Wright; captured at Gettysburg and sent to Fort Delaware and was exchanged at City Point, Virginia; captured again at Spotsylvania Courthouse, Virginia, and confined to Point Lookout Prison in Maryland and transferred to Elmira, New York, on October 11, 1864; was exchanged again at Venus Point in Savannah, Georgia, on November 15, 1864.

Simeon Wright. Son of Zechariah and Lydia Norris Wright; served in Major Smith's Home Guard in Whiteville in February of 1864 when he was nineteen.

Doctor Franklin Wright. Son of Zechariah and Lydia Norris Wright, Seventh Battalion North Carolina Junior Reserves and Company I, Third Regiment North Carolina Junior Reserves; was hospitalized at Goldsboro, North Carolina, and survived the war.

John W. Wright. Son of McLennon and Sarah Williams Wright, Company B, Seventh North Carolina Junior Reserves, which was also known as Captain John D. Kerr's Company, Fourth District Reserve Force.

The following are children of Return Page Sr. and Sarah Ann Grainger. Sarah was the granddaughter of Lt. John Grainger, who served in the Revolutionary War, and his wife, Charity Buffkin. According to the 1850 Census, they lived in Horry County.

Return Wade Hampton Page Jr.. Served in Company H, Twenty-Third South Carolina Infantry (Hatch's Coastal Rangers). Return was listed as a POW captured by Captain Rodgers on the North East Rail Road 17, May 1863 near Vicksburg, MS. He enlisted for twelve months in November of 1861. Paid $25.00 at Mt. Pleasant, SC Dec 1863.

He was detached to Ft. Sumter in January–February of 1864 and then to James Island March–May 1864, he was listed as AWOL in June of 1864 and until February 1865. He was arrested by Provo Marshall but there is no date on the document.

Abraham "Abram" Beaty Page. Brother of Return Page, Jr. and William M. Page, served in Hatch's Coastal Regiment with his brother. Abraham follows a similar history according to the records but there is no record of him being captured near Vicksburg, M.S. as Return was. Abraham was also listed as AWOL in June 1864.

William Marion Page twin of Return Page, Jr. Served in Company F, S.C., 1st Infantry Provisional Army (McCreary's). He enlisted on April 1864 at Conwayboro, SC (now Conway) and was captured near Petersburg, VA on June 22, 1864. He was exchanged November 1, 1864 at Point Lookout, MD and received at Venus Point, Savannah, GA Nov 15, 1864, no further records exist.

Samuel C. Page. Older brother of William and Return Jr. Page, Company F, (Horry Rebels), commanded by Lt. Col Thomas P Alston, First Regiment, South Carolina Infantry also known as McCreary's First Provisional Army; wounded at Gettysburg in July 1863. Listed at a hospital in Charlottesville, VA on July 12 1863, furloughed on July 24, 1863, and was back in Jackson General Hospital in Richmond, VA on October 31, 1863. He was back in the hospital again in November of 1863 and furloughed in April of 1864. I have found no evidence of him after the war thus, he may have subsequently died of the wounds received at Gettysburg.

The following are other members of my family tree:
William Henry Harrison Grainger. Father of Arabella Grainger, enlisted in the Company C, First Heavy Artillery in April 1862. He determined the war was not suited to his preference, so he deserted July 28, 1862. Thus, there is no known evidence he was ever captured or punished by authorities for his desertion.

Return Strong Worley. Brother of Alfred Martine Jonch Worley, served in Company D, Second North Carolina Artillery, Thirty-Sixth State Troops. He enlisted March 14, 1862, for the duration of the war, and he was enlisted by Captain E.B. Dudley. He was captured at Fort Fisher on January 15, 1865. He was released at Point Lookout,

Maryland, on June 3, 1865, after taking an oath of allegiance to the United States. He is listed as admitted to the CSA General Hospital Number Four in Wilmington from July 16, 1863, until July 23, 1863, furloughed to Fair Bluff.

Alfred Martine Jonch Worley. Enlisted in Captain Nathan L. Williamson's Cape Fear Regiment, Company E of Artillery. He was captured at Fort Fisher on January 15, 1865. There is no record of when he was paroled, but he lived until 1906. Dennis Worley, a descendant of Martine and an attorney in Tabor City, relates a story concerning Martine's imprisonment at a Union prisoner-of-war camp. When the Union army began paroling people, they did so alphabetically. When no one answered to the last name that started with a *B*, Martine raised his hand, took the person's identity, and was released. When released, he walked home from Maryland to Cherry Grove in Columbus County.

Absolam Benjamin Turbeville. Served as a private in Company H, Twenty-Third South Carolina Infantry, and enlisted on May 9, 1862, at James Island, South Carolina. In January and February of 1864, he was detached to Fort Sumter, South Carolina. From March until June of 1864, he was absent without leave but returned to duty on June 30, 1864. Absolam was taken prisoner as a part of the Army of Northern Virginia, Wallace's Brigade, when General Robert E. Lee surrendered his army to Lieutenant General Ulysses S. Grant on April 9, 1865. His final muster record lists him as a "Prisoner of War belonging to the Army of Northern Virginia."

George Washington Turbeville. Served in the Twenty-Third South Carolina Infantry, Company H, Hatch's Coastal Regiment and enlisted on December 11, 1861, at James Island, South Carolina. He was taken prisoner by the forces of the United States under the command of Major General J.G. Foster and paroled near Kinston, North Carolina, on December 14, 1862. He appears on a list of patients at a military hospital in Wilmington, North Carolina, on April 8, 1863, and returned to duty April 12. He also appears on a list of prisoners taken by US Captain Rodgers on North Eastern Railway on May 17, 1863.

Willis H. Turbeville. Served as a private in Company I, Thirty-First Louisiana Infantry. He died or was killed during the siege of Vicksburg. I state it this way because he is listed as sick in camp in January and February of 1863 and as captured at Vicksburg on July 4, 1863. I conclude he must have subsequently died from his illness at Vicksburg because he signed the parole on July 9, 1863.

Reuben Fowler Jr. Served in Company D, Twentieth North Carolina Regiment, Captain J.B. Stanley's Company. Died of disease at Smithfield, North Carolina, on January 5, 1862.

Calvin Turbeville. May have died of pneumonia during the battle of Williamsburg, as Kershaw's Brigade was part of General John Bankhead Magruder's command at this battle.[205]

Brazil or Braswell Strickland. Mustered into service on June 15, 1861, at Fort Caswell, Oak Island, Wilmington, North Carolina, Eighteenth Regiment North Carolina Volunteers. On June 18, 1862, he was sent to Chesapeake, US General Hospital, Fort Monroe, Virginia. The remarks state he was sent to Fort Delaware. The injury he sustained is listed as an ankle wound. He is also listed as being captured at Williamsburg on May 6, 1862, and exchanged on July 16, 1862, by a detachment of New York Volunteers. He was wounded again at the battle of Hanover Courthouse and captured once more by the Army of the Potomac on May 27, 1961. His name appears on a list of Confederates wounded in the Gaines's Hospital on June 5, 1862. Finally, he was discharged by the unreadable Act of 1862 in January or February of 1863.

David Formyduval Williamson. Served as a private in Captain L. Williamson's Company of Columbus Artillery and was mustered in on March 12, 1862. He is listed as hospitalized in Wilmington in October of 1864 and was then captured at Fort Fisher on January 15, 1865. The Columbus County books list him as a prisoner at Elmira, New York, which is consistent with the other Confederates captured at Fort Fisher. He survived and moved to the Panhandle of Florida, where he died.

Lennie or Lennirue Williamson. Enlisted on April 23, 1862, and then deserted on September 1, 1862. He survived the war and married Catherine Jane Worley.

Obadiah Williamson. Served as a lieutenant on the muster rolls of Company E of the Thirty-Sixth North Carolina State Troops. He served in Captain Nathan L. Williamson's Columbus Artillery beginning March 12, 1862. He was elected to an officer's position that same day, and his successor is listed as Hezekiah D. Williamson. He was detached to Smithfield by order of Maj. General Whiting in July–August 1864. The muster also states he was in Herbert's Brigade, Whiting's Division, Beauregard's Corps of the Army of Northern Virginia. He is listed as a prisoner of war at Point Lookout, Maryland, as captured at Bentonville, North Carolina, on March 19, 1965, and as transferred to Washington, DC, on April 3, 1865. He was released on oath on June 17, 1865.

Dallis Martin Williamson. Enlisted in N.L. Williamson's artillery, was captured at Fort Fisher, sent to Elmira, and paroled on July 11, 1865. Dallis was the son of Laban Williamson and Sarah Ann Nance. He died in Georgia in 1931.

Wright Williamson. The brother of Emery Lorenzo Williamson, served in Company D of the Thirty-Sixth State Troops when he was thirty-six years old. He was admitted to the hospital with malaria on December 24, 1864. Unsure of death, but his widow, Zylphia Strickland Williamson, applied for a pension in 1902 as a result of his service to North Carolina.

Joseph Wilbur Williamson. The brother of Emery Lorenzo Williamson, captured at Fort Fisher on January 15, 1865, when he was thirty-four years old and sent to Elmira, New York, where he died on June 21, 1865, of chronic diarrhea.

Daniel S. Williamson. The brother of Emery Lorenzo Williamson, served in Company E, Thirty-Sixth State Troops. He was thirty years old when he was captured at Fort Fisher on January 15, 1865, and died at Elmira, March 14, 1865, of chronic diarrhea. Richard H. Triebe incorrectly lists Daniel Williamson as being from Brunswick County in his book *Fort Fisher to Elmira*. Daniel may have enlisted in Brunswick, but he was a Williamson from Cerro Gordo, Columbus, and the son of my three-times-removed great-grandfather Elias Williamson.[206]

Nathan Lewis Holmes. Brother of Emery Lorenzo Williamson, served in Captain Burrell Smith's Company, Fair Bluff Volunteers, originally Company C of the Tenth Regiment and later Company C of the Twentieth Regiment. He fought at Mechanicsville, Cold Harbor,

Malvern Hill, Fredericksburg, Chancellorsville, and Gettysburg. He was captured at Gettysburg on July 1, 1862, and paroled at Point Lookout, Maryland, on February 18, 1865.

Elias Harvey Williamson. Brother of Emery Lorenzo Williamson, tried to volunteer for the Thirty-Sixth State Troops on March 12, 1862, but was rejected for being too young—he was sixteen. Thank God; otherwise, he would have died at Elmira too. The Union and the state of North Carolina took enough of the sons of Elias and Dorothy Holmes Nance Williamson as it was.

Marmadine D. Williamson. Brother of Emery Lorenzo Williamson; was wounded on July 1, 1862, promoted to sergeant on May 3, 1863, and killed at the Battle of Gettysburg on July 1, 1863. He fought at Mechanicsville, Cold Harbor, Malvern Hill, Sharpsburg, Chancellorsville, Fredericksburg, and Gettysburg.

Alonzo Williamson. Served as a private and then promoted to corporal. He enlisted May 7, 1861, at Whiteville by Captain William H. Toon's Company, Columbus County Guards No. 2, Tenth Regiment North Carolina Infantry, which became Company Koff Regiment. The Tenth subsequently became the Twentieth North Carolina Infantry by Special Order No. 222 on November 14, 1861. He was at Fort Caswell in July of 1861. He received a bounty of fifty dollars on March 1, 1862. He was captured at Gettysburg, according to the muster rolls, on July 1, 1863. However, in the *Columbus County, North Carolina Heritage* book, he is listed as wounded at Gaines' Mill and again at Pickett's Charge, captured and held prisoner at Fort Delaware, and released June 19, 1865. The muster rolls confirm he was wounded June 28, 1862, which coincides with the battle of Gaines' Mill. The rolls do also confirm he was sent to Fort Delaware, and the date written is July 1, 1863. The date of parole is also listed as June 19, 1865, on the muster rolls. My conclusion is he was part of Iverson's blunder on the first day of the battle at Gettysburg.

Alvin D.B. Williamson. Served in Company K of the Twentieth North Carolina and was enlisted by Captain Toon. He appears on a list of elected officers on April 26, 1862 as a first lieutenant but is shown as resigned on October 8, 1862. His signed letter of resignation is enclosed from the Rebel Archives, stating he feels he is unable to fulfill the duties of the office. The letter is dated September 24, 1862. Special Order 235 accepted his resignation.

Alvin must have gone back to Columbus County, as he enlisted in the Captain Oliver H. Powell's Company E of the 36th Regiment in February of 1863. This was same company started by Nathan Lewis Williamson, and then when he resigned, Powell took command. Alvin was captured at the fall of Fort Fisher and was sent to Point Lookout, Maryland. He was paroled between the dates of 12–14 May, 1865.

Hosea Williamson. Served in Company E, Artillery Thirty-Sixth State Troops and enlisted March 12, 1862. He was captured at Fort Fisher on January 15, 1865, when he was twenty years old and sent to Elmira, New York, as a prisoner. He was paroled on July 11, 1865, under General Orders Number 109 from the AGO dated June 6, 1865.[207]

Shelton Williamson. Served in the Twentieth North Carolina Infantry. He was promoted to corporal on May 2, 1862. He was wounded and disabled at Cold Harbor and was left at a hospital in Pennsylvania on July 4. He appears on a list of Rebel sick and wounded received at Decamp General Hospital in David's Island, New York Harbor, in July of 1863. David's Island was originally only a Union hospital, but it treated twenty-five thousand Confederates after the Battle of Gettysburg. He complained of a hand and side wound. Records indicate he was at Mechanicsville, Cold Harbor, Fredericksburg, Chancellorsville, and Gettysburg, wounded and disabled on July 1, 1863. Shelton died at a hospital in Petersburg, Virginia, on December 24, 1863, of tuberculosis.

Return Williamson. Enlisted in Captain Burrell Smith's Fair Bluff Volunteers. He fought at Mechanicsville, Gaines' Mill, Malvern Hill, South Mountain, Sharpsburg, and Chancellorsville. He was wounded in the shoulder at Gettysburg. He was taken prisoner but not listed as taken prisoner until July 4, 1863. He was sent to Fort McHenry, Maryland. There is no record of him being exchanged, but he was at the Episcopal Church Hospital in Williamsburg, Virginia, in August of 1863 and transferred to Farmville Hospital on August 28, 1863. Since there are no other records, the assumption is the wound ended his military stint, and he went home.

Nathan Lewis Williamson. Represented Columbus County in the North Carolina House from 1842 to 1849 and again from 1860 to 1861 and served as clerk of court for Columbus County, resigning on February 16, 1856. He formed a company known as Captain N. Williamson's Unattached Company of Artillery. This unit was mustered in at Wilmington on March 12, 1862. He was listed in Captain Lamb's Artillery at Fort Caswell but resigned his commission on September 13, 1862, and was replaced by Oliver H. Powell.

On December 1, 1886, Nathan's obituary states "he died near Cerro Gordo, Columbus County, North Carolina, brother Nathan L.

Williamson, aged seventy-four years. Our friend and brother professed faith in the Lord Jesus Christ fifty years ago. A few days before his death, when talking to a near-relative regarding his spiritual condition, he remarked, 'I feel that all my sins are forgiven, and that I am ready to see God's face and live.' [...] He leaves nine children to mourn their loss, and among this number is H.D. Williamson, Senator-elect from Columbus County to the next legislature."

Haynes Leonard Williamson. Served in Company E, Thirty-Sixth State Troops. He transferred to this company from a Captain Stephenson's Company on August 4, 1862. He was discharged because of a disability on March 21, 1864. There is no indication of the nature of the disability.

James Colon Williamson. Tried to join his father's unit on March 17, 1862. Still, he was dropped, as he was prohibited from entering by the Conscription Act passed by Congress, and he belonged to Company A of the Twentieth North Carolina. He was killed at the Battle of Gettysburg on July 1, 1863. The exact location of his remains is unknown. Many Confederates dead at Gettysburg were dug up after the battle and relocated to Hollywood Cemetery in Richmond, and this is believed to be where he is.

Joshua Robert Williamson. Served in Company E, Thirty-Sixth NC Regiment when he was nineteen years old. He was captured at Fort Fisher on January 15, 1865, and died at Elmira, New York, of congestion in the lungs on February 15, 1865.[208]

Hezekiah Dwight Williamson. Served in Captain Burrell Smith's Fair Bluff Company and, eventually, the Twentieth North Carolina

Infantry. He was promoted on March 15, 1862, and transferred to the Thirty-Sixth North Carolina. The muster rolls state he was transferred to N.L. Williamson Artillery. There are no more records for him, but the assumption is he was captured at Fort Fisher and also became a prisoner.

Hezekiah Dwight Williamson. Went from Warsaw School to enlist in the Coast Artillery in 1842 and became the first lieutenant, serving at Fort Fisher and other battles on the coast. He went into the naval stores business in Cerro Gordo after the war and, in 1875, came to this section and was prominent in Red Shirt days.

The Red Shirts were part of a Democratic campaign to oppose the interracial coalition of Republicans and Populists, which had gained control of the state legislature in the 1894 election and elected a Republican governor in 1896. Such biracial coalitions had also occurred in other states across the South, in some cases overturning or threatening White Democratic control of state legislatures. Upper-class and middle-class White populations feared the empowerment of freedmen and poor Whites. To break up the coalition, White Democrats used intimidation and outright violence to reduce Black Republican voting and regained control of the state legislature in 1896. After the Democratic win in November, the Red Shirts disappeared from public view. Because their members were primarily poor Whites, the Democratic Party of elitist Whites parted ways with the group. Thus, the prevalence of Red Shirts declined upon the inauguration of Governor Charles Brantley Aycock. In 1912, Aycock was running for the Senate, and while making a speech in Alabama on Universal Education, he spoke for a few minutes, saying, "I have always talked about education." He then stopped, threw up his hands, reeled backward, and fell dead of a heart attack.

Williamson remained in Cerro Gordo for several years, conducted successful business ventures, and accumulated suitable property, which he held until failing health required his retirement. He served in both branches of the North Carolina legislature. And he was always known as a friend of the masses, ready to help a man get on and rise in the world.[209]

Levi C. Hays. Enlisted in Company F, North Carolina Fifty-First Infantry Regiment on April 21, 1862. He mustered out on April 28, 1862, and was promoted to full private on February 1, 1863. He reenlisted to Company F, North Carolina Fifty-First Infantry Regiment on February 1, 1863.

Erastus W. Hays. Enlisted on April 20, 1862, in the district of Marion, South Carolina, and was mustered into military service as a private in Company D of the Twenty-Fifth South Carolina Volunteer Infantry—the Eutaw Regiment. He died a prisoner of war in Alexandria, Virginia, as the result of receiving a gunshot wound to his neck during the battle at Weldon Railroad, Virginia, on August 21, 1864. A year earlier, he had received an injury during his regiment's defense of Battery Wagner on Morris Island, South Carolina.

Austin Grier Hays. Enlisted in Company D, Twenty-Fifth South Carolina Infantry, Eutaw Regiment. Possibly at Fort Fisher, he appears on a list of patients at CSA Hospital Number Four in Wilmington on December 26, 1864, with the complaint of chronic diarrhea. However, he was not captured at the second battle of Fort Fisher, as records indicated, he was captured at Town Creek during the battle of Wilmington on February 12, 1865. He was sent to Point Lookout, Maryland, took an oath of allegiance to the United States, and was paroled on June 28, 1865.

Regarding the battle of Wilmington, General Johnson Hagood had burned the only bridge across Town Creek to slow down Union Major General Jacob D. Cox and entrenched on the north side of the river. Cox was eager to attempt his encircling plan that, due to Hagood's retreat at Fort Anderson, the Federals had been unable to complete. The creek was not fordable, so on February 20, Cox's troops found a single flat-bottom boat in the river and used it to ferry three brigades across the creek while the fourth brigade skirmished with Hagood as a diversion. Hagood discovered the flanking movement and decided, since his position was now untenable, to retreat to Wilmington. He left two regiments to cover his retreat. The Federals then waded through the swamp and attacked the Confederate flank, routing the two regiments and taking 375 prisoners along with two pieces of artillery. The next day, Cox rebuilt the destroyed bridge, and Schofield's artillery crossed, along with Porter's gunboats. Both were within range of the city itself.[210]

General Bragg saw the hopelessness of the situation and ordered the city abandoned. On February 21, Cox's Division continued its march toward the city. Still, it was delayed by the destroyed bridges across the Brunswick River and by Confederate cavalry, while Hoke's Division continued to hold off Terry's command. Bragg evacuated Union prisoners located there while evacuating anything of military value; he also ordered bales of cotton and tobacco burned so they would not fall into Union hands, along with storehouses, foundries, shipyards, and ships. Bragg retreated with his forces at one o'clock in the morning on the twenty-second. Cox's corps entered the city after eight that morning, with Terry's forces entering an hour later.[211]

Noah Lee. Grandson of Noah Lee Sr.; served as a private in Company B, Tenth South Carolina Infantry. He was captured near Jonesboro-Rough-and-Ready, Georgia, on September 2, 1864, and died of chronic diarrhea at Third Ward Georgia Hospital outside of Augusta, Georgia.

Nathaniel Strickland. Went to Fort Fisher to see his sick son, who was also there. He was impressed into service by the Confederate army, captured by the Union army, and sent to prison at Elmira, New York. There he died of exposure and diarrhea.

World War I
William Austin Stokes Sr. Served in Battery B, 113 Artillery, Thirtieth Division "Old Hickory Division." He appears on the list of troops leaving Brooklyn on May 27, 1918, on the HMS *Armagh*, a converted British refrigeration ship. They returned to Newport News, Virginia, on March 18, 1919, and were disbanded at Camp Jackson, South Carolina, at the end of March in 1919. The battery arrived at Toul on August 26, 1918, and was immediately marched to the regimental echelon in the Foret de la Reine. It took part in the St. Mihiel offensive, having three men wounded at Thiacourt, and from there, it marched with the regiment to its position for the Argonne offensive.

After withdrawing from the Argonne, the battery was sent with the regiment to the Meuse Plains. While occupying positions in this sector, it was stationed at a little abandoned French village called Villiers for thirteen days. This position was nearer to the German lines than the position of any other battery in the brigade. During this period, it was constantly under observation from hostile airplanes and subjected to daily shelling by the enemy without returning the fire. It was the most dangerous position occupied by the battery during the entire war, and while no one was killed there, the escapes were more than fortunate. On the night that orders had been given to retire, the infantry got out first, and for three hours, this battery was the front line of the army at this place. The Germans, in some way, got wind of this and, just as the battery was withdrawing, subjected the position to the heaviest shelling it underwent during the war.

The armistice signing found the battery in position on the heights above the Meuse Plains, and here it remained until December 7, 1918, when it took up the march with the regiment for Luxemburg and the shore of the Moselle River. The battery proceeded with the regiment on its various marches, returned with it to Le Mans, France, and thence to America and was mustered out at Camp Jackson, South Carolina, on March 28, 1919. The members of the battery who were initially from Beaufort and surrounding counties proceeded to Washington, DC, as an organization. There they received the greatest "welcome home reception" Washington had ever witnessed from the assembled citizens of the entire surrounding country. Of the original 178 men who had departed with the battery, only 110 returned to enjoy the celebration, as some had been killed and others permanently scarred from the effects of war.[212] To illustrate the staggering preparation of the war and the enormous cost of wars, consider how, during the three hours preceding H hour, the Allies expended more ammunition than both sides managed to fire throughout the four years of the American Civil War. The cost was later calculated to have been "$180 million, or $1 million per minute."[213]

Pearly S. Page. Listed as being on troop transport ship *USS Harrisburg* when it departed from France on June 17, 1919. He arrived back in Hoboken, New Jersey, on June 26, 1919. He is listed as serving in the Thirteenth Company, Third Regiment Aviation Service Mechanics.

The Third was organized at Camp Greene, Charlotte, North Carolina, on April 15, 1918.

On June 30, 1918, the Third was ordered to Camp Upton in Long Island, New York, arriving on July 1, 1918. Four days later, they left for Hoboken, New Jersey. On July 9, they departed the United States and maintained a zigzag pattern across the Atlantic and arrived in Brest, France, on July 26, 1918. On September 15, 1918, an epidemic of the Spanish influenza broke out in camp for nearly a month. The hospital was full of soldiers. The captain who had recorded this praised the camp hospital for their efficient and capable handling of the outbreak.

David Kemper Page. Departed Newport News, Virginia, on October 23, 1918, with the Nineteenth Battery OCT, ARD Camp Jackson, home listed as Gallivants Ferry, South Carolina.

Charles Return Page. Departed with Company A, Third Pioneer Infantry, Sergeant, Service on July 11, 1919, from St. Nazaire, France, and arrived in Hoboken, New Jersey, on July 23, 1919. From what I have found, he was attached to the Third, which was formerly the Fifth Massachusetts Infantry. The unit arrived at Camp Wadsworth from Camp Greene on February 8, 1918, with thirty-five officers and 559 enlisted men who were commanded by Colonel Willis W. Stover and filled to wartime strength with draftees. The regiment left Camp Wadsworth on August 17 with 3,553 officers and men.[214]

World War II
In researching the children of Nathan Lewis Williamson, I discovered his granddaughter Agnes was married to Thomas Shelby Combs, who commanded the USS *Yorktown*. Nathan's granddaughter Ferdie Elsie was

married to Samuel Ginder, who commanded the USS *Enterprise* during World War II. Both are buried at Arlington National Cemetery.

In researching this cemetery, I discovered a granddaughter of Lucinda Williamson named Ruby C. Ward (Nathan Lewis Williamson's daughter) who served in World War II as a nurse. It was a pleasant surprise to see a descendant of a Williamson had contributed to the American victory in World War II. The contribution of women is often overlooked, but they have been vital to the triumph of America.

The information about these men and their descendants was given to me by John Williamson of Davidson, North Carolina, a retired professor of biology at Davidson College. He provided me with much insight into the Williamson family, who had moved to the Pensacola, Florida, area.

These women must have met their naval spouses while they were at the naval air station, the same place where I did my water survival training for the air force. It is interesting to think that I may have walked in some of the same areas as them. In 1930, Both Ferdie and Agnes and their spouses were on the Census as living in Coronado, San Diego. Again, I have landed on the same runway in my duties with the air guard as they may have used back in the 1930s and 1940s.

Ruby C. Ward Oestreich. Attended the Lumberton Hospital School of Nursing and enlisted in the army upon graduation. She worked with the Sixty-Fifth General Hospital in England for two years as first lieutenant. During her stay, she met her future husband, Dwight, who had been admitted with an eye injury. They married in St. Louis in 1946.

Joseph Nathan Williamson. Drafted into the army and added to a Connecticut National Guard unit. He served in the Buna and Papua New Guinea campaigns. He stated that toward the end of 1944, names were placed in a coffee can, and six who were drawn out were sent home. He was the sixth name pulled from the can. When he made it back to San Francisco Bay, he took everything he had from the war and tossed it into the bay. The only memories I have of him discussing the war are when he pulled out a book he had with the unit's members and pointed to him and his friend from Georgia named Whittenburg. The unit he had served in was an artillery unit, and he was a machine gunner. He was discharged from Fort Blanton, Florida, and made his way back to Williamson's Cross Roads. He lived there until his death in 2008.

William Gray Worley. Served, but I do not know the extent of his service. Pa Joe stated he was "in love with the uniform more than the Army." He made it through the war but died in his forties.

War on Terror

Jeffrey D. Page. Joined the Air Force at age seventeen. Mom and Dad dropped me off at the bus stop in Rock Hill, and from there, my career began. I served three years at Scott Air Force Base in Illinois and three at Taegu Air Base in Korea. After ten years, I rejoined the North Carolina Air National Guard in 1998. As of this writing, I have twenty-eight years in the service. At the guard, I was in the aerial port for six years, supply for two, and thus far, fourteen years as a loadmaster on C-130s and C-17s with the 156th Airlift Squadron or 145th Operations Support Squadron. I served as a combat veteran of Afghanistan with approximately one hundred hours of flight time in the country. As of writing this, I have 1,850 hours of flight time.

Brittany Elizabeth Page. Served the past nine years as a nurse in the 156th Aero-Medical Evacuation Squadron, North Carolina Air Guard.

CHAPTER 22
American Civil War

War between the States, 1861–1865

My ancestors' grandfathers fought, bled, and died to form a "more perfect union" of states, not necessarily a nation, during the Revolutionary War against their fellow Englishmen and the British. With the few exceptions of the Dutch and French blood that had mingled into my ancestry, it is almost exclusively British. Thus, when the English-speaking people of the Carolinas went to war against England in 1776, they were fighting family. Then in 1860, the same people went to war against each other again. Most of my ancestors cast their fate with St. Andrew's cross and tried again to form another nation. Some gave the last full measure of their blood, some threw up their hands and went home or AWOL, and many others manned their positions at Fort Fisher and played a pivotal role in keeping Robert E. Lee's Army of Northern Virginia in the war by keeping the Port of Wilmington open.

As I write this, I wish I had the pleasure of asking my ancestors, "Why did you fight? Did you fight to keep slavery or because North and South Carolina called you to do so?" The only thing I can conclude from my research is that the Civil War was more complex than I originally thought. It happened for more than one particular reason. Yes, the issue of slavery and a house divided had been the decisive reasons, but why did so many, who obviously had no stake in slavery, give their life to keep another human in bondage? There must have been many who wailed and cried at the lives that were sacrificed for the war. It must be devastating to lose not one but many family members to war. With the casualty rate as high as it was, I am still amazed that the twin brothers William and Return Jr. Page made it through the war. Had Return Page not have gone missing and philandering in Horry County, I and many others would not be here now. Such are the fortunes and misfortunes of war.

Benjamin Humphries, a planter from Sunflower County, Mississippi, who would become a general in the Confederate army, summarized this duality best:

> *My nativity fixed my allegiance to Mississippi. Beneath her soil, my ancestors and my children slept in death. All I had dear on earth, family, friends, and property welded me to that soil by the strongest cement of nature. Her God was my God; her people were my people; her interests were my interests; her sympathies were my sympathies; I could not, did not deliberate after the war was inaugurated and brought to her door-sills. I cast my lot with my mother state, and as she had crossed the Rubicon, I determined to march with her armies, whether her warpath led to Rome or ruin.*[215]

Thomas Jefferson once said, "I tremble for my country when I reflect that God is just; that his justice cannot sleep forever." Indeed, the wrath of God brought the war to the United States, and poor farmers and planters alike were caught in the maelstrom. It is generally agreed 620,000 Americans died in the Civil War.[216] North Carolina had 30,000 deaths, and South Carolina had 15,000. However, recently, the number of deaths has been raised. "By combing through newly digitized census data from the 19th century, J. David Hacker, a demographic historian from Binghamton University in New York, has recalculated the death toll and increased it by more than 20 percent to 750,000."[217] This would correlate to a death rate of 7.2 million today, applying the same percentage to the current US population.

Returning to my family, I have discovered evidence some owned one to twenty slaves, but as Lincoln had pointed out, both the North and South bear responsibility for this, not just those who had come into the South's social structure by birth. Governor Zebulon Vance of North Carolina, who served as a colonel in the Twenty-Sixth North Carolina Infantry, noted North Carolina "was the last to move in the drama of secession."[218]

In February of 1861, thousands of America's people declared their intent to remain in the Union by a majority. The fall of Fort Sumter and President Lincoln's call for seventy-five thousand volunteers changed the majority of opinion in North Carolina, and she cast her fate with her Southern sisters seceding from the Union. Once the Tar Heels moved, there was no hesitation, and the state furnished one-sixth of the soldiers for the Confederacy. The major issue for North Carolina was jeopardizing its economic success, as it was not as dependent upon slavery as Deep South states. The large Yeoman farmers and Whigs (political party) in the states were not ideologically connected to slavery.[219] I think had Lincoln taken a different tactic, perhaps North Carolina, Tennessee, and Virginia would have stayed in the Union.

Some soldiers had to decide whether to support the Union and fight against relatives or to put family and state first. I honor their courage and the memory of those who died fighting.

Many of my ancestors in North Carolina laid down their farmers' coats and exchanged them for uniforms when North Carolina had abandoned the Union and cast her fortune with the other Southern states. One of these was James Colon Williamson, my three-times-removed great-grandfather's nephew. According to a historian at Gettysburg National Military Park, James was killed in action on July 1, 1863, at Gettysburg. The Twentieth North Carolinian Infantry was assigned to a brigade commanded by Brigadier General Alfred Iverson. James was with his fellow North Carolinians when the entire brigade was caught in a cross fire of Union bullets, resulting in the loss of 253 out of the 372 present for duty that day. This is an astonishing 68 percent casualty rate. In comparison, Pickett's Charge on the last day of battle, July 3, 1863, suffered slightly over 50 percent casualties.[220]

An article in the *Gettysburg Compiler* notes an elaborately coordinated assault on Oak Hill by the division of Maj. Gen. Robert E. Rodes with the brigades of Col. Edward A. O'Neal and Iverson. The attack fell apart for multiple reasons. Rodes acted somewhat hastily, seeing limited Union forces at his front and not noticing Union reinforcements were arriving from the town to augment the Union defensive line. O'Neal used only three of his four brigades and attacked in a place other than instructed. Iverson stood safely away from the melee, observing from a distance.[221] In the words of the historian of the Twenty-Third North Carolina, "Unwarned, unled as a brigade, went forward Iverson's deserted band to its doom."[222]

Writing in the *Gettysburg Compiler*, Zachary Wesley records the following:

> *When the Tar Heels got within fifty yards, the Federals rose and opened fire, knocking massive holes into the Confederate ranks. The stunning ranks then attempted to return fire before falling back into a gully over which they had previously advanced. Within twenty minutes, white handkerchiefs appeared along the edge of the gully—the Confederates were surrendering. Over 900 of Iverson's 1,384 men had been killed, wounded, or captured. Meanwhile, Alfred Iverson remained comfortably in the rear, enraged at the supposed cowardice of his men. In recalling the disastrous assault, Iverson recalled, "I saw white handkerchiefs raised, and my line of battle still lying down in position, I characterized the surrender as disgraceful, but when I found afterward that five hundred of my men were left lying dead and wounded on a line as straight as a dress parade, I exonerated [...] the survivors. The dead remained in neat, packed rows. Their boots remained in a straight line, as if they were standing in formation; the blood flowed like streams, staining the ground crimson."*[223]

In contrast to Iverson's decision to remain at the rear of the battle, a subordinate lauded Union General Henry Baxter for his gallantry in action at Oak Hill: "I wish to say one word outside of my Regiment in regard to Generals Baxter and Robinson. They were on every part of the field, encouraging and stimulating the men by their presence and bravery." The following is a detailing of the action from the Union perspective:

According to author Harry W. Pfanz:

At a range of about eighty yards, Baxter shouted, his colors and muskets rose and his brigade delivered perhaps the most killing brigade-size volley of the war, mowing down rank upon rank of North Carolina's sons, in almost perfect lines. Iverson's brigade, 1,350 men of the 5th, 12th, 20th, and 23rd

North Carolina Regiments had walked straight into the trap, leaderless. Baxter's men kept up a hot and rapid-fire on the survivors, some of whom chose to fire back, others waving handkerchiefs in an effort to surrender, but there was no escape, no moving forward, and no retreat. They were at the mercy of Baxter's men. To make matters worse for the Southerners, Cutler's men moved up and joined in on the firing. The 12th North Carolina to the far left (North) of the formation was the least bloodied yet lost over a third of its men in the ambush—a depression of ground also aided them in escaping further casualties. Baxter taking the situation in hand, shouted, "Up, boys! And give them steel!" The Yankees climbed over the wall and rushed toward Iverson's torn brigade, taking 322 prisoners. Almost twice that number lay upon the ground, killed or wounded. Baxter's brigade, in action against the North Carolinians, took three Battle Flags. Some men of Iverson's Brigade escaped, the 23rd. NC could count thirty-four men in its ranks after the fight, and it suffered 89 percent casualties in just a few moments against Baxter's men. Most of the dead lay in a perfect line, just as they fell to the first volley.[224]

Iverson earned a lasting enmity of his men and was relieved of his command by General Robert E. Lee on July 19, 1863. The historian at the Gettysburg National Military Park states the Tar Heels who were killed that day were buried on the field or at a military hospital until 1872, when an effort was made to move them to Hollywood Cemetery in Richmond, Virginia. The subsequent years from their death resulted in only 60 percent of the bodies identified. James is also one of those who will forever be unknown. Captured at Fort Fisher, James subsequently died of "congestion of the lungs" at Elmira, New York, because of the poor conditions.

In researching the camp, I have realized it is a wonder anyone survived. When rats became a problem at the prison camp, a medium-sized black dog was used to catch them. Rat meat was sold to prisoners for five cents, but few could afford it. Eventually, two Rebel soldiers from North Carolina were sent to the guardhouse for thirty days after they captured and cooked the dog. Insufficient food, extreme bouts of dysentery, typhoid, pneumonia, smallpox, inadequate medical care, and flooding of the Chemung River resulted in the deaths of almost 25 percent of the prisoners at the Elmira Prison Camp. Prisoners dubbed the camp "Hellmira." My fellow Americans took pleasure in gazing upon the Rebels as circus animals and not Americans. An observation platform with chairs and binoculars was built outside the prison camp across Water Street west of Hoffman Street. Visitors were charged ten cents apiece to look at the prisoners. Refreshments were sold to spectators while the Confederate soldiers starved. After the Civil War, a House committee that investigated the condition of prisoners in Confederate camps declared that evidence proved Confederates were determined to kill Union prisoners. However, the Union's mistreatment of its prisoners of war has been dismissed as a rumor for more than a century.[225]

Of Elmira's 12,122 detainees, 2,950 of them died—a death rate of 24.3 percent, says historian Michael Horigan in *Elmira: Death Camp of the North*. "During Elmira's 369 full days of existence," he writes, "the death rate averaged eight per day." James's and Joshua's deaths for the South resulted in James's unknown grave, but that is not the case with Joshua. John W. Jones, a former slave who arrived in Elmira via the Underground Railroad, became the sexton of Woodlawn Cemetery in 1859. He was in charge of the burial of each Confederate soldier who died during the existence of the Elmira Prison Camp and demonstrated a remarkable degree of benevolence toward the Confederates by burying them with dignity. Jones meticulously recorded and carefully attached to the lid of their coffin the name, rank, company and regiment, grave number, and date of death of every prisoner he and his staff buried. In addition, evidence has been found that he had the date of death written on a piece of paper, inserted in a tightly sealed bottle, and deposited with the remains.[226]

Sexton Jones was a very busy man, especially between September 1864 and May 1865, during which time the least number of burials a month was 208, and the greatest was 495. He was paid $2.50 to bury the Confederates. Jones employed and supervised as many as twelve men in digging the trenches, which contained the graves of the dead. To his immense credit, Sexton Jones was always present to see the burials were done correctly and reverently conducted. Thanks to his conscientious and humane efforts on behalf of these dead Confederate prisoners, their resting places were known to their grieving families and future generations. Thanks to Mr. Jones, they are not forgotten.

Jones was a slave on the Ellzey family plantation in Leesburg, Virginia. When the son of the Ellzeys' overseer, John R. Rollins, died at the prison camp, Jones arranged to send the body back to the family. A few years after the Civil War ended, Jones returned to the Ellzey family plantation, where he had been a slave, and was warmly received because of his dignified acts at Elmira Cemetery.[227] Because of his kindness, out of the almost three thousand buried at Elmira, only seven are listed as unknown.

The federal government declared the burial site a national cemetery on December 7, 1877. At war's end, prisoners received railway passes and enough money to get home. The camp was officially closed on July 5, 1865. The last Confederate prisoner left the Elmira Prison Camp on

September 27, 1865. All that remains today of Elmira Prison is a well-kept cemetery along the banks of the Chemung River.

According to author Walter Clark and an article published by the Columbus County's *New Reporter* in 1946, Corporal Alonzo Williamson of Company K of the Twentieth North Carolina was one of the first casualties of the Battle of Seven Pines when a bullet shot straight through him and hit T.F. Toon. This fact is also recorded in a state of North Carolina book entitled *The Histories of the Several Regiments and Battalions from North Carolina in the Great War 1861-1865, Volume II* on page 114.

A captain of Company K, Captain Thomas Fentress Toon distinguished himself and temporarily held the rank of brigadier general at Spotsylvania Courthouse but was reverted back to colonel when the original commander recovered from his wounds. Toon survived the war and served as mayor of Fair Bluff, North Carolina, in the lower house of the state legislature and as state superintendent of public instruction for Governor Charles Brantly Aycock. Governor Aycock committed his energy to tackle the sad state of education in North Carolina. While in office, he remained loyal to his pledge to work for universal education. When two bills to enable White people to tax themselves to improve schools for White children without improving schools for Black children were introduced in the legislature in 1901, Aycock stated he would resign if adopted. Both bills died in committee.[228]

PART V
Other Thoughts

CHAPTER 23
Returning to Those Old Bones

The Regiments

Thirty-Sixth Regiment, North Carolina Infantry. Many of my relatives fought with the Thirty-Sixth Regiment. They were also called the Cape Fear Regiment. The regiment was organized at Fort Caswell in May of 1862. Its companies were formed with men from Sampson, Cumberland, New Hanover, Columbus, Halifax, Brunswick, and Bladen Counties. The regiment was attached to the departments of North Carolina and southern Virginia and was active in defense of the Cape Fear River regions. Later in the war, eight companies were engaged at Fort Fisher, one at Fort Campbell, and one at Wilmington. In December of 1864, a detachment was also active in defense of Savannah. After the surrender of Fort Fisher, the remnant of the unit served as infantrymen at the Battle of Bentonville and surrendered with the Army of Tennessee at the end of the war. Many of this regiment were at Fort Fisher, and when it was captured, there were five Williamsons, three Stricklands, and one Coleman sent to the prison in Elmira, New York. Two of these men made it back to Columbus County.

Twentieth North Carolina Infantry Regiment. Many of my relatives also fought with the Twentieth. It was organized as the Tenth Infantry Regiment Volunteers at Smithfield and Fort Caswell. It was under the command of Colonel Alfred Iverson, son of a United States senator. Fair Bluff native Thomas Toon played a pivotal role in the company's history. The Twentieth served in North Carolina and then participated in campaigns with the Army of Northern Virginia in the Seven Days' Battles, the Maryland campaign, Fredericksburg, Chancellorsville, and Gettysburg. It surrendered with seventy-one men at Appomattox, of which only nine had weapons. The unit's original muster in 1862 was 1,012 men. The following is a take from the text of the monument at Gettysburg concerning the Twentieth:

> *July 1, 1863:* "The Brigade was one of the first of the Division in the battle. It advanced against the Union line posted behind a stone fence east of Forney Field. Its right being assailed by 2nd Brigade First Corps, and its left exposed by the repulse of O'Neal a vigorous assault by Union forces in front and on left flank almost annihilated three regiments. The 12th Regiment on the right, being sheltered by the knoll, suffered slight loss, and the remnants of the others joined Ramseur's Brigade and served with it throughout the battle."

Wingate Family Information
From the will of Ann Wingate:

> *I, Ann Wingate of the [above-mentioned] Province and County, being in my proper health and senses, thanks be to God for it, calling into mind the mortality of my body and knowing that it is appointed for all flesh once to die do make and ordain this my Last Will and*

Testament that is to say principally, and first of all I give and recommend my soul into the hands of God that gave it.

Secondly, my body to be buried in a Christian-like and decent manner at the discretion of my executors, nothing doubting but at the general resurrection I shall receive the same again by the mighty power of God. And as touching this-worldly estate wherewith, it hath pleased God to bless me in this life I give and dispose of it in the following manner and form.

I give to my well-beloved son John Wingate whom I do nominate and appoint my sole executor of this my Last Will and Testament, my negro man named Peter, likewise, my negro woman named Phillis with all my sheep and hogs, cattle excepting three cows and calves together with all my household goods except one pewter dish and three plates and one iron pot and blue colored and my wearing apparel to be equally divided between my son John's Wife and my daughter Mary Simmons. Likewise, all my horses and mares being more or less to my son John Wingate and I the said Ann Wingate do utterly disallow and revoke and disannul [sic] all other wills or forms or legacies or deeds of gift in any otherwise given or bequeathed unto any other person or persons whatsoever ratifying and confirming this and no other to be my Last Will and Testament. In Witness whereof, I have hereunto set my hand and seal in the Year of our Lord 1763. Witness: Thomas Sessions, Margaret Chicken, Hannah Wingate Children of Edward and Ann (Blount) Wingate.

It is through Ann Wingate that I am a descendant of James Blount, one of the first Virginians to move into eastern North Carolina (Chowan County) from the Isle of Wight in Virginia between 1660 and 1669.[229] The line runs from my grandfather Andrew Morgan Williamson to Isham Williamson to Rebecca Wingate and Goldsbury Flowers to John Wingate to Edward Wingate and Ann Blount, then to James Blount Jr., and finally to James Blount Sr.

Hardee Family

William Hardee Sr. applied for a pension at age sixty-five on April 4, 1821. His application says he enlisted in Captain Redin Blunt's Company and Colonel Edward Buncombe's for one year on May 3, 1776. He served until May 3, 1777, and was discharged at Halifax, North Carolina. He was in no engagement during service.[230]

Family Information

The information on all the families who appeared on the First Census of the United States in 1790 is too numerous to include. They have multiplied and spread out across the United States. However, for the sake of posterity, I have made an effort to include what I considered to be important information on what I have found:

Abraham Page might have been born in England about 1740, or he might have been the son of Thomas Page, a Quaker who'd lived in Virginia—Mary Lamb Page's birth is unknown. I have conflicting information concerning Abraham. Other researchers state he is Thomas's brother. He fought in the Revolutionary War and died during it, but I have no further details on his death. His sons and brothers wound up on the South and North Carolina border after the Revolution, in Robeson and Marion Counties. When I discovered the possibility of the Pages being Quakers, I was amazed. But the lower price of land in North Carolina and the Lord Proprietors Fundamental Constitution of 1669 for Carolina encouraged migration by granting religious freedom to all settlers. Quakers were the most numerous of the settlers to the Albemarle region, composing at least one-tenth of the population, and by the early eighteenth century, they supported monthly and quarterly meetings.[231] Nonetheless, the settlement of North Carolina by 1729 was concentrated in the northeastern corner, and what would later become Columbus County was still largely waiting for those people from that area to migrate to the southeastern corner.

DNA tests of multiple Page descendants in Marion, Robeson, and Columbus Counties indicate the Page male DNA is M-253, which is predominately found in Scandinavia. What is certain is the Pages moved from Virginia to the northeastern section of North Carolina, like many other people from Virginia, and then before or during the Revolution, they came to the South and North Carolina border area of the aforementioned counties in both states.

Anna Wright married Isaac Wright, her first cousin two times removed. Isaac died before 1910 and is listed as living with his great-granddaughter Patience. There is an interesting story concerning Anna, as told to Henry Neil Wright. There were some boys at the Wright house, and they gave Anna a fifty-cent piece to stab a butcher knife into a grave. When she did not return, they went and checked on her. She had fainted and was lying on the grave. She had stabbed the knife in the grave, but it caught on her long skirt. When she rose to walk away, the blade kept her from walking too far, and she fainted.[232]

Isaac Fowler was the son of Peter Fowler, who was the brother of John, Daniel Jr., and Elizabeth Fowler Spivey. I am a descendant of all four of these siblings. Within three of four generations, their grandchildren or great-grandchildren married into each other and created a twisted vine of relatives that only a geographical move out of southeastern North Carolina could rectify. The same was true of most of the families on both sides of my parents' ancestry.

John Turbeville's son Archibald "Archie" married Martha Fagan and moved to Covington County, Alabama, then to Texas in 1860.

He was a Methodist minister and a mason. The story is they moved to Shelby County, Texas, by way of Natchez, Mississippi. They only had daughters.

One of my cousins, who was a descendant of many of those who migrated to Alabama, Alpha Moore Champion Tatom made it through the Civil War. He is my first cousin four times removed. He is buried at Williams Chapel Cemetery, Brundidge, Pike County, Alabama. He was a Confederate veteran, born on November 21, 1840, in Daleville. He died on March 10, 1910, and was buried in Williams Chapel Cemetery in Brundidge, Alabama. Alpha was a faithful church member. At age fifteen, when he and his brothers were working on a rail fence on their lands in the Tennille area, a group of school children came by. He then saw Annie Jane Adams and declared she would be his future wife. His brothers kidded him about her being a child, but Alpha just said, "I am patient. I will wait." And wait he did. In December of 1867, he was married to Annie Jane Adams. On November 18, 1906, she was killed by a runaway mule and wagon. She was buried at Bethel in Banks, Alabama. When death comes for you, it comes in many forms.

Alpha enlisted and served in the Fifteenth of Alabama Confederate Infantry until January 6, 1862. He received a physical disability discharge near Manassas, Virginia, because his feet nearly froze. He suffered for the rest of his life from this injury. He came home but reenlisted on August 5, 1862, in Co. B, Fifty-Third Alabama Cavalry—supposedly riding horseback instead of walking. He served in the Fifty-Third until the end of the war and was discharged near Augusta, Georgia, around April or May of 1865. Speaking of the war's devastation, he told of selling wild grapes and berries to the Yankees and of dressing in a Yankee uniform and slipping through their camp and "turning out about five hundred fine Yankee horses and mules." His Confederate friends caught them after the stampede.[233]

In one battle, Alpha was shot through the collar but not injured. He had several brothers who fought in the Civil War also, and one or more of them were killed. Later, Alpha wanted to visit the old battlefields, but he never could bring himself to do it.

During the summer of 1982, I worked at Hardee's in Chester and wished I was back home in Cerro Gordo. I moved to Chester in my junior year and spent four months attending Chester High School, before the summer of 1982. I spent it not knowing anyone and not really desiring to do anything. Attending three different high schools, I left Mississippi after only a year, with an impression that friendships are transitory. The only permanent things are places and the love for those people who come in and out of your life. Dunn Swamp, which pours into Porter Swamp and then joins Cow Branch to empty into the Lumber River, is still there. There are not as many old trees from when I was young, but I always know exactly where I am when I drive through the area on Haynes Lennon Road. The old cemeteries out in the fields, those marked and unmarked, hold the remains of my family who called this area home. I have outgrown this place, but it is still a warm and familiar place for me.

Concerning changing high schools, I recommend if you change high schools, you do so at the beginning of the year and not at the end of a year. I spent the summer of 1983 working, and during the two weeks before I left for basic training, I just sat in a chair, reading *The Count of Monte Cristo*. I thought then that it would be a long journey before I would enjoy no responsibility as I did before. I was disappointed I was going to the air force when most everyone else was headed to Clemson or the University of South Carolina. However, there were no plans for me to go to college, nor was there money. I thought the air force would take care of me, and I would, in turn, do my best for the air force. In the end, I can say it was the best decision

I could have made at seventeen. Twenty-eight years of service and a potential thirty before I separate, I can agree with my friend Christine Joy B.'s statement, "Jeff, it is the only life I know." Somehow, what she said of herself back in 1985 became my reality. I did not know it would end up the way it has.

I first met Christine when I walked into the break room of the Passenger Reservation Center at Scott back in 1984. She was sitting on a couch and was reading the *St. Louis Post-Dispatch*. When I walked in, she lowered the paper, smiling, and said, "I am Chris from Chanute Air Force Base." She has remained one of the few people I have met who said, "This is where I am going," then did just that. She remains an inspiration and a fond memory in my heart. So here is a toast for her and the memories we were able to make together during that short time.

In October of 1985, on a Sunday night when Christine "Chris" showed up at my door in the dorms on base, wearing a white jacket with "ILLINI" etched on the back, we discussed many things. Perhaps, if I had paid more heed to what she had to say and seen the wisdom in her words ....

I was only nineteen, and she was between twenty-two and twenty-three. Having been an air force brat, she had many more life experiences than my experiences in Cerro Gordo or even Mississippi. She recognized the importance of having a plan and following through on that plan. We both were leaving Scott Air Force Base in December. I was on the way to Korea, and she was on the way to the University of Illinois and the Air Force Reserve Officer Training Corps (ROTC) program there. She and I had many discussions over breakfast at the local IHOP or McDonalds. She was one of the most articulate women I had known up until that point. The fall of 1985 remains one of the fondest memories I have as a young, unmarried man. I corresponded with her during my time in Korea—and after she transferred to Florida State. When I was discharged from the air force in 1988, she called my parents' house. She received that commission and married a fellow air force officer and subsequently retired from the military. Thus, everything turned out as she had planned. I am proud of her and the friendship we shared. When she told me in the waning days of December in 1985 that the air force was the only life she ever knew, I did not imagine it was becoming the only life I knew and the only one I felt comfortable being a member of. It would take me ten years to realize this, which was thirteen years after that particular conversation. I would have been wiser and wealthier had I heeded Chris's advice back in 1985. The irony in not following her advice is illustrated by the fact I could have retired at age thirty-seven. Now I am fifty-seven and presently the oldest person on flight status by about five years, at the North Carolina Air National Guard. Many of my air force friends, including Christine, are nearing their second retirement or have retired.

When the air force sent me to South Korea in 1986 for a year, I stayed almost three and came home with a wife and a daughter. I was correct on the responsibility question back in the summer of 1983. When my time was over in the air force, the three of us flew into San Francisco, then caught a bus to Travis Air Force Base. I out-processed the air force at Travis and then caught a bus back to Oakland and flew home to Charlotte.

Since returning home in 1988, I have been back to Columbus County numerous times but never imagined I would own land there. And at my age of narrowing the gap between working and retiring, I have taken on the burden and joy of a farm in Cerro Gordo. My friend Lewis Bragg asked, "Why do you not take it easy and just sit and relax?" Well, I don't know how to do that, and returning to something familiar seems the best course of action for me as I continue to grow older.

The land I own is not far from all my mom's relatives, where I grew up in the tobacco fields, or my dad's sister. Water from my land drains into Drowning Creek via Mills Branch and Cow Branch. All names are dotted on old deeds and land grants. Thus, this place seems like a fitting place for me to end my journey. I returned home in a much better position than when I had left at age fifteen. Maybe I will be forgotten by my descendants, or maybe one of them will be ignited with a passion to know what had come before and start piecing together history. Which leads me to the question, "Why the land, and why the effort into this book?" I know, one day, I will no longer be living. My bones will join my brother Patrick Wayne and grandparents Gordon and Hazel at Powell Cemetery in Fair Bluff. I will rest not far from Carl Meares and his family and all those others who made those small towns in western Columbus County a vibrant community.

What I have found is that many of my ancestors fled religious persecution in France by a Catholic king. Even in the case of many of my English ancestors, they were Quakers and fled England because of their beliefs. Many of my Scotish ancestors were driven out Scotland given that they did not desire a German king of England. So, they fled to the British colonies and became indentured servants. Few came here with wealth, and they had no intention of taking advantage of other people. They were generally ordinary people, attempting to live their lives and protect their families. When they arrived in the colonies, they were not in a Garden of Eden but rather an environment that demanded hard work, sacrifice, and perseverance. They were not saints but humans fraught with frailties and shortcomings. Ultimately, I cannot deny them, as they are all my people.

An illustration of this concept is found in an incident that occurred while I was driving home from the farm. When my wife and I entered I-74 at the Evergreen-Cerro Gordo exit, I noticed my truck leaning to the right. I immediately thought the right front tire must have been low in air pressure. Thus, I asked my wife to locate a tire place in Laurinburg, which was nineteen miles away. Then I pulled over and checked the tire. No way were we going to make it nineteen miles. I had pulled off I-74 at the Pembroke exit, and where I stopped, two men were loading a motorcycle onto a trailer. I asked, "Do you know of any tire repair places nearby?"

One of the men responded, "Oxendine is down the road, but it is closed." I then realized it was after five o'clock in the evening. The guy who had answered me added, "I have a shop. Pull down that dirt road." I drove the truck down the road and discovered his name was G. Barton. He helped me change the tire. While there, I learned he was a Lumbee, and he had been drafted in 1968 and fought in Vietnam. The other man helping him with the motorcycle had been drafted a week after he was.

I told them, "I am from Cerro Gordo; my mom is from Evergreen. She is a Williamson." He actually already knew all these things because his wife was a Cartrette from Tabor City. "Wow," was my reply. "My granddaddy's grandmother was a Cartrette. I am probably related to her." He was one of the kindest people I have ever met, and there was a possibility we were kin.

There are many others out there who are just beginning their life's journey. Just like Patience Caroline and James Hattaway and Elizabeth Cartrette and Return Page Jr. many have passed through, and many will come in the future. But this is a reminder to everyone that we can find a connection to our past that can help shape our future.

I am proud of "my people." We are not perfect, and we are not blameless, but we are brave. We do not stand on others' throats and ask that you keep your knee off your and our liberties. We cannot change what is the past and do not bear responsibility for others' offenses. I owe no one anything. I have hoed my row of dirt and weeds. To suggest otherwise is to be ignorant of the reality of bare feet, tin roofs, and poverty. Thus, here on these pages is who I am and where I come from. It is accurate and how it happened as best I know, from what records I can find. Benjamin Jowett states, "Doubt comes in the window when inquiry is denied at the door." I have tried to inquire through records and interviews the accuracy of this story, thus eliminating any doubt. However, I am also confident that memories are recollections, and time changes the emotions of events in people's lives; thus, for what it is, here it is as a record of my people and those of the Lumber River Basin and the Great Pee Dee and Little Pee Dee River Basins of North and South Carolina.

SUGGESTED READINGS

Adams-Virkus, Fredrick, Ed. *Immigrant Ancestors: A List of 2,500 immigrants to America before 1750*. Baltimore: Genealogical Publishing, 1942.

Boddie, John Bennett. *Southside Virginia Families, Volume I*. Baltimore: Clearfield Press, 2003.

Boddie, John Bennett. *Historical Southern Families, Volume IX*. Baltimore: Clearfield Publishing Co. Inc., 1971.

Boddie, William W. *A History of Williamsburg: Something About the people of Williamsburg from the First Settlement by Europeans About 1703 until 1923*. Columbia, South Carolina: The State Company, 1923.

Bordeaux, Jason. *Sons of Stephen & Millie Ann Wright who served in the Civil War, Columbus County, North Carolina*. Morrisville, North Carolina, Lulu. 2010.

Bockstruck, Lloyd de Witt. *Bounty and Donation Land Grants in British America*. Baltimore: Genealogical Publishing, 2007.

Bockstruck, Lloyd de Witt. *Revolutionary War Bounty and Land Grants Awarded by State Governments*. Baltimore: Genealogical Publishing Company, 1996.

Brayton, John A. *Order of the First Families of North Carolina, Ancestor Biographies Volume I*. Baltimore: Otter Bay Books, LLC 2017.

Brayton, John A. *Order of the First Families of North Carolina, Ancestor Biographies Volume II*. Baltimore: Otter Bay Books, LLC 2014.

Bushman, Richard L. *From Puritan to Yankee: Character and the Social Order in Connecticut 1690–1765*. Cambridge, Massachusetts: Harvard University Press, 1967.

Campbell, Wanda S. *Abstracts of Wills of Bladen County, North Carolina 1743–1900*. Greenville, South Carolina: Southern Historical Press, 1962.

Chappell, Phil E. *A Genealogical History of the Chappell, Dickie, and Other Kindred Families of Virginia 1635–1900*. Kansas City, Missouri: Hudson-Kimberly Publishing Company, 1900.

Clark, Murtie June. *Colonial Soldiers of the South, 1732–1774*. Baltimore: Genealogical Publishing Co. Inc., 1986.

Clark, Walter. *A History of the Several Regiments and Battalions from North Carolina in The Great War (1861–1865) Volume 5, Part I*. Goldsboro, North Carolina: Nash Brothers Book and Job Printers, 1901.

Clark, Walter. *Histories of the Several Regiments and Battalions from North Carolina in the Great War 1861–1865, Volume 5 Part 2, with Index*. Goldsboro, North Carolina: Nash Brothers Book and Job Printers, 1901.

Clute, J.J. *Old Families of Staten Island*. Baltimore: Clearfield Company, Inc. 2003.

Coleman, J.P. *The Robert Coleman Family from Virginia to Texas*. Salem, Massachusetts: Higginson Book Company, 1962.

Columbus County North Carolina Heritage 1808–2004, Columbus County Heritage Committee, 2004.

Corbitt, David Leroy. Ed. *Explorations, Descriptions, and Attempted Settlements of Carolina 1584–1590*. Raleigh: State Department of Archives and history, 1948.

Corbitt, David Leroy. *The Formation of the North Carolina Counties 1663–1943*. Raleigh: State Department of Archives and History, 1950.

Farmer, Margaret Pace. *One Hundred and Fifty Years of Pike County, Alabama*, Montgomery, Alabama: Brown Printing Company, 1973.

Fischer, David Hackett. *Albion's Seed: Four British Folkways in America*. Oxford University Press, 1989.

Folsom, Marcia McClintock, ed. *Approaches to Teaching Austen's "Emma."* New York: Modern Language Association of America, 2004.

Foley, Louise Pledge Heath. Ed. *Early Virginia Families Along the James River: Their Deep Roots and Tangled Branches*. Richmond, Virginia: Whittet and Shepperson, 1978.

Fowler, Glenn Dora. *Annals of the Fowler Family with Branches in Virginia, North Carolina, South Carolina, Tennessee, Kentucky, Alabama, Mississippi, California, and Texas*. Austin: Texas Historical Association, 1901.

Fowler, Ricard Gildart, *A History of the Fowler Family of Southeastern North Carolina*. Norman, Oklahoma, self-published, 1985.

Gregg, Alexander. *History of the Old Cheraws*. New York: Richardson and Company, 1867.

Hardy, Sarah Pickett. *Colonial Families of the Southern States of America: A History and Genealogy of Colonial Families Who Settled in the Colonies Prior to the Revolution*. New York: Tobias A. Wright Printer and Publisher, 1911.

Hargreaves-Mawdsley, R. *Bristol and America: A Record of the First Settlers in the Colonies of North American 1654–1685*. Baltimore: Genealogical Publishing Co. Inc. 1978.

Hathaway, James Robert Bent. *The North Carolina Historical and Genealogical Register, Volume I*. London: Franklin Classics, 2018.

Holcomb, Brent. *Bladen County, North Carolina: Abstracts of Early Deeds 1738–1804*. Greenville, South Carolina: Southern Historical Press, 1979.

Hotten, John Camden. *The Original Lists of Person of Quality, Emigrants, Religious Exiles, Political Rebels, serving men Sold for a Term of Years, Apprentices, Children Stolen, Maidens Pressed, and Others who went from Great Britain to the American Plantations 1600–1700*. London: Chatto and Windus, Publishers, 1874.

Lewis, Jerry Dale "J.D." My Neck of the Woods: *The Lewis Families of Southeastern North Carolina and northeastern South Carolina*. Baltimore: Clearfield Company, Inc., 2005.

Moss, Bobby Gilmer. *Roster of the Loyalists in the Battle of Moores Creek Bridge*. Blacksburg, South Carolina: Scotia-Hibernia Press, 1992.

Moss, Bobby Gilmer, *Roster of the Patriots in the Battle of Moores Creek Bridge*. Blacksburg, South Carolina: Scotia-Hinernia Press, 1992.

Moss, Bobby Gilmer. *Roster of South Patriots in the American Revolution*. Baltimore: Genealogical Publishing, Co. Inc., 1983.

Muster Rolls of the Soldiers of the War of 1812 Detached from the Militia of North Carolina in 1812 and 1814. Raleigh: Charles C. Raboteau at the Times office, 1851.

Page, Chares Nash. *History and Genealogy of the Page Family from the Year 1257 to the Present*. Des Moines, Iowa, no date self-published.

Page, Robert E. *House of Pages in County of Suffolk, England Viking Influence in Denmark, France, England, and Virginia*. Bloomington, Indiana: Author House, 2013.

Ramsey, Beverly A. *The Blounts of Mulberry Hill: Descendants of Captain Hames Blunt of Chowan Couty, North Carolina 1650– 1900, Volume I*. Morrisville, North Carolina, Lulu. 2009.

Ramsey, Beverly A. *The Blounts of Mulberry Hill: Descendants of Captain Hames Blunt of Chowan Couty, North Carolina 1650– 1900, Volume III*. Morrisville, North Carolina, Lulu. 2009.

Salley A.S. Ed. *Marriage Notices in the South Carolina Gazette: and Country Journal 1765–1775 and The Charlestown Gazette, 1778–1780*. Charleston: The Walker, Evans, & Cogswell Company, 1904.

Sellers, W. W. *A History of Marion County, South Carolina*. Greenville, South Carolina: Southern Historical Press, 1996.

Stifakis, Stewart. *The Compendium of the Confederate Armies: South Carolina and Georgia*. Westminster, Maryland: Heritage Books, Inc. 1995.

Styrna, Christine Ann. "Winds of War and Change: The Impact of the Tuscarora War on Proprietary North Carolina,1660-1729" (1990). Dissertations, Theses, and Masters Projects. Paper 1539623795. https://scholarworks.wm.edu/cgi/viewcontent.cgi?article=3705&context=etd.

Triebe, Richard H. *Fort Fisher to Elmira: The Fatal Journey of More than Five Hundred Confederate Soldiers*. Coastal Books, 2016.

Williamson, John Hybert and Branch, Betty Williamson. *The Williamson Family from Tatum's Township, Columbus County, North Carolina*, 2006.

Wingate, Charles E.L. *History of the Wingate Family in England and in America*. New Delhi: Isha Books, 2013.

Records of the Welsh Tract Baptist Meeting, Pecander Hundred, New Castle County, Delaware, 1701 to 1828. Wilmington, Delaware, The Historical Society of Delaware, 1904.

Standing in front of porch, from left to right: Daniel Return Page (my great-grandfather), Anna Elizabeth Hattaway (Prince) Page (my great-grandmother), Rossie Clyde Page (my great-uncle), Jessie Page (my great-uncle), Ethel Byrd (husband of Emma)

On porch, from left to right: Sereny "Renna" Page (my great-aunt who died of Scarlet fever in 1916 at age twenty-nine), Gordon Davis Page (my grandfather), Emma Victoria Page Byrd (my great-aunt)

My mother, Dollie Monteen Williamson Page

Young Jeffrey Davis Page in front of the trailer at James Monroe Powell's farm

Gordon Davis Page, Hazel Turbeville Page, (my Dad's parents) Jeffrey Davis Page, author, (baby) in front of the house at Monroe Powell's home that was rented.

Mitchell Davis Page, my father.

Uncle Mitchell (Charles Mitchell Powell, Sr., Monroe Powell's son) and my Aunt Pattie Page Powell.

ENDNOTES

1 Marcus Tullius Cicero, *Orator*, trans. G. L. Hendrickson and H. M. Hubbell (Cambridge: Harvard University Press, 1939), 395.

2 "To Acknowledge Our Ancestors Means ...," Alice Walker, Relics World: A World of Words Which Can Change Your Life, https://www.relicsworld.com/alice-walker/to-acknowledge-our-ancestors-means-we-are-aware-that-we-did-not-author-alice-walker.

3 Louis R. Harlan, ed., *The Booker T. Washington Papers, Volume 3: 1889–95* (Urbana: University of Illinois Press, 1974), 583–7.

4 The Reformers, *1599 Geneva Bible* (White Hall: Tolle Lege Press, 2016), 1157.

5 ——, 957–8.

6 "'With Malice Toward None ...': Lincoln's Second Inaugural Address," National Park Service, updated September 12, 2021, https://www.nps.gov/articles/000/-with-malice-toward-none-lincoln-s-second-inaugural.htm.

7 Norman D. Sandler, "Reagan: All the Answers Are in the Bible," February 3, 1983, https://www.upi.com/Archives/1983/02/03/Reagan-All-the-answers-are-in-the-Bible/4306413096340/.

8 William Butler Yeats, "An Irish Airman Foresees His Death," Poets.org, published 1919, https://poets.org/poem/irish-airman-foresees-his-death.

9 Lloyd Lewis, Sherman, *Fighting Prophet*, 1st ed. (San Diego: Harcourt, Brace and Company, 1932), 513.

10 Jacob D. Cox, *Military Reminiscences of the Civil War* (New York: C. Scribner's Sons, 1900), 2:531–2; and ——, *The March to the Sea* (New York: Scribner, 1892), 168.

11 C. A. Whittington, *Was the C282Y Mutation an Irish Gaelic Mutation That the Vikings Help Disseminate?* 67, no. 6 (August 2006): 1270–3, https://doi.org/10.1016/j.mehy.2006.06.013.

12 "A Million Vikings Still Live Among Us: One in 33 Men Can Claim to be Direct Descendants from the Norse Warriors," News, Daily Mail, updated March 10, 2014, https://www.dailymail.co.uk/news/article-2577003/A-million-Vikings-live-One-33-men-claim-direct-descendants-Norse-warriors.html.

13 Andy Coghlan, "Ancient Invaders Transformed Britain, But Not Its DNA," Life, NewScientist, March 18, 2015, https://www.newscientist.com/article/mg22530134-300-ancient-invaders-transformed-britain-but-not-its-dna/.

14 Stephen Leslie et al., "The Fine-scale Genetic Structure of the British Population," *Nature* 519, no. 7543 (March 2015), 309–14, https://doi.org/10.1038/nature14230.

15 Frances H. Kennedy, ed., *The Civil War Battlefield Guide*, 2nd ed. (New York: Houghton Mifflin Company, 1998).

16 National Cemetery Administration, "Woodlawn National Cemetery," Find a Cemetery, US Department of Veterans Affairs, updated February 13, 2018, https://www.cem.va.gov/cems/nchp/woodlawn.asp.

17 Tom Fagart, "From Fort Fisher, North Carolina to Elmira, New York," North Carolina Civil War and Reconstruction History Center (blog), September 11, 2018, https://nccivilwarcenter.org/from-fort-fisher-north-carolina-to-elmira-new-york/.

18 NC History Center on the Civil War, "Little Known Facts on Tar Heel Confederate Soldiers in Elmira, NY," North Carolina Civil War and Reconstruction History Center, September 11, 2018, https://nccivilwarcenter.org/little-known-facts-on-tarheel-confederate-soldiers-in-elmira-ny/.

19 Rod Gragg, *Confederate Goliath: The Battle of Fort Fisher* (Baton Rouge: Louisiana State University Press, 1994), 243.

20 William W. Sellers, *A History of Marion County, South Carolina, from Its Earliest Times to the Present, 1901* (Columbia: R. L. Bryan Company, 1902).

21 North Carolina State Center for Health Statistics and Office of Minority Health and Health Disparities, *North Carolina Minority Health Facts: American Indians* (North Carolina: State Center for Health Statistics and Office of Minority Health and Health Disparities, 2010), https://schs.dph.ncdhhs.gov/schs/pdf/AmerIndian_MHFS_WEB_072210.pdf.

22 "Henry Berry Lowry (1845–?)," Encyclopedia Entry, North Carolina History Project, https://northcarolinahistory.org/encyclopedia/henry-berry-lowry-1845/.

23 Laurence M. Hauptman, *Between Two Fires: American Indians in the Civil War* (New York: Free Press Paperbacks, 1995), 79–81.

24 George Alfred Townsend, *The Swamp Outlaws or, The North Carolina Bandits: Being a Complete History of the Modern Rob Roys and Robin Hoods* (New York: Robert M. DeWitt, 1872), http://www.freeafricanamericans.com/swamp_outlaws.htm.

25 Jason Bordeaux, "McKinnie Research," *Southeastern North Carolina Genealogical Society, Roots and Remembrances* 40, no. 1 (July/August 2022): 1–23.

26 John Bennett Boddie, *Seventeenth Century Isle of Wight County, Virginia* (Chicago: Genealogical Publishing Company, 1938).

27 John H. Williamson, "The Welsh Origins of Lewis and John Williamson of Southeastern North Carolina 1750–2019" (unpublished manuscript), 3, Microsoft Word file.

28 ——.

29 John W. Jordan, LLD, ed., *Colonial and Revolutionary Families of Pennsylvania: Genealogical and Personal Memoirs* (New York: The Lewis Publishing Company, 1911).

30 Joshua Lloyd, "371-year-old Bible Lives on in Darlington County," News, *Washington Times*, June 11, 2016, https://www.washingtontimes.com/news/2016/jun/11/371-year-old-bible-lives-on-in-darlington-county/.

31 Welsh Tract Baptist Meeting, *Records of the Welsh Tract Baptist Meeting, Pencader Hundred, New Castle County Delaware*, 1701 to 1828 (Wilmington: Historical Society of Delaware, 1904).

32 Jordan, *Colonial and Revolutionary Families*, 770–1.

33 "The Welsh Settlers During the Royal Period (1729 to 1775)," Royal Colony of South Carolina, Carolana, https://www.carolana.com/SC/Royal_Colony/sc_royal_colony_welsh.html.

34 Lloyd Johnson, "Welsh Settlers," NCPedia, State Library of North Carolina, January 1, 2006, https://www.ncpedia.org/welsh-settlers.

35 Williamson, "Welsh Origins."

36 ——.

37 Alister McGrath, "Calvin and the Christian Calling," *First Things* 94, (June/July 1999): 31–5, https://www.firstthings.com/article/1999/06/calvin-and-the-christian-calling.

38 State v. Owens, 65 N.C., App. 107, No. 8313SC227 (Nov. 15 1983), https://cite.case.law/nc-app/65/107/.

39 Jess Bidgood and Alan Blinder, "Hurricane Plunges a North Carolina Town's Future Into Debt," *New York Times*, October 11, 2016, https://www.nytimes.com/2016/10/12/us/hurricane-matthew-plunges-a-north-carolina-towns-future-into-doubt.html.

40 Martha Quillin, "Some Entire NC Towns May Become Vacant Memorials to Matthew," *News & Observer*, published April 21, 2017, updated April 10, 2018, https://www.newsobserver.com/news/politics-government/state-politics/article146002379.html?platform=hootsuite.

41 Jack Claiborne and William Price, eds., *Discovering North Carolina: A Tar Heel Reader* (Chapel Hill: The University of North Carolina Press, 1991); Milton Ready, *The Tar Heel State: A History of North Carolina* (Columbia: The University of South Carolina Press, 2006); and William S. Powell, *North Carolina Through Four Centuries* (Chapel Hill: The University of North Caroline Press, 1989).

42 Hugh Talmage Lefler and Albert Ray Newsome, *North Carolina: The History of a Southern State*, 3rd ed. (Chapel Hill: The University of North Caroline Press, 1973).

43 "History," Bladen County NC Geneology and History, Bladen County NCGenWeb, updated January 22, 2018, http://www.ncgenweb.us/bladen/bladen-county-ncgenweb.

44 Francis Butler Simkins and Charles Pierce Roland, *The South Old and New: A History 1820–1947* (New York City: Alfred A. Knopf, 1947), 13.

45 David Hackett Fischer, *Albion's Seed: Four British Folkways in America* (New York: Oxford University Press, 1989), 236–41.

46 Wikipedia, "Bere Regis," Wikipedia, the Free Encyclopedia, accessed April 24, 2019, https://en.wikipedia.org/wiki/Bere_Regis.

47 Fischer, *Albion's Seed*, 245.

48 ——, 256–60.

49 ——, 264.

50 Patricia Causey Nichols, "Language and Dialect in Early Horry County," *Independent Republic Quarterly* 3, no. 4 (fall 1979), 13–4.

51 John Blythe, "Crusoe Island and the French Revolution," *NC Miscellany* (blog), *UNC Library*, July 14, 2011, https://blogs.lib.unc.edu/ncm/index.php/2011/07/14/crusoe-island-and-the-french-revolution/.

52 Swamp Merchant, "Crusoe Island: French-Haitian Settlement in the Green Swamp of North Carolina," Restoration Systems, March 25, 2011, https://restorationsystems.com/uncategorized/swamp-people-french-haitian-aristocrats-in-the-green-swamp-of-north-carolina/.

53 Judith Glover, *The Place Names of Kent* (Hartlip: Meresborough Books, 1982).

54 Wikipedia, "Suffolk dialect," Wikipedia, the Free Encyclopedia, https://en.wikipedia.org/wiki/Suffolk_dialect.

55 Sellers, *History of Marion County*.

56 Curtis McGirt, "The Ashpole Area in the 1700s," History, Fairmont History, https://fairmontnchistory.com/history/43-the-ashpole-area-in-the-1700-s.

57 ——, "Isham Pitman," Pittman Family, Fairmont History, https://fairmontnchistory.com/families/pittman.

58 ——, "Isham Pitman," Pittman Family, Fairmont History, https://fairmontnchistory.com/families/pittman.

59 Francis B. Heitman, *Historical Register: Officers of the Continental Army* (Ann Arbor: Press of Nichols, Killam & Maffitt, 1893), 382.

60 "Capt and Commander Stephen Buckland 1742–1782," Officers, Society of the Cincinnati in the State of Connecticut, July 4, 1783, http://theconnecticutsociety.org/buckland-stephen/.

61 "Learn," Getting Started, NC Land Grant Images and Data, https://www.nclandgrants.com/q/?sbj=Page%2C%20David&cyid=11&xs=1.

62 Catherine W. Bishir, *North Carolina Architecture* (Chapel Hill: The Uiniversity of North Carolina Press, 2005), 34–5.

63 Wikipedia, "Bere Regis."

64 George R. Stewart, *Names on the Land: A Historical Account of Place-naming in the United States*, 1st ed. (New York: Random House, 1945), 21–2.

65 Horry County Historical Society, "Independent Republic Quarterly," *Independent Republic Quarterly* 41, no. 1–4 (2007): 7–8, 148.

66 ——.

67 Kennedy, *Battlefield Guide*, 170–1.

68 "Civil War Service Records for Alva Cartwright," Fold3.com, accessed August 3, 2023, https://www.fold3.com/image/81544517.

69 "Civil War Service Records for Enoch Cartwright," Fold3.com, accessed August 3, 2023, https://www.fold3.com/image/81544538.

70 "Civil War Service Records for Richard Cartwright," Fold3.com, accessed August 3, 2023, https://www.fold3.com/image/81544596.

71 "Civil War Service Records for William H. Cartwright," Fold3.com, accessed August 3, 2023, https://www.fold3.com/image/81544713.

72 "Civil War Service Records for Amos Fowler," Fold3.com, accessed August 3, 2023, https://www.fold3.com/image/83564097.

73 "Civil War Service Records for F.H. Fowler," Fold3.com, accessed August 3, 2023, https://www.fold3.com/image/83564109?terms=war,confederate,united,civil,h,f,south,carolina,america,states,fowler.

74 "Civil War Service Records for G.W. Fowler," Fold3.com, accessed August 3, 2023, https://www.fold3.com/image/83564135?terms=war,confederate,civil,carolina,g,south,united,america,w,states,fowler.

75 "Civil War Service Records for Jacob P. Fowler," Fold3.com, accessed August 3, 2023, https://www.fold3.com/image/83564167.

76 "Civil War Service Records for Peter Fowler," Fold3.com, accessed August 3, 2023, https://www.fold3.com/image/83564203.

77 "Civil War Service Records for William Fowler," Fold3.com, accessed August 3, 2023, https://www.fold3.com/image/83564237.

78 ——.

79 Harry Searles, "Battle of Big Black River Bridge (May 17,1863)," Entries, Ohio Civil War Central, updated November 13, 2017, https://www.ohiocivilwarcentral.com/entry.php?rec=145.

80 Eloise Fretz Potter and Timothy Wiley Rackley, eds., *Rackley, a Southern Colonial Family: the Descendants of Edward Rackley of Virginia: with Appendixes Treating Other Rackley Family Groups Living in the United States Before 1900* (Zebulon: E.F. Potter, 1984), https://www.familysearch.org/search/catalog/313008?availability=Family%20History%20Library.

81 Richard Gildart Fowler, *A History of the Fowler Family of Southeastern North Carolina* (Norman: R.G. Fowler, 1985), 15.

82 National Archives and Records Service General Services Administrations, *Revolutionary War Pension and Bounty–Land–Warrant Application Files* (Washington: National Archives Microfilm Publications, 1974), 47, https://www.archives.gov/files/research/microfilm/m804.pdf.

83 Fowler, *Fowler Family*, 17–8.

84 Will Graves, "Pension Acts: An Overview of Revolutionary War Pension and Bounty Land Legislation and the Southern Campaigns Pension Transcript Project," accessed September 13, 2019, https://www.ncpedia.org/anchor/searching-greener-pastures.

85 Tommy W. Rogers, "The Great Population Exodus from South Carolina 1850–1860," *South Carolina Historical Magazine* 68, no. 1 (January 1967), 14–21, https://www.jstor.org/stable/27566804.

86 Donald R. Lennon and Fred D. Ragan, "Searching for Greener Pastures: Out-migration in the 1800s and 1900s," North Carolina Museum of History, accessed November 8, 2019, https://www.ncpedia.org/anchor/searching-greener-pastures.

87 James Sturgis, "Craig, Sire James Henry: (1748–1812)," *Oxford Dictionary of National Biography*, (September 2004), https://doi.org/10.1093/ref:odnb/6572.

88 John Burgoyne and Douglas R. Cubbison, *Burgoyne, and the Saratoga Campaign: His Papers* (Norman: The University of Oklahoma Press, 2012), 332.

89 Honorable John William Fortescue, *A History of the British Army: Volume III 1763–1793: Second Part–From the Close of the Seven Years' War to the Second Peace of Paris* (London: Macmillan, 1902).

90 "Biographical Memoir of the Late General Sir James Henry Craig K.B.," in *The Royal Military Chronicle* (London: J. Davis, 1812), 3:401.

91 James Sprunt, *Chronicles of the Cape Fear River: 1660–1916*, 2nd ed. (Raleigh: Edwards & Broughton Printing Company, 1916), 137.

92 "Battle of Rockfish," North Carolina Highway Historical Marker Program, North Carolina Department of Cultural Resources, http://www.ncmarkers.com/Markers.aspx?MarkerId=F-7.

93 Beverly Tetterton, "Elizabethtown, Battle of," NCpedia, State Library of North Carolina, January 1, 2006, https://ncpedia.org/elizabethtown-battle.

94 "Henrico County, VA | Jul 1, 1862," Malvern Hill, American Battlefield Trust, https://www.battlefields.org/learn/civil-war/battles/malvern-hill.

95 Daniel Harvey Hill, "McClellan's Change of Base and Malvern Hill," in Robert Underwood Johnson and Clarence Clough Buel, eds., *Battles and Leaders of the Civil War* (New York: Thomas Yoseloff, 1956), 2, 394.

96 Edward Stanley Barnhill, *The Beatys of Kingston* (Mt. Pleasant, SC: Furlong and Sons, 1958).

97 A.S. Salley Jr., ed., *Journal of the Grand Council of South Carolina*, rev. ed. (1692; repr., London: Forgotten Books, 2019).

98 Bertrand Van Ruymbeke, *From New Babylon to Eden: The Huguenots and Their Migration to Colonial South Carolina* (Columbia: University of South Carolina Press, 2006), 32–4.

99 "The Inscriptions on the Tombstones at the Old Parish Church of St. James's Santee, near Echaw Creek," *South Carolina Historical and Genealogical Magazine* 12, no. 3 (1911): 153–8, http://www.jstor.org/stable/27575308.

100 Barnhill, The Beatys, 16.

101 ———.

102 Charles W. Barid, *History of Huguenot Emigration to American*, Vol. 2 (New York: Dodd and Mead Publishers, 1885), 102.

103 Beverley A. Ramsey, *The Blounts of Mulberry Hill: Descendants of Captain James Blount of Chowan County, NC, 1650–1900*, vol. 2 (Chowan County: B. A. Ramsey, 2009).

104 Deason Hunt, *Out of Mississippi: The John Robert Wingate Family of Nacogdoches County, Texas* (Holly Lake Ranch: Deason Hunt, 2006), 2.

105 ———, 57.

106 Michael Greshko, "Did This Spanish Shipwreck Change the Course of History?" *National Geographic*, published November 2, 2015, https://www.nationalgeographic.com/news/2015/11/151102-colombia-shipwreck-cartagena-battle-1700s/.

107 Hunt, *Out of Mississippi*, 57.

108 David Stick and Robert J. Cain, "Spanish Invasions," NCpedia, State Library of North Carolina, January 1, 2006, https://www.ncpedia.org/spanish-invasions.

109 John Paden, "Concessions and Agreement," NCpedia, State Library of North Carolina, January 1, 2006, https://www.ncpedia.org/concessions-and-agreement.

110 Ramsey, *Blounts of Mulberry Hill*, 2:2.

111 The Editors of Encyclopedia Britannica, "Culpeper's Rebellion: American Colonial History," Wars, Battles & Armed Conflicts, Encyclopedia Britannica, July 26, 2013, https://www.britannica.com/event/Culpepers-Rebellion.

112 Ramsey, *Blounts of Mulberry Hill*, 2:5.

113 ——, 2:6.

114 ——, *The Blounts of Mulberry Hill: Descendants of Captain James Blount of Chowan County, NC, 1650–1900*, vol. 1 (Chowan County: B.A. Ramsey, 2009).

115 ——, *Blounts of Mulberry Hill*, 2:7–9.

116 ——, 2:10.

117 ——, 2:12–3.

118 Jerry Dale "J.D." Lewis, "Seth Sothel: Governor of Albemarle 1682 to 1689, Governor of 'Ye Lands South and West of Cape Feare' 1690 to 1692," Carolana, accessed March 1, 2020, https://www.carolana.com/Carolina/Governors/ssothel.html.

119 ——.

120 Ramsey, *Blounts of Mulberry Hill*, 2:18.

121 ——, 2:27–31.

122 Fischer, *Albion's Seed*, 623.

123 ——, 626.

124 ——, 608.

125 "Headrights (VA-NOTES)," Va4_headrights, Library of Virginia, accessed April 26, 2019, http://www.lva.virginia.gov/public/guides/va4_headrights.htm.

126 Fischer, *Albion's Seed*, 606.

127 "Dumbarton Castle," History, Historic Environment Scotland, accessed April 29, 2019, https://www.historicenvironment.scot/visit-a-place/places/dumbarton-castle/history/.

128 Ben Johnson, "The History of the Border Reivers," History of Scotland, Historic UK: The History and Heritage Accommodation Guide, https://www.historic-uk.com/HistoryUK/.

129 Charles Mosley, ed., *Burke's Peerage, Baronetage and Knightage*, vol. 3, 107th ed. (Wilmington: Burke's Peerage, 2003).

130 Sir Walter Scott, *Minstrelsy of the Scottish Border*, vol. 1 (Charleston: BiblioBazaar, 2007).

131 "Border Reivers–Border Reiver Names," Tom Moss Border Reivers, Rose Cottage Publications, www.reivershistory.co.uk/reiver-names.html.

132 "Tories," Encyclopedia Entry, North Carolina History Project, https://northcarolinahistory.org/encyclopedia/tories/.

133 Forrest King, "Descendants of Matthew Strickland (1648–1696) Through Four Generations," PDF, https://www.alliedfamilies.com/uploads/1/3/1/8/13181256/6__k_-_m_strickland_stricklin.pdf.

134 Joseph Barlow Felt, *The Annals of Salem: From Its First Settlement* (Salem: W. & S.B. Ives, 1827), 197–8.

135 "Huguenots: History and Massacre," Timeline 1501–1600, Christianity.com, https://www.christianity.com/church/church-history/timeline/1501-1600/huguenots-driven-out-of-france-11630022.html.

136 "Huguenot History," Huguenot Society of Great Britain and Ireland, https://www.alliedfamilies.com/uploads/1/3/1/8/13181256/6__k_-_m_strickland_stricklin.pdf..

137 "Clan History," Clan Colquhoun International, https://www.clancolquhoun.com/how/.

138 "Huguenots: Their History and Massacre," Timeline 1501–1600, Christianity.com, https://www.christianity.com/church/church-history/timeline/1501-1600/huguenots-driven-out-of-france-11630022.html.

139 John Bennett Boddie, *Historical Southern Families* (Baltimore: Clearfield Company, 1993), 5:247–8.

140 Sellers, *History of Marion County*, 192.

141 Editorial, *Charleston Daily Courier (Charleston, S.C.) 1852–1873*, April 11, 1872.

142 Sellers, *History of Marion County*, 425–7.

143 ——, 178.

144 Agnes Leland Baldwin, *First Settlers of South Carolina, 1670–1700* (Easley: Southern Historical Press, 1985).

145 George Cabell Greer, Early Virginia Immigrants, 1623–1666 (Richmond: W.C. Hill Printing Company, 1912).

146 National Archives and Records Service General Services Administrations, Revolutionary War Pension, 47.

147 Charles Francis Stein Jr., *Origin and History of Howard Country Maryland* (Ellicott City, MD: Howard County Historical Society, 1972).

148 John McLeod Williamson, "Abstracts of Earliest Columbus County North Carolina Deeds," abstract (Columbus County Courthouse, 1990), 3:97.

149 Lewis Palmer, *Genealogical Record of the Descendants of John and Mary Palmer of Concord, Chester (Now Delaware) Co., PA; Especially Through Their Son, John Palmer Jr., and Sons-in-law, William and James Trimble: With Notes of Ancestry, or Information, of Many of the Families With Whom They Intermarried* (Philadelphia: J.B. Lippincott and Company, 1875), 312.

150 Leslie Stephen, ed., *Dictionary of National Biography* (London: Smith, Elder & Co., 1886).

151 Harry Speight, "In wild Langstrothdale," in *Upper Wharfedale: Being a Complete Account of the History, Antiquities and Scenery of the Picturesque Valley of the Wharfe, from Otley to Langstrothdale*, 1st ed. (London: Elliot Stock, 1900), 491.

152 Robert "Bob" Fulghum, *Fulgham-Fulghum Family Facts*, no. 73 (Winter/Spring 2013), https://homepages.rootsweb.com/~fulghum/newsletters/FFFAN_Issue73.pdf.

153 Nell Marion Nugent, *Cavaliers and Pioneers: Abstracts of Virginia Land Patents and Grants, 1623–1666* (Baltimore: Genealogical Publishing Company, 1963).

154 "Virgina, US, Marriages of the Northern Neck of Virginia, US, 1649–1800," Birth, Marriage & Death, Ancestry, https://www.ancestry.com/search/collections/5063/.

155 Sellers, *History of Marion County*, 170.

156 ——, 197.

157 Jerry Dale "J.D." Lewis, *My Neck of the Woods: The Lewis Families of Southeastern North Carolina and Northeastern South Carolina*, 2nd ed. (Baltimore: Clearfield Publishing, 2009).

158 Roderick L. Carmichael, *The Scottish Highlander Carmichaels of the Carolinas* (Washington, DC: The Compiler, 1935); Frank Adams, *The Clans, Septs and Regiments of the Scottish Highlands*, 8th ed., reviewed by Sir Thomas Innes of Learney (Baltimore: Genealogical Publishing Company, 1970); and Sellers, *History of Marion County*, 480–4.

159 Mary Lewis Stevenson, *William Lewis of Horry County, South Carolina* (Columbia: The R.L. Bryan Company, 1960).

160 Christine Ann Styrna, "The Winds of War and Change: The Impact of the Tuscarora War on Proprietary North Carolina, 1660–1729" (master's thesis, 1990), 251, https://dx.doi.org/doi:10.21220/s2-x07a-1777.

161 Stevenson, *William Lewis of Horry County*.

162 ——, 189.

163 ——, 192.

164 Sellers, *History of Marion County*, 480.

165 Stevenson, *William Lewis of Horry County*, 123.

166 Alexander Gregg, *History of the Old Cheraws: Containing an Account of the Aborigines of the Pedee, the First White Settlements, Their Subsequent Progress, Civil Changes, the Struggle of the Revolution, and Growth of the Country Afterward; Extending from about A.D. 1730 to 1810, with Notices of the Families and Sketches of Individuals* (New York: Richardson and Company, 1867).

167 "Pension Application of Nathanial Whittington S9527," (PDF), transcribed by Will T. Graves, Southern Campaigns American Revolution Pension and Rosters, June 12, 1920, http://revwarapps.org/s9527.pdf.

168 Nugent, *Cavaliers and Pioneers*; and Potter and Rackley, *Southern Colonial Family*.

169 "Declaration of Elizabeth Spivey, widow of Edmund Spivey for Revolutionary War Pension under the Act of July 4th, 1836, R10,002," Fold3.com, accessed August 1, 2023, https://www.fold3.com/file/30879907/edmund-spivey-revolutionary-war-pensions?terms=north,war,us,spivey,revolutionary,carolina,united,america,states.

170 Zachary Taylor Fulmore, *Annals of the Ashpole Community: 1750–1814* (Philadelphia: S.R. Fulmore Publisher, 1992).

171 Murtie June Clark, *Colonial Soldiers of the South, 1732–1774* (Baltimore: Genealogical Publishing Company, 1986), 763.

172 Bobby Gilmer Moss, *Roster of the Patriots in the Battle of Moores Creek Bridge* (Blacksburg: Scotia-Hibernia Press, 1992), 78.

173 Daughters of the American Revolution, *Lineage Book of National Society of the Daughters of the American Revolution*, 166 vols. (Washington DC: National Society of the Daughters of the American Revolution, 1890–1939).

174 J.D. Lewis, "The American Revolution in South Carolina: Bowling Green," Carolana, accessed January 13, 2020, https://www.carolana.com/SC/Revolution/revolution_bowling_green.html.

175 Bobby Gilmer Moss, *The Roster of South Carolina Patriots in the American Revolution* (Baltimore: Genealogical Publishing Company, 2009), 989.

176 ——.

177 ——, 428.

178 ——.

179 Peter Wilson Coldham, *The Complete Book of Emigrants: 1607–1660* (Baltimore: Genealogical Publishing Co., 1987).

180 John Franklin Worley, *The Worley Clan: A Gathering of Some of the Descendants of Nicholas Worley of Duplin County, North Carolina, Particularly the Family of His Son, Nicholas Worley of Columbus County, North Carolina* (Atlanta: J.F. and V.P. Worley, 1979).

181 ——, *South Carolina Patriots*, 942.

182 "Pension Application of Theophilus Coleman R2162," (PDF), transcribed by Will T. Graves, Southern Campaigns American Revolution Pension and Rosters, November 26, 2010, https://revwarapps.org/r2162.pdf.

183 David S. Heidler, "The American Defeat at Briar Creek, 3 March 1779," *Georgia Historical Quarterly* 66, no. 3 (fall 1982): 317–31, https://www.jstor.org/stable/40580932.

184 Joshua B. Howard, "'Things Here Wear a Melancholy Appearance': The American Defeat at Briar Creek," *Georgia Historical Quarterly* 88, no. 4 (winter 2004): 477–98, https://www.jstor.org/stable/40584769.

185 Heidler, "American Defeat."

186 J.D. Lewis, "The American Revolution in North Carolina: Thomas Owen," Carolana, accessed December 12, 2019, https://www.carolana.com/NC/Revolution/patriot_leaders_nc_thomas_owen.html.

187 ——, "The American Revolution in North Carolina: Captains," Carolana, accessed December 12, 2019, https://www.carolana.com/NC/Revolution/nc_patriot_military_captains.html.

188 ——, "The American Revolution in North Carolina: Revolution Hoods," Carolana, accessed December 12, 2019, https://www.carolana.com/NC/Revolution/revolution_hoods_creek.html.

189 "Pension Application of Theophilus Coleman R2162," (PDF), transcribed by Will T. Graves, Southern Campaigns American Revolution Pension and Rosters, November 26, 2010, https://revwarapps.org/r2162.pdf.

190 ——, "The American Revolution in North Carolina: Revolution Brown Marsh," Carolana, accessed December 12, 2019, https://www.carolana.com/NC/Revolution/revolution_brown_marsh.html.

191 *The Roster of the North Carolina Troops in the Continental Army: Thomas, Abishai; Catlin, Lynde; Mifflin, Benjamin*, Colonial and State Records of North Carolina, Documenting the American South, (Philadelphia, 1971), 16:1138, https://docsouth.unc.edu/csr/index.php/document/csr16-0699.

192 Elmer D. Johnson, "Armstrong, James," NCpedia, 1979, https://www.ncpedia.org/biography/armstrong-james.

193 J.D. Lewis, "The American Revolution in North Carolina: Capt. Joseph Thomas Rhodes," Carolana, accessed December 12, 2019, https://www.carolana.com/NC/Revolution/patriots_nc_capt_joseph_thomas_rhodes.html.

194 ——, "The American Revolution in North Carolina: Eutaw Springs," Carolana, accessed February 12, 2020, https://www.carolana.com/SC/Revolution/revolution_battle_of_eutaw_springs.html.

195 The North Carolina Daughters of the American Revolution, *Roster of Soldiers from North Carolina in the American Revolution with an Appendix Containing a Collection of Miscellaneous Records* (Durham: The North Carolina Daughters of the American Revolution, 1932), 362.

196 "Pension Application of Absalom Powell, Sr. R8401," (PDF), transcribed by Will T. Graves, Southern Campaigns American Revolution Pension and Rosters, September 18, 2009, http://revwarapps.org/r8401.pdf.

197 ——.

198 Sam Starnes, "Amis, Thomas," (blog), NCpedia, accessed September 26, 2022, https://www.ncpedia.org/amis-thomas.

199 "Pension Application of Absalom Powell, Sr. R8401," (PDF), transcribed by Will T. Graves, Southern Campaigns American Revolution Pension and Rosters, September 18, 2009, http://revwarapps.org/r8401.pdf.

200 ———.

201 "Gasque's Battalion of South Carolina Militia," Marion County 1812, War of 1812, accessed September 26, 2022, https://sciway3.net/proctor/marion/military/marion_war1812_gasque.html.

202 Sellers, *History of Marion County*, 126.

203 North Carolina Adjutant-general Department, *Muster Rolls of the Soldiers of the War of 1812, Detached from the Militia of North Carolina in 1812 and 1814* (Amazon: Ulan Press, 2012), 26.

204 ———, 94.

205 D. Augustus Dickert, *History of Kershaw's Brigade, with Complete Roll of Companies, Biographical Sketches, Incidents, Anecdotes, Etc.* (Newberry: Elbert H. Aull, 1899).

206 Richard H. Triebe, *Fort Fisher to Elmira: The Fatal Journey of More Than Five Hundred Confederate Soldiers* (Columbia: Coastal books, 2016), 381.

207 ———.

208 ———, 382.

209 LeRae Umfleet, *1898 Wilmington Race riot Report: 1898 Wilmington Race Riot Commission* (PDF), Research Branch, Office of Archives and History, North Carolina Department of Cultural Resources, https://citeseerx.ist.psu.edu/viewdoc/download?doi=10.1.1.692.7610&rep=rep1&type=pdf.

210 Chris E. Fonvielle Jr., *The Wilmington Campaign: Last Rays of Departing Hope* (Campbell: Savas Publishing Company, 1997), 386, 390–3, 402–12.

211 ———, 415–29.

212 A.L. Fletcher, *History of the 113th Field Artillery 30th Division* (Raleigh: The History Committee of the 113th F.A., 1920), 157–8.

213 Carlo D'Este, *Patton: A Genius for War* (New York: Harper Collins, 1995), 254.

214 "Skeletonized New York National Guard Regiments Reorganized as Pioneer Infantry," Tent and Trench Appendix B, Jonathan Brooke and the Spartanburg County Historical Association, http://www.schistory.net/campwadsworth/unitsnon.html.

215 Jeff T. Giambrone, *Images of America: Remembering Mississippi's Confederates* (Charleston: Arcadia Publishing, 2012), 19.

216 Simkins and Roland, *The South Old and New*, 113.

217 Guy Gugliotta, "New Estimate Raises Civil War Death Toll," *New York Times*, April 12, 2012, https://historum.com/t/new-estimate-raises-civil-war-death-toll.40246/.

218 Walter Clark, *Histories of the Several Regiments and Battalions from North Carolina in the Great War 1861–1865* (Goldsboro: Nash Brothers Book and Job Printers, 1901), 5:465.

219 ———, 5:466.

220 Harry W. Pfanz, *Gettysburg—Culp's Hill and Cemetery Hill* (Chapel Hill: The University of North Carolina Press, 1993).

221 ———, *Gettysburg—The First Day* (Chapel Hill: The University of North Carolina Press, 2001).

222 Stephen W. Sears, *Gettysburg* (New York: Houghton Mifflin Company, 2003).

223 Zachary Wesley, "A Slaughter Forgotten: A Reflection on the Wayside on Iverson's Assault," Alfred Iverson, *Gettysburg Compiler*, May 11, 2018, https://gettysburgcompiler.org/tag/alfred-iverson/.

224 Pfanz, *First Day*.

225 "John W. Jones," Essential Understandings, Friends of the Thomas Balch Library, https://web.archive.org/web/20110624003730/http://www.balchfriends.org/Glimpse/JJones.htm.

226 The Chemung County Historical Society, "Elmira Prison Camp: Civil War 1864–1865," Elmira Prison Camp, Chemung County History, Elmira, New York, https://www.chemunghistory.com/elmira-prison-camp; Washington B. Traweek, "Recollections of Washington B. Traweek: Escaping Elmira," Personal Information, Elmira Prison Camp Online Library, https://www.angelfire.com/ny5/elmiraprison/traweek.html; and Diane Janowski, In Their Honor: Soldiers of the Confederacy, The Elmira Prison Camp (Elmira: New York History Review Press, 2009); and Ray Finger, "20 Facts About Elmira's Civil War Prison Camp," Star-Gazette, updated February 22, 2016, 7:30 a.m. ET, https://www.stargazette.com/story/news/local/2014/07/26/elmira-civil-war-prison-camp/13191117/.

227 Ray Finger, "20 facts about Elmira's Civil War prison camp," Star Gazette, July 26, 2014, accessed August 2, 2023, https://www.stargazette.com/story/news/local/2014/07/26/elmira-civil-war-prison-camp/13191117/.

228 Maud Thomas Smith, "Toon, Thomas Fentress," NCpedia, 1996, https://www.ncpedia.org/biography/toon-thomas-fentress.

229 Mattie Erma E. Parker, "Blount (Blunt), James," (blog), NCpedia, accessed April 8, 2022, https://www.ncpedia.org/biography/blount-blunt-james.

230 "William Hardee Sr.'s Pension Application," Horry County Historical Society, https://webtrees.mstevetodd.com/tree/M%20Steve%20Todd/media-download?xref=M1330&fact_id=ff3e93c37cedae2f9886419f73ce4fb5&disposition=inline&mark=0..

231 Lindley S. Butler, "Quakers," (blog), NCpedia, accessed April 8, 2022, https://www.ncpedia.org/quakers.

232 Henry Neil Wright, *Isaac Wright and His Descendants from Stephen Wright of Southeastern North Carolina* (Smithfield: Smithfield Herald, 2009), 88.

233 John Allan Wyeth, MD, LLD, *Life of Lieutenant-General Nathan Bedford Forrest* (New York: Harper and Brothers Publishers, 1908).

BIBLIOGRAPHY

"A Million Vikings Still Live Among Us: One in 33 Men Can Claim to be Direct Descendants from the Norse Warriors." News. Daily Mail. Updated March 10, 2014. https://www.dailymail.co.uk/news/article-2577003/A-million-Vikings-live-One-33-men-claim-direct-descendants-Norse-warriors.html.

"Battle of Rockfish." North Carolina Highway Historical Marker Program. North Carolina Department of Cultural Resources. http://www.ncmarkers.com/Markers.aspx?MarkerId=F-7.

"Biographical Memoir of the Late General Sir James Henry Craig K.B." In *The Royal Military Chronicle*, 3:401. London: J. Davis, 1812.

"Border Reivers–Border Reiver Names." Tom Moss Border Reivers. Rose Cottage Publications. www.reivershistory.co.uk/reiver-names.html.

"Capt and Commander Stephen Buckland 1742–1782." Officers. Society of the Cincinnati in the State of Connecticut. July 4, 1783. http://theconnecticutsociety.org/buckland-stephen/.

"Civil War Service Records for Alva Cartwright." Fold3.com. Accessed August 3, 2023. https://www.fold3.com/image/81544517.

"Civil War Service Records for Enoch Cartwright." Fold3.com. Accessed August 3, 2023. https://www.fold3.com/image/81544538.

"Civil War Service Records for Richard Cartwright." Fold3.com. Accessed August 3, 2023. https://www.fold3.com/image/81544596.

"Civil War Service Records for William H. Cartwright." Fold3.com. Accessed August 3, 2023. https://www.fold3.com/image/81544713.

"Civil War Service Records for Amos Fowler." Fold3.com. Accessed August 3, 2023. https://www.fold3.com/image/83564097.

"Civil War Service Records for F.H. Fowler." Fold3.com. Accessed August 3, 2023. https://www.fold3.com/image/83564109?terms=war,confederate,united,civil,h,f,south,carolina,america,states,fowler.

"Civil War Service Records for G.W. Fowler." Fold3.com. Accessed August 3, 2023. https://www.fold3.com/image/83564135?terms=war,confederate,civil,carolina,g,south,united,america,w,states,fowler.

"Civil War Service Records for Jacob P. Fowler." Fold3.com. Accessed August 3, 2023. https://www.fold3.com/image/83564167.

"Civil War Service Records for Peter Fowler." Fold3.com. Accessed August 3, 2023. https://www.fold3.com/image/83564203.

"Civil War Service Records for William Fowler." Fold3.com. Accessed August 3, 2023. https://www.fold3.com/image/83564237.

"Clan History." Clan Colquhoun International. https://www.clancolquhoun.com/how/.

"Declaration of Elizabeth Spivey, widow of Edmund Spivey for Revolutionary War Pension under the Act of July 4th, 1836, R10,002." Fold3.com. Accessed August 1, 2023. https://www.fold3.com/file/30879907/edmund-spivey-revolutionary-war-pensions?terms=north,war,us,spivey,revolutionary,carolina,united,america,states.

"Dumbarton Castle." History. Historic Environment Scotland. Accessed April 29, 2019. https://www.historicenvironment.scot/visit-a-place/places/dumbarton-castle/history/.

"Gasque's Battalion of South Carolina Militia." Marion County 1812. War of 1812. Accessed September 26, 2022. https://sciway3.net/proctor/marion/military/marion_war1812_gasque.html.

"Headrights (VA-NOTES)." Va4_headrights. Library of Virginia. Accessed April 26, 2019. http://www.lva.virginia.gov/public/guides/va4_headrights.htm.

"Henrico County, VA | Jul 1, 1862." Malvern Hill. American Battlefield Trust. https://www.battlefields.org/learn/civil-war/battles/malvern-hill.

"Henry Berry Lowry (1845–?)." Encyclopedia Entry. North Carolina History Project. https://northcarolinahistory.org/encyclopedia/henry-berry-lowry-1845/.

"History." Bladen County NC Geneology and History. Bladen County NCGenWeb. Updated January 22, 2018. http://www.ncgenweb.us/bladen/bladen-county-ncgenweb.

"Huguenot History." Huguenot Society of Great Britain and Ireland. https://www.huguenotsociety.org.uk/history.html#:~:text=Women%20were%20imprisoned%20and%20their,the%20court%20of%20the%20Czars.

"Huguenots: History and Massacre." Timeline 1501–1600. Christianity.com. https://www.christianity.com/church/church-history/timeline/1501-1600/huguenots-driven-out-of-france-11630022.html.

"Learn." Getting Started. NC Land Grant Images and Data. https://www.nclandgrants.com/q/?sbj=Page%2C%20David&cyid=11&xs=1.

"Pension Application of Absalom Powell, Sr. R8401." PDF. Transcribed by Will T. Graves. Southern Campaigns American Revolution Pension and Rosters. September 18, 2009. http://revwarapps.org/r8401.pdf.

"Pension Application of Nathanial Whittington S9527." PDF. Transcribed by Will T. Graves. Southern Campaigns American Revolution Pension and Rosters. June 12, 1920. http://revwarapps.org/s9527.pdf.

"Pension Application of Theophilus Coleman R2162." PDF. Transcribed by Will T. Graves. Southern Campaigns American Revolution Pension and Rosters. November 26, 2010. https://revwarapps.org/r2162.pdf.

"Skeletonized New York National Guard Regiments Reorganized as Pioneer Infantry." Tent and Trench Appendix B. Jonathan Brooke and the Spartanburg County Historical Association. http://www.schistory.net/campwadsworth/unitsnon.html.

"The Inscriptions on the Tombstones at the Old Parish Church of St. James's Santee, near Echaw Creek." *South Carolina Historical and Genealogical Magazine* 12, no. 3 (1911): 153–8. http://www.jstor.org/stable/27575308.

"The Welsh Settlers During the Royal Period (1729 to 1775)." Royal Colony of South Carolina. Carolana. https://www.carolana.com/SC/Royal_Colony/sc_royal_colony_welsh.html.

"To Acknowledge Our Ancestors Means …." Alice Walker. Relics World: A World of Words Which Can Change Your Life. https://www.relicsworld.com/alice-walker/to-acknowledge-our-ancestors-means-we-are-aware-that-we-did-not-author-alice-walker.

"Tories." Encyclopedia Entry. North Carolina History Project. https://northcarolinahistory.org/encyclopedia/tories/.

"Virgina, US, Marriages of the Northern Neck of Virginia, US, 1649–1800." Birth, Marriage & Death. Ancestry. https://www.ancestry.com/search/collections/5063/.

"William Hardee Sr.'s Pension Application." Horry County Historical Society. https://webtrees.mstevetodd.com/tree/M%20Steve%20Todd/media-download?xref=M1330&-fact_id=ff3e93c37cedae2f9886419f73ce4fb5&disposition=inline&mark=0. .

"'With Malice Toward None …': Lincoln's Second Inaugural Address." National Park Service. Updated September 12, 2021. https://www.nps.gov/articles/000/-with-malice-toward-none-lincoln-s-second-inaugural.htm.

Adams, Frank. *The Clans, Septs and Regiments of the Scottish Highlands*. 8th ed. Reviewed by Sir Thomas Innes of Learney. Baltimore: Genealogical Publishing Company, 1970.

Baldwin, Agnes Leland. *First Settlers of South Carolina, 1670–1700*. Easley: Southern Historical Press, 1985.

Barid, Charles W. *History of Huguenot Emigration to American, Vol. 2*, 102. New York: Dodd and Mead Publishers, 1885.

Barnhill, Edward Stanley. *The Beatys of Kingston*. Mt. Pleasant, SC: Furlong and Sons, 1958.

Bidgood, Jess, and Alan Blinder. "Hurricane Plunges a North Carolina Town's Future Into Debt." *New York Times*. October 11, 2016. https://www.nytimes.com/2016/10/12/us/hurricane-matthew-plunges-a-north-carolina-towns-future-into-doubt.html.

Bishir, Catherine W. *North Carolina Architecture*, 34–5. Chapel Hill: The Uiniversity of North Carolina Press, 2005.

Blythe, John. "Crusoe Island and the French Revolution." *NC Miscellany* (blog). *UNC Library*. July 14, 2011. https://blogs.lib.unc.edu/ncm/index.php/2011/07/14/crusoe-island-and-the-french-revolution/.

Boddie, John Bennett. *Historical Southern Families*, 5:247–8. Baltimore: Clearfield Company, 1993.

——. *Seventeenth Century Isle of Wight County, Virginia*. Chicago: Genealogical Publishing Company, 1938.

Bordeaux, Jason. "McKinnie Research." *Southeastern North Carolina Genealogical Society, Roots and Remembrances* 40, no. 1 (July/August 2022): 1–23.

Burgoyne, John, and Douglas R. Cubbison. *Burgoyne, and the Saratoga Campaign: His Papers*, 332. Norman: The University of Oklahoma Press, 2012.

Butler, Lindley S. "Quakers." NCpedia (blog). Accessed April 8, 2022. https://www.ncpedia.org/quakers.

Carmichael, Roderick L. *The Scottish Highlander Carmichaels of the Carolinas*. Washington, DC: The Compiler, 1935.

Cicero, Marcus Tullius. *Orator*, 395. Translated by G. L. Hendrickson and H. M. Hubbell. Cambridge: Harvard University Press, 1939.

Claiborne, Jack, and William Price, eds. *Discovering North Carolina: A Tar Heel Reader*. Chapel Hill: The University of North Carolina Press, 1991.

Clark, Murtie June. *Colonial Soldiers of the South, 1732–1774*, 763. Baltimore: Genealogical Publishing Company, 1986.

Clark, Walter. *Histories of the Several Regiments and Battalions from North Carolina in the Great War 1861–1865*, 5:465. Goldsboro: Nash Brothers Book and Job Printers, 1901.

Coghlan, Andy. "Ancient Invaders Transformed Britain, But Not Its DNA." Life. NewScientist. March 18, 2015. https://www.newscientist.com/article/mg22530134-300-ancient-invaders-transformed-britain-but-not-its-dna/.

Coldham, Peter Wilson. *The Complete Book of Emigrants: 1607–1660*. Baltimore: Genealogical Publishing Co., 1987.

Cox, Jacob D. *Military Reminiscences of the Civil War*, 2:531–2. New York: C. Scribner's Sons, 1900.

———. *The March to the Sea*, 168. New York: Scribner, 1892.

D'Este, Carlo. *Patton: A Genius for War*, 254. New York: Harper Collins, 1995.

Daughters of the American Revolution. *Lineage Book of National Society of the Daughters of the American Revolution*, 166 vols. Washington DC: National Society of the Daughters of the American Revolution, 1890–1939.

Dickert, D. Augustus. *History of Kershaw's Brigade, with Complete Roll of Companies, Biographical Sketches, Incidents, Anecdotes, Etc.* Newberry: Elbert H. Aull, 1899.

Editorial. *Charleston Daily Courier (Charleston, S.C.) 1852–1873*. April 11, 1872.

Fagart, Tom. "From Fort Fisher, North Carolina to Elmira, New York." North Carolina Civil War and Reconstruction History Center (blog). September 11, 2018. https://nccivilwarcenter.org/from-fort-fisher-north-carolina-to-elmira-new-york/.

Felt, Joseph Barlow. *The Annals of Salem: From Its First Settlement*, 197–8. Salem: W. & S.B. Ives, 1827.

Finger, Ray. "20 Facts About Elmira's Civil War Prison Camp." *Star-Gazette*. Updated February 22, 2016, 7:30 a.m. ET. https://www.stargazette.com/story/news/local/2014/07/26/elmira-civil-war-prison-camp/13191117/.

Finger, Ray. "20 facts about Elmira's Civil War prison camp." Star Gazette. July 26, 2014. Accessed August 2, 2023. https://www.stargazette.com/story/news/local/2014/07/26/elmira-civil-war-prison-camp/13191117/.

Fischer, David Hackett. *Albion's Seed: Four British Folkways in America*, 236–41. New York: Oxford University Press, 1989.

Fletcher, A.L. *History of the 113th Field Artillery 30th Division*, 157–8. Raleigh: The History Committee of the 113th F.A., 1920.

Fonvielle, Chris E., Jr. *The Wilmington Campaign: Last Rays of Departing Hope*, 386, 390–3, 402–12. Campbell: Savas Publishing Company, 1997.

Fortescue, Honorable John William. *A History of the British Army: Volume III 1763–1793: Second Part—From the Close of the Seven Years' War to the Second Peace of Paris*. London: Macmillan, 1902.

Fowler, Richard Gildart. *A History of the Fowler Family of Southeastern North Carolina*, 15. Norman: R.G. Fowler, 1985.

Fulghum, Robert "Bob." *Fulgham-Fulghum Family Facts*, no. 73 (Winter/Spring 2013). https://homepages.rootsweb.com/~fulghum/newsletters/FFFAN_Issue73.pdf.

Fulmore, Zachary Taylor. *Annals of the Ashpole Community: 1750–1814*. Philadelphia: S.R. Fulmore Publisher, 1992.

Giambrone, Jeff T. *Images of America: Remembering Mississippi's Confederates*, 19. Charleston: Arcadia Publishing, 2012.

Glover, Judith. *The Place Names of Kent*. Hartlip: Meresborough Books, 1982.

Gragg, Rod. *Confederate Goliath: The Battle of Fort Fisher*, 243. Baton Rouge: Louisiana State University Press, 1994.

Graves, Will. "Pension Acts: An Overview of Revolutionary War Pension and Bounty Land Legislation and the Southern Campaigns Pension Transcript Project." Accessed September 13, 2019. https://revwarapps.org/revwar-pension-acts.htm.

Greer, George Cabell. *Early Virginia Immigrants, 1623–1666*. Richmond: W.C. Hill Printing Company, 1912.

Gregg, Alexander. *History of the Old Cheraws: Containing an Account of the Aborigines of the Pedee, the First White Settlements, Their Subsequent Progress, Civil Changes, the Struggle of the Revolution, and Growth of the Country Afterward; Extending from about A.D. 1730 to 1810, with Notices of the Families and Sketches of Individuals*. New York: Richardson and Company, 1867.

Greshko, Michael. "Did This Spanish Shipwreck Change the Course of History?" *National Geographic*. Published November 2, 2015. https://www.nationalgeographic.com/news/2015/11/151102-colombia-shipwreck-cartagena-battle-1700s/.

Gugliotta, Guy. "New Estimate Raises Civil War Death Toll." *New York Times*. April 12, 2012. https://www.nytimes.com/2012/04/03/science/civil-war-toll-up-by-20-percent-in-new-estimate.html.

Harlan, Louis R., ed. *The Booker T. Washington Papers, Volume 3*: 1889–95, 583–7. Urbana: University of Illinois Press, 1974.

Hauptman, Laurence M. *Between Two Fires: American Indians in the Civil War*, 79–81. New York: Free Press Paperbacks, 1995.

Heidler, David S. "The American Defeat at Briar Creek, 3 March 1779." *Georgia Historical Quarterly* 66, no. 3 (fall 1982): 317–31. https://www.jstor.org/stable/40580932.

Heitman, Francis B. *Historical Register: Officers of the Continental Army*, 382. Ann Arbor: Press of Nichols, Killam & Maffitt, 1893.

Hill, Daniel Harvey. "McClellan's Change of Base and Malvern Hill." In *Battles and Leaders of the Civil War*, 2, 394. Edited by Robert Underwood Johnson and Clarence Clough Buel. New York: Thomas Yoseloff, 1956.

Horry County Historical Society. "Independent Republic Quarterly." *Independent Republic Quarterly* 41, no. 1–4 (2007): 7–8, 148.

Howard, Joshua B. "'Things Here Wear a Melancholy Appearance': The American Defeat at Briar Creek." *Georgia Historical Quarterly* 88, no. 4 (winter 2004): 477–98. https://www.jstor.org/stable/40584769.

Hunt, Deason. *Out of Mississippi: The John Robert Wingate Family of Nacogdoches County, Texas*, 2. Holly Lake Ranch: Deason Hunt, 2006.

Janowski, Diane. *In Their Honor: Soldiers of the Confederacy, The Elmira Prison Camp*. Elmira: New York History Review Press, 2009.

Johnson, Ben. "The History of the Border Reivers." History of Scotland. Historic UK: The History and Heritage Accommodation Guide. https://www.historic-uk.com/HistoryUK/HistoryofScotland/The-Border-Reivers/.

Johnson, Elmer D. "Armstrong, James." NCpedia. 1979. https://www.ncpedia.org/biography/armstrong-james.

Johnson, Lloyd. "Welsh Settlers." NCPedia. State Library of North Carolina. January 1, 2006. https://www.ncpedia.org/welsh-settlers.

Jordan, John W., LLD, ed. *Colonial and Revolutionary Families of Pennsylvania: Genealogical and Personal Memoirs*. New York: The Lewis Publishing Company, 1911.

Kennedy, Frances H., ed. *The Civil War Battlefield Guide*, 2nd ed., 170–1. New York: Houghton Mifflin Company, 1998.

King, Forrest. "Descendants of Matthew Strickland (1648–1696) Through Four Generations." PDF. https://www.alliedfamilies.com/uploads/1/3/1/8/13181256/6__k_-_m_strickland_stricklin.pdf.

Lefler, Hugh Talmage, and Albert Ray Newsome. *North Carolina: The History of a Southern State*, 3rd ed. Chapel Hill: The University of North Caroline Press, 1973.

Lennon, Donald R., and Fred D. Ragan. "Searching for Greener Pastures: Out-migration in the 1800s and 1900s." North Carolina Museum of History. Accessed November 8, 2019. https://www.ncpedia.org/anchor/searching-greener-pastures. .

Leslie, Stephen, Bruce Winney, Garrett Hellenthal, Dan Davison, Abdelhamid Boumertit, Tammy Day, Katarzyna Hutnik, Ellen C. Royrvik, Wellcome Trust Case Control Consortium 2, International Multiple Sclerosis Genetics Consortium, Daniel Falush, Colin Freeman, Matti Pirinen, Simon Myers, Mark Robinson, Peter Donnelly, and Walter Bodmer. "The Fine-scale Genetic Structure of the British Population." *Nature* 519, no. 7543 (March 2015), 309–14. https://doi.org/10.1038/nature14230.

Lewis, Jerry Dale "J.D." "Seth Sothel: Governor of Albemarle 1682 to 1689, Governor of 'Ye Lands South and West of Cape Feare' 1690 to 1692." Carolana. Accessed March 1, 2020. https://www.carolana.com/Carolina/Governors/ssothel.html.

———. "The American Revolution in North Carolina: Thomas Owen." Carolana. Accessed December 12, 2019. https://www.carolana.com/NC/Revolution/patriot_leaders_nc_thomas_owen.html.

———. "The American Revolution in North Carolina: Captains." Carolana. Accessed December 12, 2019. https://www.carolana.com/NC/Revolution/nc_patriot_military_captains.html.

———. "The American Revolution in North Carolina: Revolution Hoods." Carolana. Accessed December 12, 2019. https://www.carolana.com/NC/Revolution/revolution_hoods_creek.html.

———. "The American Revolution in North Carolina: Revolution Brown Marsh." Carolana,. Accessed December 12, 2019. https://www.carolana.com/NC/Revolution/revolution_brown_marsh.html.

———. "The American Revolution in North Carolina: Capt. Joseph Thomas Rhodes." Carolana. Accessed December 12, 2019. https://www.carolana.com/NC/Revolution/patriots_nc_capt_joseph_thomas_rhodes.html.

———. "The American Revolution in North Carolina: Eutaw Springs." Carolana. Accessed February 12, 2020. https://www.carolana.com/SC/Revolution/revolution_battle_of_eutaw_springs.html.

———. "The American Revolution in South Carolina: Bowling Green." Carolana. Accessed January 13, 2020. https://www.carolana.com/SC/Revolution/revolution_bowling_green.html.

———. *My Neck of the Woods: The Lewis Families of Southeastern North Carolina and Northeastern South Carolina*, 2nd ed. Baltimore: Clearfield Publishing, 2009.

Lewis, Lloyd. *Sherman, Fighting Prophet*, 1st ed., 513. San Diego: Harcourt, Brace and Company, 1932.

Lloyd, Joshua. "371-year-old Bible Lives on in Darlington County." News. *Washington Times*. June 11, 2016. https://www.washingtontimes.com/news/2016/jun/11/371-year-old-bible-lives-on-in-darlington-county/.

McGirt, Curtis. "Isham Pitman." Pittman Family. Fairmont History. https://fairmontnchistory.com/families/pittman.

———. "The Ashpole Area in the 1700s." History. Fairmont History. https://fairmontnchistory.com/history/43-the-ashpole-area-in-the-1700-s.

McGrath, Alister. "Calvin and the Christian Calling." *First Things* 94, (June/July 1999): 31–5. https://www.firstthings.com/article/1999/06/calvin-and-the-christian-calling.

Mosley, Charles, ed. *Burke's Peerage, Baronetage and Knightage*. Vol. 3. 107th ed. Wilmington: Burke's Peerage, 2003.

Moss, Bobby Gilmer. *Roster of the Patriots in the Battle of Moores Creek Bridge*, 78. Blacksburg: Scotia-Hibernia Press, 1992.

———. *The Roster of South Carolina Patriots in the American Revolution*, 989. Baltimore: Genealogical Publishing Company, 2009.

National Archives and Records Service General Services Administrations. *Revolutionary War Pension and Bounty–Land–Warrant Application Files*, 47. Washington: National Archives Microfilm Publications, 1974. https://www.archives.gov/files/research/microfilm/m804.pdf.

National Cemetery Administration. "Woodlawn National Cemetery." Find a Cemetery. US Department of Veterans Affairs. Updated February 13, 2018. https://www.cem.va.gov/cems/nchp/woodlawn.asp.

NC History Center on the Civil War. "Little Known Facts on Tar Heel Confederate Soldiers in Elmira, NY." North Carolina Civil War and Reconstruction History Center. September 11, 2018. https://nccivilwarcenter.org/little-known-facts-on-tarheel-confederate-soldiers-in-elmira-ny/.

Nichols, Patricia Causey. "Language and Dialect in Early Horry County." *Independent Republic Quarterly* 3, no. 4 (fall 1979), 13–4.

North Carolina Adjutant-general Department. *Muster Rolls of the Soldiers of the War of 1812, Detached from the Militia of North Carolina in 1812 and 1814*, 26. Amazon: Ulan Press, 2012.

North Carolina State Center for Health Statistics and Office of Minority Health and Health Disparities. *North Carolina Minority Health Facts: American Indians*. North Carolina: State Center for Health Statistics and Office of Minority Health and Health Disparities, 2010. https://schs.dph.ncdhhs.gov/schs/pdf/AmerIndian_MHFS_WEB_072210.pdf.

Nugent, Nell Marion. *Cavaliers and Pioneers: Abstracts of Virginia Land Patents and Grants, 1623–1666*. Baltimore: Genealogical Publishing Company, 1963.

Paden, John. "Concessions and Agreement." NCpedia. State Library of North Carolina. January 1, 2006. https://www.ncpedia.org/concessions-and-agreement.

Palmer, Lewis. *Genealogical Record of the Descendants of John and Mary Palmer of Concord, Chester (Now Delaware) Co., PA; Especially Through Their Son, John Palmer Jr., and Sons-in-law, William and James Trimble: With Notes of Ancestry, or Information, of Many of the Families With Whom They Intermarried*, 312. Philadelphia: J.B. Lippincott and Company, 1875.

Parker, Mattie Erma E. "Blount (Blunt), James." NCpedia(blog). Accessed April 8, 2022. https://www.ncpedia.org/biography/blount-blunt-james.

Pfanz, Harry W. Gettysburg—*Culp's Hill and Cemetery Hill*. Chapel Hill: The University of North Carolina Press, 1993.

———. *Gettysburg—The First Day*. Chapel Hill: The University of North Carolina Press, 2001.

Potter, Eloise Fretz, and Timothy Wiley Rackley, eds. *Rackley, a Southern Colonial Family: the Descendants of Edward Rackley of Virginia: with Appendixes Treating Other Rackley Family Groups Living in the United States Before 1900*. Zebulon: E.F. Potter, 1984. https://www.familysearch.org/search/catalog/313008?availability=Family%20History%20Library.

Powell, William S. *North Carolina Through Four Centuries*. Chapel Hill: The University of North Caroline Press, 1989.

Quillin, Martha. "Some Entire NC Towns May Become Vacant Memorials to Matthew." *News & Observer*. Published April 21, 2017. Updated April 10, 2018. https://www.newsobserver.com/news/politics-government/state-politics/article146002379.html?platform=hootsuite.

Ramsey, Beverley A. *The Blounts of Mulberry Hill: Descendants of Captain James Blount of Chowan County, NC, 1650–1900*. 2 vols. Chowan County: B. A. Ramsey, 2009.

Ready, Milton. *The Tar Heel State: A History of North Carolina*. Columbia: The University of South Carolina Press, 2006.

Rogers, Tommy W. "The Great Population Exodus from South Carolina 1850–1860." *South Carolina Historical Magazine* 68, no. 1 (January 1967), 14–21. https://www.jstor.org/stable/27566804.

Salley, A.S. Jr., ed. *Journal of the Grand Council of South Carolina*. London: Forgotten Books, 2019. First published 1692.

Sandler, Norman D. "Reagan: All the Answers Are in the Bible." February 3, 1983. https://www.upi.com/Archives/1983/02/03/Reagan-All-the-answers-are-in-the-Bible/4306413096400/.

Scott, Sir Walter. *Minstrelsy of the Scottish Border*. Vol. 1. Charleston: BiblioBazaar, 2007.

Searles, Harry. "Battle of Big Black River Bridge (May 17,1863)." Entries. Ohio Civil War Central. Updated November 13, 2017. https://www.ohiocivilwarcentral.com/entry.php?rec=145.

Sears, Stephen W. *Gettysburg*. New York: Houghton Mifflin Company, 2003.

Sellers, William W. *A History of Marion County, South Carolina, from Its Earliest Times to the Present, 1901.* Columbia: R.L. Bryan Company, 1902.

Simkins, Francis Butler, and Charles Pierce Roland. *The South Old and New: A History 1820–1947,* 13. New York City: Alfred A. Knopf, 1947.

Smith, Maud Thomas. "Toon, Thomas Fentress." NCpedia. 1996. https://www.ncpedia.org/biography/toon-thomas-fentress.

Speight, Harry. "In wild Langstrothdale." In *Upper Wharfedale: Being a Complete Account of the History, Antiquities and Scenery of the Picturesque Valley of the Wharfe, from Otley to Langstrothdale,* 491. 1st ed. London: Elliot Stock, 1900.

Sprunt, James. *Chronicles of the Cape Fear River: 1660–1916,* 137. 2nd ed. Raleigh: Edwards & Brought on Printing Company, 1916.

Starnes, Sam. "Amis, Thomas." NCpedia (blog). Accessed September 26, 2022. https://www.ncpedia.org/amis-thomas.

State v. Owens. 65 N.C. App. 107. No. 8313SC227. Nov. 15 1983. https://cite.case.law/nc-app/65/107/.

Stein, Charles Francis Jr. *Origin and History of Howard Country Maryland.* Ellicott City, MD: Howard County Historical Society, 1972.

Stephen, Leslie, ed. *Dictionary of National Biography.* London: Smith, Elder & Co., 1886.

Stevenson, Mary Lewis. *William Lewis of Horry County, South Carolina.* Columbia: The R.L. Bryan Company, 1960.

Stewart, George R. *Names on the Land: A Historical Account of Place-naming in the United States,* 21–2. 1st ed. New York: Random House, 1945.

Stick, David, and Robert J. Cain. "Spanish Invasions." NCpedia. State Library of North Carolina. January 1, 2006. https://www.ncpedia.org/spanish-invasions.

Sturgis, James. "Craig, Sir James Henry: (1748–1812)." *Oxford Dictionary of National Biography.* September 2004. https://doi.org/10.1093/ref:odnb/6572.

Styrna, Christine Ann. "The Winds of War and Change: The Impact of the Tuscarora War on Proprietary North Carolina, 1660–1729." Master's thesis, 1990, 251.

Swamp Merchant. "Crusoe Island: French-Haitian Settlement in the Green Swamp of North Carolina." Restoration Systems. March 25, 2011. https://restorationsystems.com/uncategorized/swamp-people-french-haitian-aristocrats-in-the-green-swamp-of-north-carolina/.

Tetterton, Beverly. "Elizabethtown, Battle of." NCpedia. State Library of North Carolina. January 1, 2006. https://ncpedia.org/elizabethtown-battle.

The Chemung County Historical Society. "Elmira Prison Camp: Civil War 1864–1865." Elmira Prison Camp. Chemung County History, Elmira, New York. https://www.chemunghistory.com/elmira-prison-camp.

The Editors of Encyclopedia Britannica. "Culpeper's Rebellion: American Colonial History." Wars, Battles & Armed Conflicts. Encyclopedia Britannica. July 26, 2013. https://www.britannica.com/event/Culpepers-Rebellion.

The North Carolina Daughters of the American Revolution. *Roster of Soldiers from North Carolina in the American Revolution with an Appendix Containing a Collection of Miscellaneous Records,* 362. Durham: The North Carolina Daughters of the American Revolution, 1932.

The Reformers. *1599 Geneva Bible,* 1157. White Hall: Tolle Lege Press, 2016.

The Roster of the North Carolina Troops in the Continental Army: Thomas, Abishai; Catlin, Lynde; Mifflin, Benjamin, 16:1138. Colonial and State Records of North Carolina. Documenting the American South. Philadelphia, 1971. https://docsouth.unc.edu/csr/index.php/document/csr16-0699.

Townsend, George Alfred. *The Swamp Outlaws, or, The North Carolina Bandits: Being a Complete History of the Modern Rob Roys and Robin Hoods*. New York: Robert M. DeWitt, 1872. http://www.freeafricanamericans.com/swamp_outlaws.htm.

Traweek, Washington B. "Recollections of Washington B. Traweek: Escaping Elmira." Personal Information. Elmira Prison Camp Online Library. https://www.angelfire.com/ny5/elmiraprison/traweek.html.

Triebe, Richard H. *Fort Fisher to Elmira: The Fatal Journey of More Than Five Hundred Confederate Soldiers*, 381. Columbia: Coastal books, 2016.

Umfleet, LeRae. *1898 Wilmington Race riot Report: 1898 Wilmington Race Riot Commission*. PDF. Research Branch, Office of Archives and History. North Carolina Department of Cultural Resources. https://citeseerx.ist.psu.edu/viewdoc/download?doi=10.1.1.692.7610&rep=rep1&type=pdf.

Van Ruymbeke, Bertrand. *From New Babylon to Eden: The Huguenots and Their Migration to Colonial South Carolina*, 32–4. Columbia: University of South Carolina Press, 2006.

Welsh Tract Baptist Meeting. *Records of the Welsh Tract Baptist Meeting, Pencader Hundred, New Castle County Delaware, 1701 to 1828*. Wilmington: Historical Society of Delaware, 1904.

Wesley, Zachary. "A Slaughter Forgotten: A Reflection on the Wayside on Iverson's Assault." Alfred Iverson. *Gettysburg Compiler*. May 11, 2018. https://gettysburgcompiler.org/tag/alfred-iverson/.

Whittington, C.A. *Was the C282Y Mutation an Irish Gaelic Mutation That the Vikings Help Disseminate?* 67, no. 6 (August 2006): 1270–3. https://doi.org/10.1016/j.mehy.2006.06.013.

Wikipedia. "Bere Regis." Wikipedia, the Free Encyclopedia. Accessed April 24, 2019. https://en.wikipedia.org/wiki/Bere_Regis.

———. "Suffolk dialect." Wikipedia, the Free Encyclopedia. Accessed April 24, 2019. https://en.wikipedia.org/wiki/Suffolk_dialect.

Williamson, John H. "The Welsh Origins of Lewis and John Williamson of Southeastern North Carolina 1750–2019." Unpublished manuscript, 3. Microsoft Word file.

Williamson, John McLeod. "Abstracts of Earliest Columbus County North Carolina Deeds." Abstract, 3:97. Columbus County Courthouse, 1990.

Worley, John Franklin. *The Worley Clan: A Gathering of Some of the Descendants of Nicholas Worley of Duplin County, North Carolina, Particularly the Family of His Son, Nicholas Worley of Columbus County, North Carolina*. Atlanta: J.F. and V.P. Worley, 1979.

Wright, Henry Neil. *Isaac Wright and His Descendants from Stephen Wright of Southeastern North Carolina*, 88. Smithfield: Smithfield Herald, 2009.

Wyeth, John Allan, MD, LLD. *Life of Lieutenant-General Nathan Bedford Forrest*. New York: Harper and Brothers Publishers, 1908.

Yeats, William Butler. "An Irish Airman Foresees His Death." Poets.org. Published 1919. https://poets.org/poem/irish-airman-foresees-his-death.

ACKNOWLEDGMENTS

Thank you to Warren Publishing's team for your encouragement, guidance, patience, and hard work. To the president Mindy Kuhn and vice president and editor-in-chief Amy Ashby, you saw potential in my book years ago, and I will forever be grateful to you. To Warren's managing editor and my developmental editor and writing coach Melissa Long, and my copy editor Angela Meyers, thank you for your skills and thoroughness. To the marketing director Lacey Cope, thank you for your assistance with marketing.

Thank you to Eddie Leekota Williamson, Dollie Monteen Williamson Page, Mitchell Davis Page, Bobbi Jean Page Lunsford, and Patti Sue Page Powell for sharing your memories and family stories with me.

Thank you to my wonderful wife, Diane M. Triggs, for all your love and words of encouragement.

Finally, thank you to everyone whose assistance I have received during the five-year journey of writing and researching this book. We made it!

www.ingramcontent.com/pod-product-compliance
Lightning Source LLC
Chambersburg PA
CBHW030101170426
43198CB00009B/450